Redemption and the Merchant God

Northwestern University Press
Studies in Russian Literature and Theory

Series Editors
Robert Belknap
Caryl Emerson
Gary Saul Morson
William Mills Todd III
Andrew Wachtel

Redemption and the Merchant God

DOSTOEVSKY'S ECONOMY OF
SALVATION AND ANTISEMITISM

Susan McReynolds

NORTHWESTERN UNIVERSITY PRESS / EVANSTON, ILLINOIS

Northwestern University Press
www.nupress.northwestern.edu

Printed in the United States of America

10 9 8 7 6 5 4 3 2 1

ISBN: 978-0-8101-2787-6

**The Library of Congress has cataloged the
original, hardcover edition as follows:**

McReynolds, Susan.
    Redemption and the merchant god : Dostoevsky's economy of salvation and
antisemitism / Susan McReynolds.
        p. cm. — (Studies in Russian literature and theory)
    Includes bibliographical references and index.
    1. Dostoyevsky, Fyodor, 1821–1881—Religion. 2. Dostoyevsky, Fyodor, 1821–
1881—Criticism and interpretation. 3. Jews in literature. 4. Antisemitism in
literature. 5. Jesus Christ—Crucifixion. I. Title. II. Series.
PG3328.Z7R4259 2008
891.733—dc22   2007035877

To my parents, Peter and Rosemarie McReynolds

Contents

Acknowledgments

The research and writing of this book were partly funded by a generous grant from the Alice Kaplan Institute for the Humanities at Northwestern University and by an individual research grant from the University Research Grants Committee.

I am deeply grateful for the support and inspiration many people have provided over the years. The roots of this project go back to my first encounters with Dostoevsky under the guidance of Bill Todd. He mentored these ideas through every phase, and they would not have developed to completion without his patience, wisdom, and commitment. Sander Gilman generously offered insights that prompted profound revaluation of the project at several critical junctures. His feedback and encouragement were indispensable.

Any new work on Dostoevsky owes a significant debt to the remarkable tradition of Dostoevsky scholarship in the United States, Europe, and Russia. The members of the International Dostoevsky Society bring infectious passion to their study of Dostoevsky's life and works, and they energized this composition. I owe a special debt to the work and example of Ulrich Schmid, an inspiring Dostoevsky scholar and leader in the international community. Here in the United States, several people must be singled out for special thanks: Caryl Emerson, Robin Feuer Miller, Donna Orwin, and Nina Perlina. Our stimulating exchanges and their encouragement made a tremendous difference.

The Northwestern University Slavic Department is the home of extraordinary individuals who contributed to this book. Clare Cavanagh and Séamas O'Driscoll gave generously of their time, insight, and friendship through the long process. The intellectual energy and friendship of Andrew and Elizabeth Wachtel sustained the work through difficult times. Gary Saul Morson tirelessly mentored the writing process; he has been an inspirational friend and mentor, nothing short of an intellectual lodestar.

Note on the Text

We are following a modified Library of Congress transliteration system in this volume. To make the text more readable to a general audience, first and last names ending in –ii have been changed to –y, such as Dostoevsky or Merezhkovsky rather than Dostoevskii or Merezhkovskii. We have also, for the sake of readability, collapsed –iia endings to –ia. Names are given in their standard English form when one exists. Bibliographical references follow the standard Library of Congress transliteration system.

Abbreviations of Works by Fyodor Dostoevsky

BK   Fyodor Dostoevsky. *The Brothers Karamazov*. Edited by Ralph E. Matlaw. Translated by Constance Garnett. New York: W. W. Norton, 1976.

CP   Fyodor Dostoevsky. *Crime and Punishment*. Translated by Constance Garnett, with an introduction by Joseph Frank. New York: Bantam Classic, 1987.

D   Fyodor Dostoevsky. *Demons*. Translated and annotated by Richard Pevear and Larissa Volokhonsky. New York: Vintage Classics, 1995.

I   Fyodor Dostoevsky. *The Idiot*. Translated and with an introduction by David Magarshack. London: Penguin, 1955.

MHD   Fyodor Dostoevsky. *Memoirs from the House of the Dead*. Edited by Ronald Hingley. Translated by Jessie Coulson. Oxford: Oxford University Press, 1965; 1992 edition.

PF   Fyodor Dostoevsky. *Poor Folk*. Translated and with an introduction by Robert Dessaix. Ann Arbor, Mich.: Ardis, 1982.

Pss   Fyodor Dostoevsky. *Polnoe sobranie sochinenii v tridtsati tomakh*. 30 vols. Edited by V. V. Vinogradov, G. M. Fridlender, and M. B. Khrapchenko. Leningrad: Nauka, 1972–90.

WD   Fyodor Dostoevsky. *A Writer's Diary*. 2 vols. Translated and annotated by Kenneth Lantz, with an introduction by Gary Saul Morson. Evanston, Ill.: Northwestern University Press, 1994.

WN   Fyodor Dostoevsky. *Winter Notes on Summer Impressions*. Translated by David Patterson. Evanston, Ill.: Northwestern University Press, 1988.

Redemption and the Merchant God

Speaking with the Devil

> We are still discovering Dostoevsky's spiritual
> heritage; we are still trying to crack the riddles
> he posed, still trying to solve the problems
> he presents; our understanding of Dostoevsky
> is still incomplete—and one can say this with
> utmost certainty, despite the large volume of
> literature on Dostoevsky and his influence on
> the world.
> —V. V. Zen'kovskii

DOSTOEVSKY CONTINUES to pose riddles. The an-
tisemitism that casts a shadow over his later years, for example, still requires
elucidation.[1] How could the author of *The Brothers Karamazov* also be the
source of the slurs against the Jews contained in the *Diary of a Writer,* or
indeed allow belief in the possibility of ritual murder into his great novel
through the mouth of Alyosha Karamazov? Alyosha's attitude is significant, for
the novel establishes him as a moral authority, one to whom other characters
look for guidance. "You are my conscience now," Liza Khokhlakova tells him.
"Perhaps I want to be healed by you," Ivan says to Alyosha before launching
into his rebellion against God. "Is it true that at Passover the Yids steal and kill
children?" Liza asks Alyosha, to which he replies, "I don't know."[2]

Dostoevsky contains other paradoxes as well; one of the most important concerns his relationship to Christianity. Often hailed as a deeply
Christian artist, he is just as frequently cited as an example of a skeptical
thinker whose ruthless questioning can undermine even the firmest religious convictions.[3] His relationship to Christianity has been highly contested,
by Dostoevsky himself and by generations of readers. "Critics inside and
outside Russia have been arguing for over a century about whether or not
Dostoevsky was a Christian," Steven Cassedy notes.[4] Today most readers can
agree that Dostoevsky was indeed a Christian, but his relationship to official
Russian Orthodox doctrine still inspires debate. "Dostoevsky was a confessed
Orthodox Christian, but his relationship with official Orthodoxy remains
unclear," George Pattison and Diane Oenning Thompson concede.[5] Gary
Rosenshield advances a widely held view when he describes Dostoevsky's

relationship to Orthodox theology as one characterized by sharp differences. Dostoevsky's writings, Rosenshield explains, contain many examples of "heretical divergences from Orthodox practice and doctrine."[6]

The teachings of Father Zosima, for example, are often taken to be the Christian core of Dostoevsky's art; yet even here, in the portrait of Zosima, critics agree that Dostoevsky does not conform to Orthodox theology. Rosenshield points to "some of the religious views and practices of Father Zosima" as instances that "diverge from Orthodoxy and even owe a great deal to the Western literary tradition."[7] "Father Zosima's thought is shot through with undeniably pantheistic, Franciscan, Pietistic, Utopian Socialist, Hegelian historicist and sentimental humanitarian elements," Rosenshield maintains.[8] Roger B. Anderson emphasizes the mythic and pantheistic aspects of Zosima's beliefs; Sven Linnér shows that Zosima diverges significantly from his ostensible prototype, the Russian *starets*, or elder, and instead conforms more to models found in Rousseau, Hugo, and other Western authors.[9] Arkady Dolinin advances the view that some of Dostoevsky's most cherished visions of the ideal future are even devoid of God. Dostoevsky sympathetically depicts "somehow with particular profundity, the human dream of constructing a life on earth without God," Dolinin observes.[10] Dostoevsky vociferously rejected any attempt to substitute other ideals for Christ as doomed to failure. Yet, in Dolinin's view, the artist actually adumbrates a God with attributes "taken from the image of the God-man and transmitted to someone who is not yet clearly envisioned, the embodiment of human ideals that Kirillov calls the man-god."[11]

Dostoevsky's own testimony adds to the complexity. The primary qualities of his spiritual life, Dostoevsky consistently asserted, were doubt and the longing for faith rather than the experience of faith. One of the most important documents in this regard is the now famous letter he sent to N. D. Fonvizina in 1854. Writing from the Siberian city of Omsk shortly after his release from prison, Dostoevsky confesses that he experiences minutes when "you thirst, like 'parched grass,' for faith." "I will tell you about myself," he proposes to Fonvizina, "that I am a child of the century, a child of unbelief and doubt to this time and even (I know this) to the bitter end. What terrible torments this longing to believe has cost me and continues to cost me; the more arguments against it (*the longing for faith*), the stronger it becomes in me."[12] Even when he implies that he has, in fact, acquired faith, Dostoevsky emphasizes—with great pride—the inextricable relationship between faith and doubt in his soul. No one else, he boasts in the notebooks from the last year of his life, has dared to express "the atheistic point of view" so boldly. "It is clear that I do not believe in Christ and preach Him like a child, but that my *hosanna* has passed through a great *furnace of doubt*," he insists (*Pss*, 15:425). "Throughout his life and literature," Avril Pyman wryly observes, "this furnace was kept well-stoked."[13]

4

Such complexity prompts scholars such as Malcolm Jones to conclude that neither faith nor doubt ever gained a final victory in Dostoevsky's writings. "Both extremes," Jones maintains, "persisted to the end."[14] Many other readers have been unable or unwilling to tolerate the possibly irresolvable nature of Dostoevsky's relationship to faith, however. "Some read Dostoevsky perhaps too religiously, seeing him as a prophet and messenger of God to the exclusion of some of the complexities of his work," Pattison and Thompson observe.[15] Much post–Soviet Russian Dostoevsky criticism displays a pronounced tendency toward establishing the artist as an authoritative Orthodox thinker, whose fiction can be used as a guide to theological doctrine. In his foreword to *F. M. Dostoevsky and Orthodoxy*, Valery Alekseev refers to the writer as "God's chosen one," "the Orthodox thinker and prophet Fedor Mikhailovich Dostoevsky," and enthuses, "Truly he possessed the gift of the prophet and therefore today helps us reach the main secrets of the existence of God and man."[16]

The urge to respond to Dostoevsky as a prophet or theological authority has deep roots in the Anglo-American tradition as well. In his thorough study of Dostoevsky's reception in England, Peter Kaye describes Maurice Baring as "an apostle for Russian literature and culture" in general and Dostoevsky in particular. Baring, Kaye explains, exhorted the English "to seek spiritual and Christian truth from Dostoevsky."[17] More recently, Pattison and Thompson have made the highly problematic suggestion that Christian readers may be the best interpreters of Dostoevsky. Discussing the growing tendency to approach Dostoevsky's novels as affirmations of Christian faith, they assert, "The devout approach, then, is not necessarily illegitimate," for "there are some things one understands only when one believes."[18] The desire to treat Dostoevsky "as a latter-day Messiah" has elicited criticism from other readers, however.[19]

Dostoevsky himself betrayed ambivalent feelings about the desire to adopt what Pattison and Thompson call "a reverential attitude" toward his writings.[20] On the one hand, there can be no denying that he cultivated the status of a prophet, especially in works such as his enormously popular and influential *Diary of a Writer.* On the other hand, there is clear evidence that he also resisted the formation of what Victor Ehrlich calls "the oracular school in Dostoevsky criticism," which "seeks to reduce the staggering complexity of the Dostoevsky universe to edifying or inspirational messages."[21] In 1878, Moscow University students wrote Dostoevsky, asking him to explain how they should understand contemporary events. "If you want to do me a great favor," Dostoevsky responded in an April 1878 letter, "then please, for the love of God, do not consider me some kind of teacher or instructor from above" (*Pss*, 30.1:25).

The possibility that Dostoevsky lived in limbo—that he tried but "never really succeeded in extricating himself from the torture chamber of doubt and unbelief that are part of the modern consciousness"—has prompted another branch of readers to impose a different kind of finality on him, by stabilizing him as a clear *unbeliever.*[22] This tendency is not much in evidence today but was a significant strand of scholarship from the earliest days of Dostoevsky reception through the 1960s. One of Dostoevsky's prominent early twentieth-century English readers, J. Middleton Murry, goes so far as to assert that Alyosha Karamazov "is not a Christian. He has passed beyond the Christian revelation."[23] Perception of Dostoevsky as un- or even anti-Christian is frequently expressed as enthusiasm for Ivan Karamazov.[24] We find Alyosha's faith unconvincing, William Hamilton argues, but we can "receive Ivan with a terrible kind of delight. Here is a true gift to us all, perhaps Dostoevsky's supreme gift. Ivan's picture of himself we immediately recognize as a self-portrait; the God that is dead for him is dead for us."[25]

There are many arguments against imposing either kind of finality on Dostoevsky. Irving Howe makes a convincing case against approaching Dostoevsky as a religious authority, or, by extension, against trying to pin an anti-Christian message onto the artist. Howe cautions that "to read Dostoevsky primarily as a religious or social prophet—and one with a formulated prophecy—is invariably to rob him of those tensions which are the bone and blood of his art."[26] Two of the most important tensions running through Dostoevsky's life and writings—the tensions between his humanism and antisemitism, faith and doubt—are obscured if we try to force him into a role better suited to a priest or a theologian than to a complex artist, or if we try to see Christianity resolved for him in the other fashion, as decisively repudiated.

The riddle of Dostoevsky's antisemitism, I believe, is linked to this vexed question of his relationship to Christian faith. As many other readers have realized, Dostoevsky's hatred of the Jews problematizes his status as a Christian. Vladimir Soloviev, for example, argued that Dostoevsky's prejudice represented a betrayal of his most cherished Christian values.[27] The relationship between Dostoevsky's antisemitism and Christian faith may be much more complex than simple opposition, however. In this study, I identify several specific forms of anxiety about Christianity running throughout Dostoevsky's writings. These Christian anxieties, I show, were important sources of his lifelong vacillation between faith and doubt. His concerns about Christianity, I go on to argue, did more than trap Dostoevsky in a kind of permanent spiritual oscillation; they also contributed to the emergence of antisemitism in his last years as a kind of response or solution to "the torture chamber of doubt and unbelief."[28]

If Dostoevsky ever did extricate himself from his tormenting doubts, he accomplished this not through positive affirmation of Christian doctrine but through his invention of the Jews, who came to function as a reassuringly separate embodiment of aspects of Christianity he had difficulty accepting. The sources of Dostoevsky's puzzling antisemitism can be understood by examining his anxieties about Christianity, which center on the nature of Christian salvation.[29]

Dostoevsky's doubts about Christianity, I will argue, are focused on the Crucifixion as a vehicle of redemption. These anxieties about redemption through the Crucifixion were so profound that they generated a longing for certainty that prompted him to invent the Jews as the repository of what he found objectionable about his Christian faith. Finding a guarantee of salvation as a member of a chosen people elected to defeat the Jewish Antichrist was one consequence of a lifelong preoccupation with the problem of resurrection. Dostoevsky never did achieve stable faith; but he did acquire the certainty of belief in a clear, firm, reassuring Jewish–Russian Christian opposition. At the end of his life, firm conviction as to the irreconcilable difference between what he called the Jewish and Russian ideas was functioning as substitute for faith in the doctrines of the church.

There are very few values or beliefs Dostoevsky held consistently throughout his complicated life, but there are some, and they are essential for understanding the ambivalence about Christianity that produced his mature antisemitism. An approach adequate to the complexity of Dostoevsky's antisemitism must study the big picture, the long evolution of topics that at first have no overt connection to the Jews in his writings. Dostoevsky's most cherished values included his love of children, his implacable resistance against the infringement of utilitarianism into moral life, and his determination to hold all authorities, even the most vaunted, to the most stringent *individual* ethical code. These principles form the core of what he considered to be Christian faith.

First of all, Dostoevsky believed in the sanctity of children.[30] The sensitivity to the suffering of the "insulted and injured" for which he is justly famous (and which makes his antisemitism all the more troubling) centers on children. Dostoevsky's writings, Boris Tikhomirov asserts, contain a "highly original view of the *absolute value* of children in Christianity"; this emphasis on children, Tikhomirov points out, "is some distance from Church orthodoxy."[31]

Second, Dostoevsky opposed utilitarianism. He strenuously objects to the belief that human life and experience can be reduced to quantifiable, comparable units that make utilitarian calculations about suffering and benefits possible. He affirms instead the utter *incommensurability* of human life and actions, the belief that some things are unquantifiable and incomparable. The groups he associates with the crude application of cost-benefit analysis to human life vary—at different points in his life he ascribes it to socialism, the West in general, and finally the Jews—but he always abominates it as one of the worst moral errors into which humanity has strayed.

Finally, and connected to his love of children and allegiance to the principle of incommensurability, Dostoevsky consistently rejected the view that some entities or authorities are not bound by the same moral strictures to which individuals are subject. The spectacle of suffering children or other innocents, frequently justified through recourse to utilitarian arguments and the claim that some higher authorities, such as states or societies, enjoy moral immunity, provokes Dostoevsky's moral outrage. Dostoevsky, I will show, invites readers to perceive parallels between earthly and divine forms of authority that claim the right to transgress the moral law.

I uncover Dostoevsky's haunting fear that accepting redemption through the Crucifixion implicates the Christian in each of these moral errors. My close readings of key passages reveal that Dostoevsky struggled with a heretical perception of the Crucifixion as a child sacrifice, with the suspicion that it is based in the utilitarian logic he abhorred, and with the belief that it represents an impermissible violation of individual morality, which forbids killing for any reason.[32] For Dostoevsky's major characters, and for the "character" of Russia in the *Diary of a Writer,* the process of acquiring faith—the possibility of redemption from agonizing doubt into certainty— entails clarifying their relationship to these moral dilemmas posed for their creator by the Crucifixion.[33]

The very concept of God's ontological otherness is subjected to critical scrutiny in Dostoevsky's writings. By rejecting the claim of secular authorities to transcend the moral law and suggesting similarities among *all* forms of transgressive authority, Dostoevsky challenges God's right to sacrifice his son. Over the years, through complex forms of articulation in his novels, Dostoevsky gradually expresses the view that a willingness to trade in the suffering of children or other innocents lies at the basis of the Crucifixion. He eventually identifies this willingness as the essence of what he calls the "Jewish idea." The God of the Crucifixion finally becomes associated with a real Jewish authority figure, Benjamin Disraeli, orchestrating the sacrifice of innocents in the Balkans for the sake of peace and prosperity in Western Europe in the *Diary.*

Dostoevsky's discomfort with the Crucifixion clearly makes him a heretic, one whose views are at odds with the teachings of the Russian Orthodox or indeed any Christian church.[34] The subject of this book is not Christian theology or even measurement of Dostoevsky's divergence from official doctrine, but rather a meticulous reconstruction of Dostoevsky's own idiosyncratic understanding of the Crucifixion and how this unique perspective contributed to the development of his antisemitism. His heretical understanding of the Crucifixion, I will show, prompted Dostoevsky to affect a theological shift: he exonerates the Christian God-Father of what was to him an unforgivable trespass against morality, God's sacrifice of his child to benefit others, by transferring this guilt to the Jews. My reconstructive project leads to the conclusion that Dostoevsky's subjective experience of Christianity came to diverge sharply from Christian doctrine and, tragically, formed the basis of his mature antisemitism.

Dostoevsky's heretical understanding of the Crucifixion is the source of views that place him most definitively outside the teachings of any Christian church. It also places his lifelong struggle for faith in a new light. When scholars discuss Dostoevsky's quest for belief, they frequently identify the conflict between reason and faith as the primary source of his spiritual suffering. The fifth and final volume of Joseph Frank's biography of Dostoevsky, for example, approaches *The Brothers Karamazov* primarily as a fictional exposition of the dialogue between faith and reason the artist experienced in his own soul. There is another source of spiritual anxiety that is at least as important for understanding Dostoevsky's art, however. His doubts spring not only from the corrosive effects of reason but also from his increasingly heretical apprehension of the Crucifixion.

Why mature Dostoevsky, the artist of Christian humanism, develops an antisemitic obsession now becomes evident: his antisemitism emerges as his heretical ideas ripen. For much of his life, Dostoevsky paid little attention to the Jews. During the long stretch of time from 1846 (the year *Poor Folk* was published) through 1876 (the first year the *Diary* was issued as an independent monthly), he shows no interest in Jewish affairs. But he was always tormented by the problem of resurrection through Christ; it is no exaggeration to say that his life and writings are in fact haunted by the problem of redemption through Christ on the cross. As he awaited what would turn out to be his mock execution on Semenovsky Square in 1849, he apparently murmured, *"Nous serons avec le Christ"* ("We will be with Christ"), to which the radical atheist Nikolai Speshnev, likewise awaiting the firing squad, replied, *"Un peu de poussiere"* ("a bit of dust"). The "burden of Speshnev's words," Jones notes, the possibility of death as annihilation rather than resurrection, "refused thereafter to go away."[35]

Through close analysis of Dostoevsky's novels and the *Diary of a Writer,* I show that he suffered from profound discomfort with the Crucifixion as a vehicle of redemption. The Crucifixion provokes Dostoevsky through what he perceives to be its combination of Christ's voluntary self-sacrifice and the pathos of a child victim sacrificed by his father. As Dostoevsky's heretical notions mature, Christ's willing self-sacrifice is gradually eclipsed, and the role played by God the Father in the Crucifixion becomes increasingly sinister.

Over the years, Dostoevsky comes to the never explicitly stated belief that the God of the Crucifixion is a bad Jewish utilitarian whose presence within Christianity is intolerable. Either God must be expelled from Christianity, which then becomes heretically focused on Christ the Son, or some way must be found to cleanse God of the qualities Dostoevsky abhors, by projecting them onto someone else. At times, Dostoevsky pursues both tactics. He heretically reduces Christianity to love of Christ alone, and he invents the Jews as the embodiment of those qualities he perceives but cannot tolerate in Christ's father.[36] Dostoevsky gradually excludes a perceived willingness to sacrifice children or innocents from Christianity and projects it onto the Jews.

The child Christ held in his mother's arms in Raphael's *Madonna and Child*, the painting Dostoevsky loved so much that he placed it above his writing desk; the son who goes to the garden of Gethsemane to find out what his father has planned for him and who asks if the cup of suffering can pass from his lips; the baby Jesus of so much Russian and Western devotional art—adoration of this child Christ is at the center of Dostoevsky's spirituality. Dostoevsky finds God the Father's willingness to subject this child to so much suffering—to sacrifice him for the benefit of others—difficult to bear and difficult to tolerate within Christianity.

"The works of Dostoevsky," Thompson has observed, "comprise the greatest body of representations of Christ in modern fiction."[37] I explicate an aspect of how Christ is conceived in Dostoevsky's writings that remains unexplored: as the child victim of a bad father and a bad Jew. "O yes, he gave his son," the Grand Inquisitor complains about the God of the Crucifixion in Dostoevsky's notes for *The Brothers Karamazov*, "that is an argument of terrible power, an eternal argument, a terrible argument" (*Pss*, 15:230). The opinions of the Grand Inquisitor don't necessarily belong to Dostoevsky, but Dostoevsky frequently allows even his most problematic characters to express views close to his own. The relationship between Dostoevsky and the Grand Inquisitor is much more intimate in the author's notebooks, where this quotation occurs, than in the final novel; in the notebooks for *The Brothers Karamazov*, the Grand Inquisitor voices a number of concerns that Dostoevsky clearly shared. The bitterness about the child-sacrificer God of the Crucifixion expressed by the Grand Inquisitor was not foreign to Dostoevsky.

Persistent ambivalence about the Crucifixion leads Dostoevsky to search for alternative means of salvation. In addition to projecting what he doesn't like about Christianity onto the Jews, he makes those aspects of the Crucifixion he *can* affirm into what he calls the "Russian idea." For Dostoevsky, the Crucifixion is not just the sacrifice of a son by a father who claims the right to kill on the grounds that he transcends individual morality and is doing it to benefit humanity; it is also a transcendent act of self-sacrifice. Disentangling Christ's self-sacrifice from God's sacrifice of his son—distinguishing between what Dostoevsky comes to perceive as giving oneself and trafficking in others—becomes a primary concern for the characters of Dostoevsky's novels and for Russia in his journalism.

Dostoevsky comes to the conclusion that we can't redeem ourselves by benefiting from God's sacrifice of his son, but rather we have to become like Christ by performing our own self-sacrificial feats. I trace the evolutionary process by which Dostoevsky gradually defines Christianity as consisting exclusively of *imitatio Christi,* specifically the reenactment of Christ's self-sacrifice. "The highest happiness," Dostoevsky writes in his notebooks in April 1864, while the corpse of his first wife lay on the table, is to "destroy this *I,* wholly give it up to each and all absolutely and selflessly. . . . This is the paradise of Christ. All of history and humanity is simply the development, struggle, striving and achievement of this ideal" (*Pss,* 20:172). This conviction is presented to the public in *Winter Notes on Summer Impressions* and the *Diary.* In *Winter Notes,* Dostoevsky asserts that the capacity for self-sacrifice represents the height of personal development. "To voluntarily lay down one's life for the sake of all, to go to the cross or to the stake for the sake of all, can be done only in the light of the strongest development of the personality."[38]

There are compelling reasons why any discussion of the relationship between Dostoevsky's faith and antisemitism must pay close attention to the *Diary of a Writer.* It stands in direct relationship to his final novel: the *Diary* can be read as a semiautobiographical companion to *The Brothers Karamazov.* It occupies an unusual place in his thinking about salvation as well, serving as one of Dostoevsky's most compelling stories of the struggle for redemption. A collection of fiction, historical and cultural essays, and political commentary, the *Diary* was published as a column in the conservative journal the *Citizen* over the course of 1873 and then as an independent monthly in 1876 and 1877. Dostoevsky interrupted publication to write *The Brothers Karamazov;* one special issue, a reprint of and commentary about Dostoevsky's Pushkin Speech, appeared in August 1880. He resumed the *Diary* in 1881; the January issue appeared several days after his death. He intended to publish the *Diary* as a book, as it is now available.[39]

Dostoevsky adopts a unique relationship to his *Diary* readers and claims to speak in a personal voice. He offered the *Diary* as a responsive guide to contemporary life, addressing topics of national concern each month, and as a conversation with his readers, a dialogue in which he occasionally claims to step out from behind his fictional narrators and speak in his own voice. In December 1877, he announced that he would be suspending publication of the *Diary* in order to devote himself to the novel that became *The Brothers Karamazov.* The public clamored for him to continue publishing the *Diary.* "Perhaps I shall venture to put out one issue and speak

with my readers once more," he writes in response to the public outcry; "I
have been putting out my little periodical for myself as much as for others,
after all, from a compelling need to express myself in our curious and most
peculiar age."[40] "To those who wrote to tell me that I am abandoning my
publication at a most exciting time," he continues, "I would reply that a year
from now there may ensue a time that may be even more exciting and more
distinctive, and then we shall serve the good cause together once more. I
write together, because I plainly regard my many correspondents as my coworkers" (*WD*, December 1877, 1264).

The boundaries between *The Diary of a Writer* and *The Brothers
Karamazov* were blurry for Dostoevsky; they evolved together in his creative imagination. "In this year of rest from the *deadlines* of publication," he
explains in December 1877, "I truly intend to devote all my time to a literary work that has imperceptibly and involuntarily been taking shape within
me over these two years of publishing the *Diary*" (*WD*, December 1877,
1264).[41] His biographer Konstantin Mochulsky discusses the *Diary* as a labo-
ratory for *The Brothers Karamazov*.[42] The boundaries between the *Diary*
and *The Brothers Karamazov* were blurry for Dostoevsky's original readers
as well; Dostoevsky encouraged them to perceive intimate connections linking the two works.[43] The novel and journal, so intertwined with each other
in their genesis and original reception, can be legitimately approached as a
kind of superwork.

The *Diary* associates Orthodox Russia with the redemptive imitation
of Christ's self-sacrifice. Locating the essence of Russia and Christianity in
the concept of self-sacrifice is something that can be found during various
periods of Dostoevsky's work. He frequently insists that Christianity and the
Russian idea permit only the shedding of one's own blood, not that of others.
We witness him working out the distinction between sacrificing the self or
others over many years in his notebooks. His notes for the 1881 *Diary* assert an essential difference between giving one's own life and shedding the
blood of others. "Blood. 'Only that is strong, where blood flows.' Only the
scoundrels have forgotten that strength is only with those whose blood flows,
not with those who shed blood. There it is—the law of blood on earth" (*Pss*,
27:46). Russia, he writes in the *Diary*, spearheads a "union" founded in the
"regeneration of people through the true principles of Christ," the principles
of self-sacrifice and service (*WD*, June 1876, 530).

The Russian people, Dostoevsky argues in the *Diary*, offer the world
a pure gift, one untainted by the elements of child sacrifice, utilitarian exchange logic, or trespass against individual morality that he fears contami-
nate the Crucifixion. Dostoevsky specifies that the Russian understanding of Christianity is Christ-centered and manifests itself in self-sacrificial
service.[44] "In Russian Christianity—real Russian Christianity—there is not

12

even a trace of mysticism; there is only love for humanity and the image of Christ; those are its essentials, at least," Dostoevsky argues in the *Diary* (*WD*, September 1876, 631).

Dostoevsky does at least two heretical things in the *Diary*: he focuses on Christ to the exclusion of God; and by the end of his life he has begun to marginalize Christ as well, even the Christ of independent, self-willed self-sacrifice. In the *Diary*, Dostoevsky begins to associate free, voluntary self-giving with the Russian people even more than with Christ. They begin to emerge as a vehicle of salvation in their own right and threaten to eclipse Christ as an object of veneration.[45]

From the standpoint of the official church, of course, there is little left of Christianity if one rejects the Crucifixion or tries to replace it with something else. Yet Dostoevsky had an uncanny ability to believe that he was upholding Christianity even as he undermined it, as scholars such as Valentina Vetlovskaia have pointed out. "Dostoevsky was never a proponent of traditional Christianity," Vetlovskaia asserts; he "was traveling his own paths, far from traditional Christianity."[46] Dostoevsky simply refused to perceive his heretical divergence from Christian theology and equated his own views with true doctrine, "naming them Christian and sincerely believing that they in fact represented Christianity."[47] He maintained allegiance to what he believed was the essence of Christianity—the principle of self-sacrifice—which to him was more fundamental to the spirit of Christianity than the Crucifixion.

Belief in a human capacity for self-sacrifice is one of Dostoevsky's most cherished ideas; he advances it as his own in works like *Winter Notes* and the *Diary* and turns to it for comfort at moments of grief, as at Maria Dmitrievna's death. This idea, so precious to Dostoevsky, the essence of his Russian Christian idea, is also one that he ascribes to ambiguous characters such as Raskolnikov, Stavrogin, and Ivan Karamazov in their early stages of development in his notebooks. Nikolai Stavrogin, the antihero of *Demons* and one of Dostoevsky's most enigmatic and disturbing creations, begins as a mouthpiece for some of the author's most cherished beliefs. "The morality of Christ in two words," the character evolving into Stavrogin says in Dostoevsky's notes for *Demons*: "it's the idea that the happiness of the individual is the free and intentional renunciation of the self, if only it would be better for others" (*Pss*, 11:193).

Stavrogin, the apotheosis of will who eventually takes his own life, echoes words Dostoevsky had put forth as his own for readers in 1863 in *Winter Notes*. There Dostoevsky had declared, "Sacrifice of the self for the sake of all is, in my opinion, a sign of the very highest development of personality, of the very height of its power, the highest form of self-mastery, the greatest freedom of one's own will" (*WN*, 49). Characters such as

Raskolnikov, Ivan, and Stavrogin, who become Dostoevsky's most famous rebels against God, begin in his notes and thoughts as those to whom he gives his most precious beliefs and intimate fears.

The final forms they assume in Dostoevsky's novels are quite different from how they are initially conceived in his notebooks, but these characters still betray their genetic connection to Dostoevsky: they struggle with the same problems of resurrection and distinguishing between self- and other-sacrifice, between appropriate and inappropriate vehicles of redemption, that preoccupy their creator. Dostoevsky allows these characters to explore various objections to Christian faith, and in the process reveals profound sympathy with their objections.[48] The anxieties and questions these characters experience lead nowhere good for them; for Dostoevsky, they lead ultimately to antisemitism.

The many connections linking the most compelling characters of Dostoevsky's novels with what eventually becomes the Russian Christian idea he articulates in the *Diary* warrant further study. Examining the dialogue he creates among his novels and essays reveals that Dostoevsky's most problematic characters—his spiritual rebels—express some of his most intimate concerns about Christianity. "My *hosanna* has passed through a great *furnace of doubt,* as the devil says in my novel," the quotation from Dostoevsky's 1880 notes continues. Dostoevsky speaks with the devil—or the devil speaks for Dostoevsky—in complex ways. The perception that "Dostoevsky rather too frequently gave all the best lines to the devil" gains new significance when we study his rebellious characters together with the character of Christian Russia in the *Diary.*[49]

Portraying the Russian people as a vehicle of salvation, an alternative to the Crucifixion, is a goal that runs through Dostoevsky's writings but is never fully realized until the *Diary.* Some of the most important stations or episodes on the way to the articulation of the Russian idea in the *Diary* involve Dostoevsky's spiritual rebels. Over the years, Dostoevsky gradually came to believe in the messiahship of the Russian people. Some of the earliest expressions of this view are voiced by Myshkin and Stavrogin. The world may experience "resurrection by Russian thought alone, by the Russian God and Christ" Myshkin proclaims.[50] "Through this people all humanity will be saved, and the final idea will be brought into the world, and the kingdom of heaven," the Prince, as Stavrogin is originally known, proclaims about the Russian people in the notes for *Demons* (*Pss,* 11:132).[51]

Along with the figure evolving into Shatov, Stavrogin/the Prince repeatedly questions whether faith is possible. "The question now is: who can believe?"; "Is it possible to believe?" Stavrogin/the Prince demands (*Pss,* 11:178). "The question is, is it possible to believe in Orthodoxy?" he asks together with Shatov (*Pss,* 11:177). "What is to be done?" Shatov inquires, to which the Prince replies, "It's necessary to accomplish a great feat [*Nado sdelat' velikii podvig*]" (*Pss*, 11:177).

Inventing the Russian and Jewish ideas is Dostoevsky's great feat. "The desire for a noble feat [*zhazhda podviga*]," he writes in his 1876–77 notebooks; "They ask what Christianity is—that's what it is." The possibility of faith, of redemption from tormenting doubt to serenity and certitude, comes to depend on distinguishing Russians from Jews, Christ from his father, and bypassing the Crucifixion on the way to salvation. In his progression toward this feat—articulating the difference between the Russian and Jewish ideas—Dostoevsky is greatly assisted by his spiritually ambiguous characters, figures such as Raskolnikov, Stavrogin, and Ivan Karamazov.

Clarifying the nature of Dostoevsky's mature antisemitism, especially as it gains expression in the *Diary*, can shed new light on his earlier works. Mature Dostoevsky insists on the importance of maintaining a strict distinction between Russians and Jews. His preoccupation with this distinction originates in concerns that are present in his earliest writings. There is no antisemitism in Dostoevsky's early works, but there are concerns about Christianity that eventually contribute to the development of his Jew hating, and there are elements of what he will later call "the Jewish idea." The negative qualities Dostoevsky eventually ascribes to the Jews can be discerned in his earliest writings, where they preoccupy him and produce extreme discomfort but are not yet "Jewish." On the contrary, the qualities later Dostoevsky will condemn as "Jewish" are frequently shown to be features of Christian characters in his early works.

The Russian and Jewish ideas oppose each other in the *Diary* as universality and particularity, self-sacrificial service and the exploitation of others. "The national Russian idea," Dostoevsky writes in the *Diary*, is "the unity of all humanity" (*WD*, January 1877, 830). Russians long for "*worldwide union in the name of Christ*" and "service to the whole of mankind" (*WD*, January 1881, 1351; June 1876, 524). Russian desire for brotherly unity is opposed by the Jews, however; "the Jew preserves all of his distinctiveness" and is characterized by "alienation and estrangement on the level of religious dogma; no intermingling" (*WD*, March 1877, 913, 910).

Russians exhibit "selfless love for their unfortunate and oppressed brethren," and their guiding idea is "the notion of sacrifice" (*WD*, July/August 1876, 597, 598). "Russia's whole power," he argues, "and her whole future mission lie in her self-denying unselfishness" (*WD*, June 1876, 525). The Russian dedicates himself to the defense of the world's weak and oppressed, whereas the Jew obeys the command to "destroy the others or enslave or exploit them" (*WD*, March 1877, 910). The Jewish "spirit is imbued precisely with this merciless attitude toward everyone who is not a Jew, this disrespect for every tribe and for every human creature who is not a Jew," Dostoevsky complains (*WD*, March 1877, 913).

"What if it weren't the Jews who numbered three million in Russia but the Russians, and what if there were eighty million Jews?" Dostoevsky asks *Diary* readers.

> Now how would they transform the Russians, and how would they treat them? . . . Would they not turn them directly into slaves? Even worse: would they not strip them utterly bare? Would they not massacre them altogether, exterminate them completely, as they did more than once with alien peoples in times of old in their ancient history? (*WD*, March 1877, 909)

He answers these questions for readers, explaining that the Jews are already a global scourge. Over in America, he writes, the Jews "have already thrown themselves en masse onto the many liberated Negroes and have already got them in their clutches in their usual style via the well-known and eternal 'pursuit of gold'" (*WD*, March 1877, 906). He confides that he foresaw this scenario years ago, when the slaves were first liberated; back then he thought to himself, "Now the Negroes have been liberated from their slavery, they still won't come off unscathed because the Jews, who are so numerous in the world, will at once fling themselves on this fresh little victim" (*WD*, March 1877, 906).

The Jews confront Christian society with a problem, Dostoevsky claims. They are "armed with laws and principles entirely opposed to the idea by which the entire European world has developed until now" (*WD*, March 1877, 912). "The final word of humanity about this great tribe still remains to be said," he believes, for the question remains: "To what extent are they themselves capable of serving the new and beautiful cause of *genuine* brotherly unity with people who are alien to them by religion and blood?" (*WD*, March 1877, 910, 918). He implies that they are not. "The Christian idea of salvation only through the closest moral and brotherly union of people," he contends, is threatened as "the top level of Jews gains a stronger and surer hold over humanity and strives to mold the world to its image and essence" (*WD*, March 1877, 915). "Europe is everywhere on the eve of collapse, a general, terrible collapse," he warns (*WD*, 1880, 1319). The Jews control the stock exchanges and the credit, he contends, adding that "they are the ones who control the whole of international politics as well, and what will happen hereafter is, of course, known only to the Jews themselves; their reign, their complete reign, is drawing nigh!" (*WD*, March 1877, 914).

The challenge posed by Dostoevsky's Russian chauvinism and Jew hating has elicited a variety of responses from his readers. Two primary strategies for containing the significance of his antisemitism have evolved: apologetics and something that can be called "separation criticism"—the attempt to separate Dostoevsky's antisemitism from his art.

Dostoevsky's chauvinism and antisemitism are sometimes dismissed as the puzzling but essentially meaningless intrusion of a biographical enigma into literary texts. Murray Krieger's impatience with Myshkin's nationalist outbursts in *The Idiot* illustrates the urge to apologetic dismissal. Dostoevsky recklessly "lets himself go" with "Myshkin's momentary invective" in *The Idiot,* Krieger complains. "When Dostoevsky gets off on the problems of Roman Catholicism and of Russianness, he seems to lose all aesthetic presence and ventriloquizes freely. I cannot, then, take this passage seriously, as being more than an errant insertion in this book that is so full of them," he maintains.[52]

One of the most recent apologetic discussions of Dostoevsky's antisemitism is found in Cassedy's study of Dostoevsky's religion. "Lord knows," Cassedy concedes, "there's plenty of evidence in his nonfictional writings, not just his letters, to support the view he hated the Jews as a group."[53] Many of the references to Jews are "quite nasty," Cassedy acknowledges, "almost nasty enough to pass for the remarks of a *pogromchik.*"[54] After making these concessions, however, Cassedy cites two curious arguments against taking Dostoevsky's antisemitism seriously: some of Dostoevsky's remarks were made to powerful individuals whom he was trying to please, and he had some Jewish friends.

Referring to a letter Dostoevsky writes Konstantin Pobedonostsev, in which Dostoevsky deplores an alleged "Judaizing" of Germany, Cassedy writes, "We must take into account Dostoevsky's reader. Is there any possibility that Dostoevsky made these hateful remarks simply because he felt they would please his notoriously conservative friend?"[55] If someone made hateful remarks about African Americans in a letter to David Duke, would this context lessen their significance? This apologetic strategy is also undermined by the fact that Dostoevsky expressed vehemently antisemitic views in letters to unremarkable private citizens as well as to high-ranking officials such as Pobedonostsev.[56]

As for the argument that having some cordial personal relations with individuals from a minority group somehow inoculates one from prejudice, history refutes this argument so thoroughly that one is surprised to encounter it here. The apologetic tenor of Cassedy's discussion is neatly contained in an analysis of the *Diary* piece "The Funeral of a Universal Man." Here Cassedy points to Dostoevsky's occasional use of the word "Jew" instead of "Yid" as an exonerating factor: "Dostoevsky even uses the word *evrei* (the more polite word for Jew) throughout this entry."[57]

Other readers try to limit the significance of Dostoevsky's unpalatable views by pursuing separation criticism, claiming that the antisemitism is confined to his journalism. A strict line allegedly separates the belligerent antisemite of the essays from the Christian humanist of the novels. *Dostoevsky and the Christian Tradition,* for example, begins with the assertion that Dostoevsky the Christian can be appreciated separately from Dostoevsky the chauvinist. "Sympathy with Dostoevsky's Christian aspirations does not entail succumbing to his political and nationalist prejudices, to what Bakhtin called 'the small Dostoevsky,'" Pattison and Thompson assert.[58] The idea of two Dostoevskys has a long history; it was propagated by D. S. Merezhkovsky and David Zaslavsky, among others.[59]

This containment strategy concedes that antisemitism and chauvinism play significant roles in Dostoevsky's journalism but denies them importance for the novels. "Despite the anti-Semitic obsession raging throughout his journalistic works," Nathan Rosen asserts, "Dostoevsky the creative artist was not inspired by it in any of his great novels."[60] Jones advances the view that Dostoevsky's national messianism "seems to cast little light on what is original and insightful in Dostoevsky's major fiction and to have little in common with those qualities which have established him as a world-ranking author." Noting that "most non-academic admirers of Dostoevsky" have not found his ideas about Russian messianism interesting, Jones believes "there are good reasons why this is so":

> In the first place there is their strident, didactic, nationalist tone, at times tinged by anti-Semitism; in the second, they display no intellectual originality and, some would say, lack intellectual integrity. . . . One is irritated by tireless assertions of Russia's excellence, and by his bitter complaints that this excellence cannot be understood by Western Europeans.[61]

"The public Dostoevsky was a Christian," A. Boyce Gibson acknowledges, "and in his later years a Christian propagandist—but the artist calls it all in question."[62] Sergei Hackel argues that "Dostoevsky the journalist" attempted to "sidestep the complexity of his novelistic world" in his journalism, with the result that his nonfictional works are read today "more out of scholarly curiosity than in awe of a great writer, whose stature they tend to diminish."[63]

Trying to quarantine Dostoevsky's antisemitism behind a kind of cordon sanitaire is illegitimate, however.[64] He is one of those instructive figures who debunks what Vadim Rossman, in a recent study of antisemitism and the Russian intelligentsia, calls "the liberal myth of the incompatibility of anti-Semitism with true intelligence and high Russian moral standards."[65] The most serious flaw in this belief that art is incompatible with certain ideologies, Gary Saul Morson points out, is that it is simply untrue.[66] Dostoevsky's prejudice and artistry develop in tandem: the development of his antisemitism and Russian messianism coincides with the arc of his creative talent. "I hate Europe," he writes to his niece Sofia Ivanova from Dresden in 1871, on the threshold of his most productive decade. "If only you knew what mortal loathing, to the point of hatred, Europe has aroused in me these four years" (*Pss*, 29.1:161).

Examining the relationship between what seems to be lowest and highest in Dostoevsky's writings—his prejudices and the heights of religious and philosophical questioning to which he soars—leads to the conclusion that they are intimately connected. Antisemitic Russian messianism grows in importance to become an essential element of Dostoevsky's heretical Christian faith; the artist, Christian heretic, and antisemite become linked. By entertaining the possibility that his art and animus are interconnected, this study yields new readings of his novels, gains new appreciation of the Christian experience as embodied in one of the world's greatest artists, and traces the emergence of antisemitism from Dostoevsky's Christian anxieties.

PART I

"I Am Not an Expert at Lulling to Sleep":

The Struggle Between Faith and Doubt

in Dostoevsky's Writings

DOSTOEVSKY'S AMBIVALENCE about salvation through the Crucifixion had several consequences. It decreed that his spiritual life would be one of constant oscillation between doubt and affirmation; it affected his reception by his contemporaries; and it shaped the plots of his writings, both his novels and his journalism. Preoccupation with the problem of resurrection runs throughout Dostoevsky's life and work. Longing for salvation drives the life stories of Dostoevsky himself and his primary characters, who undertake impassioned quests to discover the potential bases of transformation, the catalysts that could enable individuals and whole communities to overcome sin and begin anew. What T. A. Kasatkina writes about *Crime and Punishment* probably applies to Dostoevsky's entire output: like *Crime and Punishment,* Dostoevsky's essays and novels alike are "about resurrection, about how resurrection takes place and the circumstances under which it is impossible."[1]

At times, Dostoevsky seems to triumph over his doubts and conveys a sense of certainty. He can be emphatic about the absolute, exclusive truth of Christianity. To the anonymous mother of an eight-year-old boy who writes him in 1878 seeking advice about child rearing, he advises:

Acquaint him with the Gospels, teach him to believe in God strictly according to the law. This is a sine qua non, otherwise he won't be a good person, but will at the very best turn into a sufferer, or in the bad case into an indifferent fat man [*zhirnyi chelovek*], and even worse. You won't think of anything better than Christ, believe it. (*Pss,* 30.1:17)

Readers responded to this confidence Dostoevsky could project. Many turned to him as someone who could restore faith, and we witness Dostoevsky enthusiastically playing this role in his letters. "You see before you a sick soul, who has found a confessor," writes the painter E. F. Iunge, daughter of Dostoevsky's friend and court lady-in-waiting A. I. Tolstaia (*Pss,* 30.1:329). Iunge exemplifies a significant category of Dostoevsky's contemporary readers, for whom he was a kind of iconic representative of faith. "As long as there is at least one man, with convictions, believing, loving, not an egoist—what a great consolation that is in difficult moments," she writes her mother of Dostoevsky (*Pss,* 30.1:330).

"You write that they have destroyed your faith in Christ," Dostoevsky responds to an anonymous young woman who writes him in spiritual despair. "But why didn't you first of all ask yourself: who are these people who reject Christ as Savior?" I'm not saying they are bad people, he explains, just appallingly ignorant about things they presume to judge, arrogant, and flighty. "You are not the first to lose faith," he says, and enigmatically assures her: "I know many negators who in the end turned with their whole being to Christ" (*Pss,* 30.1:140).

Yet the same man who writes so reassuringly about negators eventually embracing Christ also betrays an ambivalent attitude toward the possession of faith. When corresponding with readers such as Konstantin Pobedonostsev and Nikolai Liubimov, he worries that he has not made Father Zosima, his representative of Christianity, convincing enough; but when other readers believe he has portrayed faith successfully, he objects. Pobedonostsev was disturbed by the "power and energy" of Ivan Karamazov's "atheistic positions." He complains to Dostoevsky, "An answer" to Ivan's challenge "hasn't yet appeared, but . . . is necessary." After reading the critique of God's world put forth by Ivan and the Grand Inquisitor, Pobedonostsev writes Dostoevsky in August 1879: "Your 'Grand Inquisitor' made a strong impression on me. I haven't read much else that is so powerful. But I waited—from where will there be a rebuff, objection and clarification—and it hasn't come yet" (*Pss,* 15:491).

The refutation, Dostoevsky assures him, will come "as the last words of the dying elder," Zosima's homily of faith and acceptance of God's creation, seeming injustice and all. Liubimov, who edited *The Brothers Karamazov* for publication in the *Russian Messenger,* proofread and critiqued each installment. Like Pobedonostsev, he frequently objected to the vigor of the novel's critique of God and expressed his concerns to Dostoevsky. "It is for this theme," the affirmation of faith, Dostoevsky assures him, "that the entire novel is being written" (June 1879, *Pss,* 30.1:68).

Despite such assurances to readers like Pobedonostsev and Liubimov, however, Dostoevsky knew that the primary quality of his spiritual life was struggle or conflict. When other readers reported that they found stable faith portrayed in his art, Dostoevsky objected. Some of the first readers of *The Brothers Karamazov* accused him of presenting simplistic portraits of secure believers in figures such as Father Zosima and Alyosha Karamazov. He responds to their objections by emphasizing his doubts and the strength of the case against God he makes through Ivan Karamazov and the Grand Inquisitor. "The scoundrels tease about my *uneducated* and retrograde belief in God," he complains. "These blockheads can't imagine such a powerful denial of God as the one put in the Grand Inquisitor and the preceding chapter. . . . Their stupid nature can't even imagine such a powerful negation as what I passed through," he boasts (1880–81 notebooks, *Pss*, 27:48).

Dostoevsky took special pride in his love for Christ alone, even a Christ outside of the truth. The strength of his doubts and his special access to the spirit of atheism played a similar role in his spiritual life—like love of Christ, they too were points of jealous pride and identity for Dostoevsky. The novelist and former schoolteacher L. A. Ozhigina carried on a brief correspondence with Dostoevsky; her letters are no longer extant, but we have one of his. In a curious exchange, she apparently accords him the power to instill faith, but he rejects this ascription. "You think I'm one of those people who save hearts, settle souls, drive away grief?" Dostoevsky asks her. "Many people write me this—but I know for certain that I am more capable of instilling disillusionment and disgust. I am not an expert at lulling to sleep, although I've tried it sometimes. But some creatures simply need to be lulled" (February 1878, *Pss*, 30.1:9).

In mature works like "The Peasant Marey" (published in the February 1876 *Diary*), Dostoevsky composes a spiritual biography for himself according to which he experienced a decisive spiritual transformation while in prison in the early 1850s. His writings from the period immediately after his release from prison, however, contradict the narrative Dostoevsky composed for himself decades later. Instead of the conclusive conversion to popular Christianity Dostoevsky later claimed to have experienced, we find an existence characterized by ongoing struggle and illness, apparently spiritual as well as physical. In the famous 1854 letter to Fonvizina that declares his allegiance to Christ, post–prison camp Dostoevsky also confesses to being in a state of anticipation.

> I am in some kind of expectation of something; it is as though I am still sick now, and it seems to me that soon, very soon something decisive must happen, that I am approaching a crisis in my life, that I seem to have ripened for something and that there will be something, maybe quiet and clear, maybe terrible [*groznoe*], but in any case inevitable. But perhaps all this is my sickly deliriums [*bol'nye bredni*]! (*Pss*, 28.1:177)

Confessions like these seriously undermine Dostoevsky's later claim to have undergone a decisive conversion experience in prison.

To the end of his life, Dostoevsky embraced what he calls "duality." "You write about your duality [*dvoistvennost'*]," he replies to Iunge. "This is why you are dear to me, because exactly the same thing as this *split* [*razdvoenie*] in you exists in me as well, and has been in me all my life. It is a great torment [*muka*], but at the same time a great pleasure [*naslazhdenie.*]" He recommends faith in Christ as a solution—though not a completely effective one—to this duality, and he tellingly confesses the necessity of accepting the desire to believe as a substitute for belief itself. "Do you believe in Christ and his promises?" he asks Iunge. "If you believe (or very much want to believe), then give yourself to him completely, and the torments from this duality will be greatly softened, and you will receive a spiritual solution [*iskhod dushevnyi*], and that is the most important thing" (*Pss*, 30.1:147).

Many of Dostoevsky's original Russian readers identified irresolvable spiritual tension as the defining feature of his art. Unlike Iunge, these readers perceived a permanent oscillation between faith and doubt at the core of Dostoevsky's work. Writing in the *Literary Journal*, Dostoevsky's contemporary V. K. Petersen claims to discern a "constant fight" in Dostoevsky's soul (*Pss*, 15:508). Dostoevsky, Petersen writes, is "an extremely interesting type of man who believes in spite of the most despairing doubts," someone "eternally doubting and daring to look deeply into the abyss of negation" (*Pss*, 15:508–9).

Other early Russian readers suspect that if Dostoevsky's writings do contain any resolution to the problem of faith, it is in favor of doubt. E. F. Tiutcheva, daughter of the poet Tiutchev and a lady-in-waiting for the imperial family, believed that Dostoevsky's words were remarkably effective at communicating objections to religion but inadequate to the task of restoring faith. "Dostoevsky took on a too difficult task," she maintains. "Expose the sore, put it on display—that can be done, but who will heal it?" she asks Pobedonostsev (October 1879, *Pss*, 15:495). Not a writer like Dostoevsky, she answers: "The dark spirit of temptation and high-handed doubt isn't banished with words [*slovopreniiami*], but with prayer and fasting" (*Pss*, 15:495). Another contemporary, the Slavophile I. V. Pavlov, agrees with Tiutcheva's conclusion. The "stench of the abysmal fall" is portrayed in *The Brothers Karamazov* "with stunning, troubling clarity," whereas Christian ideals "come out dim and pale" in comparison, Pavlov fears (*Pss*, 15:499).

Dostoevsky was well aware that his novel could be interpreted as a victory for Ivan. "Until the end of the novel," he concedes, "it is possible to understand these ideas and positions incorrectly" (i.e., as a victory for Ivan). "And just as I feared, that's what happened," he writes, regarding the reactions of Liubimov and Mikhail Katkov, the conservative editor of the *Russian Messenger* (*Pss*, 30.1:70). Regarding Zosima's homily, he admits, "I tremble for it in this sense: will it be a sufficient answer. All the more because it's not a direct answer to the positions previously expressed (in the Grand Inquisitor and before), to the specific points, but only oblique."[2]

Many of Dostoevsky's readers, including some of the most prominent, do in fact believe that Ivan's rebellion overshadows Zosima's faith. The editors of Dostoevsky's collected works, for example, write, "In spite of

Pobedonostsev's desires and the subjective intentions of Dostoevsky himself," nonetheless "a certain unstable equilibrium between *pro et contra* is constructed" (*Pss,* 15:492). "As far as the reader is concerned," they contend, "the ideas and aesthetic effect created on him by the rebellious chapters were so powerful that they not infrequently unquestionably overshadowed the impression created by Zosima's homily."[3]

Far from enjoying newfound faith, the man who emerged from Siberian prison was tormented by the difficulty of regeneration. Shortly after being released, Dostoevsky writes in the 1854 letter to Fonvizina, "The most unbearable misfortune is when you yourself become unjust, evil, foul; you recognize all this, you reproach yourself—but you cannot master yourself. I experienced this" (*Pss,* 28.1:177). His notebooks from 1864 express similar frustration. "The tragedy of the underground," Dostoevsky confides in his notebooks, consists of "the consciousness of something better and the impossibility of achieving that something." "What is there to support those who wish to reform themselves?" he asks. "Consolation, faith? There is consolation from no one, faith in no one!" (*Pss,* 16:329).

Salvation is difficult for the characters of Dostoevsky's novels. The underground man fails to escape from his mouse hole through the hope held out by Liza's love; Raskolnikov's moral rebirth seems unconvincing to many readers; Myshkin reverts to idiocy; Ivan Karamazov seems to succumb to madness and a possibly fatal illness; the direction of Dmitry Karamazov's spiritual development is in question at the end of the novel. Death by suicide or murder, or perdition through emigration and conversion to Catholicism befall major characters of *Crime and Punishment, The Idiot, Demons,* and *The Brothers Karamazov.*[4]

Dostoevsky's novels betray contradictory impulses; they seem fissured by tension between the urge to portray the attainment of Christian faith— salvation from sin into new life—and the ambiguity of what actually gets represented. *Crime and Punishment,* to take one of the novels as an example, clearly wants to be the story of Raskolnikov's resurrection. When the novel begins, Raskolnikov is trapped in his coffinlike garret, seeking a way out. "He did not know what to do with himself to escape from his wretchedness," we are told. "He longed to forget himself all together, to forget everything, and then to wake up and begin life anew."[5] The epilogue asserts that Raskolnikov rises to a new life on the banks of a Siberian river with Sonia at his side, but many find his alleged resurrection unconvincing. The conclusion seems "implausible" to many readers, Philip Rahv writes.[6] Joseph Frank likewise faults the attempt to portray Raskolnikov's regeneration as a failure. Raskolnikov's "adoption of a new set of values," he writes, "is brushed in too rapidly and too perfunctorily to be really successful."[7]

Robin Feuer Miller analyzes "a quintessentially Dostoevskian development" shaping the evolution of *The Idiot* from notes to final publication, a development that reveals the depth of Dostoevsky's fears about the difficulty of regeneration. Dostoevsky's starting point when he sets out to write the novel, Miller explains, is the "conviction that true goodness arises out of the abyss of human evil and suffering." Yet he seems incapable of portraying a spiritual reversal from sin to salvation: "In the novel, however, no character undergoes such a far-reaching development."[8] The early plans for action are "linear ones—where development and permanent changes in the characters occur—whereas the overall shape of the novel itself, in contrast to the notes, is a zigzag or a circle."[9]

The problem of redemption becomes increasingly acute in Dostoevsky's writings after *Crime and Punishment* and *The Idiot*. Raskolnikov's ambiguous ending, Frank writes,

> would be a story that to preoccupy Dostoevsky throughout the remainder of his creative life. For time and again we shall see him returning to the challenge of creating a regenerated Raskolnikov—of creating, that is, a highly educated and spiritually developed member of Russian society who conquers his egoism and undergoes a genuine conversion to a Christian morality of love.[10]

Like *Crime and Punishment*, Dostoevsky's other major novels can be read as failed (or at least unconvincing to many) redemption narratives. Characters such as Gorianchikov (the narrator of *Notes from the House of the Dead*), Raskolnikov, Myshkin and other characters from *The Idiot*, and Stavrogin long for moral resurrection, but many readers believe they never achieve it.

Frank identifies education, egoism, and high culture as primary obstacles to resurrection facing Dostoevsky's characters. There may be another, perhaps even more fundamental reason for this failure or difficulty, however: Dostoevsky's heretical ambivalence about the Crucifixion as a vehicle of redemption. Dostoevsky may be incapable of portraying a convincing resurrection in his novels because he cannot fully endorse the vehicle of redemption his fictional characters would have to use.

He would have to find a different kind of character—a community or corporate body rather than an individual—that could use a different vehicle of redemption. He succeeds at this in the *Diary*. The difficulty of redemption for the characters of Dostoevsky's novels can be contrasted to the relative ease with which salvation is achieved by the national community in Dostoevsky's essays. For characters in *The Idiot*, Miller writes, "One development is usually cancelled out in the next scene by a reverse oscillation; heroes and heroines do not really change—they vacillate"; but Russia follows a clear path to salvation in the *Diary*.[11] Pessimism about the possibility of rebirth for individuals in Dostoevsky's novels stands in sharp contrast to his journalism's optimism about immanent communal regeneration for Russia and Russians.

History is one of the foremost theaters of Dostoevsky's religious imagination, providing him with a stage for the drama of Christian redemption. He believed that the problem of redemption was at the center of historical processes. Dostoevsky praises Victor Hugo for propagating the idea of "*restoration* [*vosstanovlenie*]" as "the historical necessity of the nineteenth century."[12] Perhaps, Dostoevsky muses, this historically necessary restoration will "finally be fully embodied, whole, clearly and powerfully, in some great work of art" (*Pss*, 20:28). The narrative Dostoevsky weaves for Russia in *Time, Epoch,* and the *Diary* can be read as one of Dostoevsky's responses to this challenge.

In the *Diary* and essays such as the "Subscription Announcement for the Journal *Time* for 1861" and the "Series of Essays on Russian Literature" published in *Time,* Dostoevsky composes a plot for Russia that revolves around the same dilemmas faced by his novelistic characters. The *Diary* is a familiar Dostoevskian tale of the quest for moral resurrection in a fallen world, a tale in which Russia and Dostoevsky himself play complex heroes, struggling between rebellion against and submission to God in their attempts to reform themselves. The generically different redemption plots of his novels and essays exist in dialogue with each other, provoking, qualifying, and reflecting on each other.[13] If we read only his fictional narratives of individual spiritual biography, to the exclusion of the national-historical narratives in his journalism, we are left with a truncated appreciation of the range of Dostoevsky's artistry and ideas.

Understanding Dostoevsky as a Christian artist is difficult without considering the *Diary*; it is of central importance to the phenomenon of Dostoevsky as a spiritual mentor. Iunge writes to her mother in 1880 of the spiritual consolation the *Diary* provided, especially during the Balkan War. "He speaks so directly, so loudly about his faith with such burning words!" she enthuses; "I would like to go and say 'thank you'—thank you, that he thought and expressed things that were filling the soul and tormenting me" (*Pss*, 30.1:330).

The *Diary* is a key text in the struggle for faith that animates the novels as well. It distinguishes itself among Dostoevsky's works as the text in which this struggle becomes autobiographical, communal, and interactive, taking the spiritual dilemmas developing in the novels and making them Dostoevsky's, Russia's, and the reader's own. Our appreciation of the challenges faced by characters like Raskolnikov, Ippolit Terentiev, Stavrogin, and Ivan Karamazov is significantly enriched when we read their stories together with Russia's story in the *Diary*.

29

Overcoming sin and rising to new life, the intergeneric dialogue about redemption suggests, may be difficult as an individual, but easier for members of a messianic nation. Dostoevsky expresses millennial hopes in the *Diary.* "Something fateful, awesome, and—most importantly—near at hand is certainly looming over Europe," he tells readers (*WD,* September 1877, 1123). "The great Russian is only now beginning to live, only now rising up to utter his word, perhaps to the whole world" (*WD,* May 1873, 474). "So many problems will finally be solved . . . so many matters that were utterly insolvable, given the former course of events, will now be settled; the face of Europe will be so altered; so many new and progressive things will begin in human relationships, that, perhaps, there is no cause for spiritual anguish and excessive fear over this last convulsion of old Europe on the eve of its great and certain renewal" (*WD,* September 1877, 1125).

"Someone is knocking," Dostoevsky writes in the September 1877 issue of the *Diary,* "someone, a new man, with a new word, wants to open the door and come in" (*WD,* September 1877, 1127). "Who will come in?" he asks. "Will it be an entirely new man, or will it once more be someone like all of us, the old homunculi?" (*WD,* September 1877, 1126). A new Russian man is about to emerge, he assures his readers, for the nation is on the brink of a new life.

> Everyone senses that something decisive has begun, that there is somehow going to be a resolution of an issue from the past—a long, drawn-out issue from the past—and that a step is being taken toward something quite new, toward something that means a sharp break with the past, that will renew and resurrect the things of the past for a new life and . . . that it is Russia who is taking this step! (*WD,* April 1877, 929)

Redemption is easier for the nation than for individuals because Russia can save itself through an alternative vehicle of salvation, not the Crucifixion. Individuals in Dostoevsky's novels have two options: either they can accept salvation through Christ on the cross, which is dissatisfying because to Dostoevsky it means implicating oneself in moral quandaries, or they can rebel against the offer of salvation through Christ, which leads to madness and ruin for themselves and others. Russia, however, has a third option beyond moral compromise or the disasters consequent to the sin of rebellion. Russia can bypass the Crucifixion and yet maintain allegiance to Christ by performing its own act of self-sacrificial service to humanity.

Chapter Two

"He Gave His Son": The Problem of the
Crucifixion as Child Sacrifice in Dostoevsky

Oh yes, he gave his son, sent him himself to
be crucified . . . Oh, that is an argument of
terrible power, an eternal argument.
—Dostoevsky (*Pss*, 15:230)

INQUISITOR: What is happiness bought with?
What flood of blood, baseness, and bestiality,
impossible to bear? They don't speak about
that. O, the crucifixion—that is a terrible
argument.

INQUISITOR: God as a merchant. I love
humanity *more than you.*
—Dostoevsky (*Pss*, 15:230)

ONE HERETICAL PERSPECTIVE on Christianity
that can be discerned running throughout Dostoevsky's works is given con-
cise expression by the Grand Inquisitor, that complex figure who stands in
such enigmatic relationship to the author. The Grand Inquisitor's characterization of God as a merchant and the Crucifixion as a "terrible argument"
summarizes a view of Christianity that evolves over the years in Dostoevsky's
writings. Some of Dostoevsky's most important characters, including Russia
in the *Diary*, are called on to define their relationship to a merchant God
presiding over an economy of salvation in which child sacrifice circulates
between God and his adult customers as a kind of redemptive currency. The
Soviet critic V. V. Ermilov contends that *The Brothers Karamazov* reveals an
alleged "amorality" in Christianity; the novel, Ermilov argues, makes it appear that Christ has purchased the "right to torment children" because "he
redeemed all sins."[1] Pattison and Thompson dismiss Ermilov's contention as
a "distortion."[2] This certainly is a distortion of Christianity, but does it really
misrepresent the anxieties about Christianity that permeate Dostoevsky's
oeuvre? This is a question that cannot be so easily dismissed.

The existence of this salvational economy leads to several endings in

Dostoevsky's writings. How a character responds to the suffering of children, Robert Louis Jackson points out, is a moral litmus test. Ivan and Alyosha Karamazov display opposite reactions. The suffering of children acquires very different meaning in the plots of the two brothers, Jackson writes: "The suffering and death of a child . . . in both discourses inspires radically different conclusions on the part of the speakers."[3] Dostoevsky's positive characters—representatives of Christian faith such as Sonia Marmeladova, Tikhon, Alyosha Karamazov, and Zosima—accept child sacrifice as the ultimate price of their relationship to God. "It is through children that the soul is cured," Myshkin says (*I*, 90), and Christian faith is in fact often acquired in Dostoevsky's novels by accepting the suffering of children. Dostoevsky's first and last novels are built on dead children. Little Nelli, the self-sacrificing child martyr of *The Insulted and Injured,* and Ilyusha Snegirov, the pathetic dying child of *The Brothers Karamazov,* perish so that others may be reconciled and live.

Alyosha Karamazov embraces Ilyusha's sacramental death as the basis of a new community of boys that forms around him; Zosima's beatific faith, especially as propounded through his reading of Job, accepts the use of dead children as the basis of one's reconciliation with God (the nature of Zosima's faith will be the subject of detailed analysis in chapter 11). Spiritual resurrection takes place literally over the bodies of dead children such as Nelli and Ilyusha, or before the specter of dead children, as in *Crime and Punishment,* where Sonia's faith consists of accepting the possibility that her little siblings could die as a result of her acquiescence to the will of Providence.

Dostoevsky's creative biography is, among other things, a quest to make sense of Christianity as a religion of child sacrifice, a creed that thanks and praises its God for the performance of what would be abominable if committed by an individual. Over the course of his search for an ethical framework within which Nelli's reluctant self-sacrifice becomes comprehensible and justified—on the way from Nelli to Ilyusha—Dostoevsky portrays Christian faith in ways that reveal lasting, never-resolved ambivalence.

Ambivalence about reconciling oneself to the sacrificial death of children produces two other responses to the "terrible argument" of the Crucifixion. The rebellions of characters such as Raskolnikov, Ippolit Terentiev, Stavrogin, and Ivan Karamazov, I will show, are at least partly inspired by dissatisfaction with the merchant God and his traffic in innocents; so is Russia's Christian mission to the Balkans in the *Diary.* The *Diary's* vision of redemption as a gift, not a sacrificial exchange, given by the Russian people to the world, represents a successful resolution to the dilemma that proves insoluble for the characters of Dostoevsky's novels.

For Dostoevsky, real children are associated with Christ in complex ways; his love of Christ and love of children are closely intertwined. Children and Christ are at the center of his spirituality, as critics such as William Rowe remind us. "Dostoevsky preferred Christ even to the Truth and placed children closest to Christ," Rowe writes.[4] Because of the close connections linking Christ and children for Dostoevsky, examining his experiences of and ideas about real children can illuminate his experience of Christianity. It can also illuminate characters such as Raskolnikov, Stavrogin, and Ivan Karamazov in new ways. Like Dostoevsky himself, Jones reminds us, his "metaphysical nihilists are haunted by the image of Christ" and suffering children.[5]

The Christian, Dostoevsky believes, must protect children. "To Dostoevsky," Rosenshield writes, "there can be no greater crime than that committed against an innocent child. And thus our greatest responsibility before God is to protect children."[6] Dostoevsky upholds the rights of children against any authority, even the most sacred.[7] He welcomed the establishment of a Society for the Protection of Children and expressed outrage when an editorial in the *Warsaw Diary* criticized the principle of defending children as an infringement on the sacred authority of the family.

> I just read the article where the editors stand for the torture of children. They mock the idea of a society for the protection of children. Standing up for tortured children—to them that means destroying the family. What an absurdity! That family, where the parents smear a four-year-old girl with feces . . . is that family really something sacred [*razve sviatynia*], isn't it already destroyed? (*Pss,* 30.1:141)

In February 1880, he replied to a request that he read at a charity function: "I agree to read for the evening, as long as it is to benefit children" (*Pss,* 30.1:143).

The character evolving into Stavrogin in the notes for *Demons* tells Shatov that other ideologies, such as science, not only do not protect children, but even condone child abuse. "If scientific means, for example, turn out to be insufficient for feeding and life becomes crowded, then they will throw babies [*mladentsev*] into the outhouse or eat them," he tells Shatov; "it will certainly be so, especially if science says so" (*Pss,* 11:181). This early version of Stavrogin declares that Christianity distinguishes itself from other worldviews through its allegiance to children. "Giving yourself to Christianity, you will never reconcile yourself to the burning of infants [*mladentsev*]," the Prince declares (*Pss,* 11:181–82).

Dostoevsky in the *Diary* and some of his most compelling characters express the view that children enjoy special spiritual status. According to the *Diary* and Zosima, children are the guiltless pledge of the reality of goodness, the possibility of love, and the connection between humanity and the divine. Zosima tells the monks gathered around him to "love children especially, for they, too, are sinless, like angels, and live to bring us to tenderness and the purification of our hearts and as a sort of example for us" (*BK,* 319).

"We ought not to exalt ourselves above children," Dostoevsky admonishes *Diary* readers; "we are worse than they. And if we teach them something to make them better, then they also teach us much and also make us better by our very contact with them. They humanize our souls by their mere presence in our midst" (*WD*, January 1876, 379). Ivan maintains that children exist outside the adult community. "Children while they are quite little—up to seven, for instance—are so remote from grown-up people; they are different creatures, as it were, of a different species" (*BK*, 219).

Loving children is of paramount spiritual and even social/civic importance; children play a crucial mediatory role between human society and the divine. "How can we not love them?" Dostoevsky asks *Diary* readers.

> If we cease loving children, then whom will we be able to love thereafter, and what will become of us? Remember also that it was only for the children and their little golden heads that our Savior promised to shorten "the times and the seasons" for us. For their sake the torments of the regeneration of human society into a more perfect one will be shortened. (*WD*, July/August 1877, 1059–60)

Passages like this have inspired readers to comment on the remarkable role children play in Dostoevsky's spiritual vision. "It is precisely in the child, according to Dostoevsky, that there arises (and perhaps, on the contrary, comes undone?) an important kind of 'knot,' tying together the interrelations between God and mankind," Tikhomirov observes.[8]

In his private writings, Dostoevsky expresses the view that children elevate adults spiritually and provide meaning to life. "How good that you have them," he responds to his friend Anna Filosofova's July 1879 letter about her children, "they so humanize existence in the highest sense. Children are a torment [*Detki—muka*], but they are necessary, without them there is no goal in life" (*Pss*, 30.1:78). Having children is one of life's greatest consolations, he tells Anna Grigorevna at a difficult moment. "Don't be gloomy," he exhorts her; "there are some a thousand times worse off than us, and we can still be happy, at least because of the children" (*Pss*, 29.2:42).

There is also a disturbing dimension to the mediatory role children play, to the fact that souls are cured, as Myshkin puts it, through children. Zosima urges the monks gathered around him, "Take yourself up, and make yourself responsible for all the sins of men," but the role of suffering for the sins of others usually falls on children in Dostoevsky's writings (*BK*, 320). Children frequently function as sacrificial victims in his novels, where "the 'child-victim' is subjected, primarily as a passive sacrifice, to the adult world's cruelty and injustice," Rowe writes.[9]

The deep connection between suffering children and crucified Christ for Dostoevsky has been clear to his readers. His writings advance "the idea of the child as an earthly 'substitute' for Christ," Tikhomirov asserts.[10] Suffering children in Dostoevsky have been recognized as instantiations of the Passion. Rimvydas Silbajoris likens the children at Ilyusha's funeral to the apostles and says that this scene of child survivors united around their love for a dead child is Dostoevsky's final answer to Ivan's religious doubts. "The final passage in the novel can be understood as representing in symbolic terms the whole content of Dostoevsky's doctrine on children," Silbajoris writes. "The injured child Iljusha becomes the symbolic equivalent of the dead Christ, while Alyosha personifies the resurrection of Christ's living word of love."[11]

Dostoevsky's suffering children thus call on readers, Russia in the *Diary,* and Dostoevsky's characters to define their relationship to the use of children as a vehicle of redemption, to accept or reject the Crucifixion as a form of child sacrifice. For Ivan, Alyosha, and Dmitry Karamazov, as well as for Zosima, some readers believe, the possibility of Christian faith depends on how one reacts to suffering children. "All four characters stand transfixed before the spectacle of a suffering child," Miller writes; "for all four the possibility for religious faith is inextricably intertwined with the reality of such suffering."[12] Dostoevsky himself claimed that Ilyusha's death, and the boys' reconciliation with it, was the core of the novel. In April 1880, he writes Liubimov that Alyosha's speech at the little boy's funeral "reflects the meaning of the whole novel" (*Pss,* 15:446).

Dostoevsky's novels impress some readers with a guilt-free, even joyful acceptance of the use of dead children to benefit others. The twelve surviving schoolboys benefit from Ilyusha's death, Silbajoris writes; their memory of their dead friend provides them with "something to hold against the apparent meaninglessness of the universe. This fact exists *because* Iljusha suffered and died."[13] "The suffering of the child," Jackson writes of Ilyusha, "is ultimately a basis for union and harmony, both in an immediate and higher sense."[14] Rowe contends that "the function of Ilyusha's death is to end the novel on a note of hope."[15]

Viacheslav Ivanov believes that "the final section of *The Brothers Karamazov* contains such a sublime glorification of the heroic child-martyr that we are entirely consoled, and bless his obscure sacrifice as a source of immeasurable comfort."[16] "So long as the memory of Ilyusha remains alive in each of these children whom it has brought into a covenant together," Ivanov writes, "it will preserve each of them from despair and collapse."[17] Alyosha, Miller writes, founds a "living church"—the brotherhood of boys gathered around him—"cemented by the very mortar that Ivan had earlier so eloquently refused to accept—the unjustified suffering of a child." Alyosha "is the architect, the builder, of precisely such an edifice, to which we, he, and the boys do mutually consent." Despite "the sadness of events," Miller concludes, the novel is "hauntingly optimistic." The boys gathered around Alyosha "accept themselves and their brotherhood, though their edifice does stand upon a child's tears," and we, too, "accept the stone of the dead child."[18]

But is this significance of children—their status as sacrificial offerings that accomplish the redemption of others—really something that is portrayed so positively in Dostoevsky's novels? And is such an understanding of children even Christian? There must be countertendencies in the novels to have inspired reactions such as that of Albert Camus. Camus, who played the role of Ivan in a production of *The Brothers Karamazov* staged in Algiers in 1937, appropriates that character's rejection of the dead child as a cornerstone of faith. "Even on my death bed," Dr. R exclaims in *The Plague*, "I do not accept this world of God's, where they torture children."[19] Tikhomirov, for one, believes that understanding children this way—as substitutes for the sacrificial Christ of the Passion, who play a special mediatory role between humanity and God—represents a rebellious departure from Christian doctrine.

"A question arises," Tikhomirov writes: "what kind of *Biblical basis* is there for such a view of the child?"[20] Not only is there no biblical basis for this view, Tikhomirov replies, but Dostoevsky has even accomplished a kind of "contamination" of Orthodox doctrine and scriptural sources. Regarding Zosima's contention that children are sinless like angels, Tikhomirov observes, "Such a view of the child stands in a certain defiance of the Orthodox representation of human nature in its condition after Original Sin."[21] In his attempt to persuade Sonia to reject God, Raskolnikov points to the fact that Petersburg's children are violated morally and physically. Acknowledge what happens to children here in Petersburg, Raskolnikov demands of her: "Children can't remain children. There are seven-year-old perverts and thieves. But children are the image of Christ: 'Theirs is the kingdom of God'" (*CP*, 307). This passage contains a "significant . . . alteration of the quotation from the Gospels," Tikhomirov points out. The Gospels say "of such" is the kingdom of God, indicating a much broader category of inheritors, not "theirs" (i.e., exclusively children). "But above all, what merits attention is the highly unusual view of the child as . . . an *icon* of Christ; 'But children are the image of Christ.' There is nothing close to this in the cited Gospel story of 'Christ's encounter with the children,'" Tikhomirov points out. "Apparently here Dostoevsky (and his hero) are giving an original interpretation," Tikhomirov concludes.[22]

When it comes to the treatment of children, Tikhomirov believes, Dostoevsky is prepared to scrutinize God himself:

In his "eschatological scenario," Dostoevsky endows *children* with exceptional significance. The most agonizing, but salvational "regeneration of human society into a more perfect one," the very character of the transition from the time of "great sorrows" to the millennial kingdom of Christ is, in the view of the writer, conditional upon *attitudes to children.* Whose attitude? That, it seems, both of adult humanity and the God of Providence.[23]

His profound love of children and conviction that they play a unique role in humanity's redemption narrative embolden Dostoevsky to place the attitudes of God himself under examination.

Concern with children and the desire to write about them form the basis of Dostoevsky's major novels. *Crime and Punishment* began as a novel about families and children. In June 1865, he writes to A. A. Kraevsky, editor of *Notes of Fatherland,* offering him a new work and requesting an advance. "My novel is called *The Drunkards,*" he writes, "and will deal primarily with the present problem of alcoholism. It will not only expose the question but present it in all its branches, particularly the depiction of families, the education of children under such conditions, etc., etc." (*Pss,* 28.2:127). The first notes for *The Adolescent,* from February through April 1874, conceive the work as a "novel about children, solely about children and a child-hero" (*Pss,* 15:406). The notes from August 1874 show the novel evolving into a story about fathers and children.

The *Diary of a Writer* and *The Brothers Karamazov* evolved together in Dostoevsky's imagination as works primarily about children. When Soloviev inquired as to what his proposed *Diary* would be about, Dostoevsky replied, "Something about children—about children in general, about children with fathers, children without fathers especially, about children at Christmas parties, without Christmas parties, about child criminals. . . . Of course, these are not some kind of strict etudes or reports, but just some warm words and indications" (*Pss,* 30.1:72).

Dostoevsky launches the first issue of the *Diary* as an independent monthly in January 1876 by professing an interest in children and commitment to writing about them. "There was a Christmas tree and a children's party at the Artists' Club, and I went to have a look at the children," he writes (*WD,* January 1876, 301–2). This opening issue of the independent *Diary* tells readers about an ongoing project that eventually becomes *The Brothers Karamazov.* "Even formerly I always watched children, but now I pay particular attention to them. For a long time now I have had the goal of writing a novel about children in Russia today, and about their fathers too, of course, in their mutual relationship of today. . . . I will take fathers and children from every level of Russian society I can and follow the children from their earliest childhood" (*WD*, January 1876, 302).

Work toward *The Brothers Karamazov* began in Dostoevsky's March 1876 notebooks as a novel called *Fathers and Children* (*Pss*, 17:6–8, 430–35). "A year ago I almost began my *Fathers and Children*," Dostoevsky tells *Diary* readers, "but I held back, and thank God I did, for I was not ready" (*WD*, January 1876, 302). The process of getting ready included writing the *Diary* and contacting people with knowledge about children. In March 1878, he writes the pedagogue V. V. Mikhailov:

> *I'm counting on you.* What interests me particularly in your letter is that you love children, have lived among children a great deal, and do so even now. Here, then, is my request, dear Vladimir Vasilyevich: I have conceived and soon will start writing a large novel where, among other things, children, particularly youngsters aged approximately seven to fifteen, will play a great role. . . . I am studying them and have studied them all my life, and love them dearly, and have children myself . . . [thus] the observations of a man like you will be very valuable to me. . . . So write me about children—*everything you know.* (*Pss*, 30.1:12)

Defending his decision to devote his energies to the *Diary* rather than fiction, he writes M. A. Aleksandrov in March 1876:

> Preparing to write one very big novel, I planned to immerse myself especially in the study not of reality itself—I am already acquainted with that—but with the details of the present. One of the most important tasks in this present, for me, for example, is the young generation, and along with that—the modern Russian family, which, I have a feeling, is by no means what it was twenty years ago. (*Pss*, 29.2:78)

Dostoevsky's notebooks from this period reveal a preoccupation with children, especially their suffering. His notes from 1877 contain the entry: "Children. The torture of children (why didn't you help?)" (*Pss*, 15:410). Among the very earliest entries in the notes for *Brothers Karamazov*, we read: "Find out about child labor in factories. About gymnasiums, life in gymnasiums"; "In the orphanage"; "About Pestalozzi, about Frebel. The essay by Lev Tolstoy about modern school curriculum in *Notes of the Fatherland*" (*Pss*, 15:199).

Composition of *The Brothers Karamazov* coincided with the death of a child, Dostoevsky's son Alyosha in May 1878. Dostoevsky recriminated himself for the child's death; he apparently could not escape feeling at least partly responsible for Alyosha's death from epilepsy, the disease the child inherited from his father. In his grief, Dostoevsky spent a week at Optyna Pustyn' with Soloviev. Serious work on *The Brothers Karamazov* began on his return home in July 1878. The death of a child is thus the basis of the novel biographically as well as structurally. "I put much of myself and what is mine into it," Dostoevsky writes to I. S. Aksakov of the novel (*Pss,* 30.1:214).

Dostoevsky's love of children communicated itself to his readers. As Liubimov edited the chapter "Little Boys" for the April 1880 installment of the novel in the *Russian Messenger,* he wrote Dostoevsky, "This part is splendidly done (you love children very much). I'm sure it will create a strong impression" (*Pss,* 15:440). Pobedonostsev, who was troubled by the force of Ivan's critique, was equally disturbed by the representation of child abuse. "I'm waiting for the issue of *The Russian Messenger* to appear, to find out the conclusion of the conversations about faith between the Karamazov brothers," Pobedonostsev writes Dostoevsky in June 1879. "It is a very powerful chapter—but why did you portray the torture of children that way!" (*Pss,* 15:427).

"I bawled reading the peasant woman's story of the dead child," Iunge writes her mother. She continues, "Yesterday evening I read about the torture of children and the 'Grand Inquisitor,' I couldn't read any more, and I tossed and turned until morning, thinking about all this and composing a letter to Dostoevsky" (*Pss,* 30.1:330). A. I. Tolstaia showed her daughter's letter to the Dostoevskys; Anna Grigorevna read it aloud before her husband, and it made a strong impression on him. Tolstaia reported back to her daughter that "he repeated over and over that I must not forget to convey his thankfulness to you, that you understood his novel *Karamazovs* so deeply, and to tell you, that no one has read it with such comprehension as you" (*Pss,* 30.1:329).

There are indications that children continued to preoccupy Dostoevsky until he died and that they would have stood at the center of future works. The pedagogue and writer A. M. Slivitsky, who attended the Pushkin celebrations, recalls Dostoevsky addressing a group of young people. "I'll write *Children* and then die," Slivitsky recounts Dostoevsky saying (*Pss,* 15:486). "According to Dostoevsky's conception, the novel *Children* would be the continuation of *The Brothers Karamazov,*" Slivitsky writes. "The children of the preceding novel would be the main heroes" (*Pss,* 15:486).

The problem of suffering children in Dostoevsky, these stand-ins for crucified Christ, is linked to the problem of theodicy. In contrast to earlier periods of Dostoevsky scholarship, there is currently a critical consensus that his works affirm the value or rightness of suffering children as reenactments of the Passion; this critical view appears to be linked to a general consensus regarding a larger problem of theodicy, or God's apparent authorship of injustice.

The dilemma posed by the merchant God and his terrible argument of child sacrifice is more familiar in Dostoevsky criticism as the problem of theodicy. Frank identifies the "tragic confrontation" between "the age-old imperatives of the Christian faith" and "man's ambition to change the world for the better" as the central theme of *Crime and Punishment*. I would extend this observation: conflict between the desire to correct injustice and acceptance of what Frank calls Christian imperatives is a central theme of all Dostoevsky's works, including his journalism.

Redemption is frequently accomplished in Dostoevsky's writings by clarifying how we relate to innocent suffering and the authorities behind it. Jackson writes that Christians in Dostoevsky's world have to accept the existence of injustice.[24] Raskolnikov and Ivan, Jackson believes, are guilty of insisting on a moral absolute; Dostoevsky shows this to be un-Christian, Jackson claims. Raskolnikov's father is repudiated because he is "indifferent to good and evil" in the dream of the beaten horse, but the Christian, while not yielding to evil, must accept it.[25] Sonia, for example, accepts the possibility that Providence decrees the death of her siblings.

The assumption that Christianity and intervention against injustice are in conflict, shared here by Frank and Jackson, reveals the persuasiveness of one strand in Dostoevsky's fiction. This strand running throughout his novels comes to define Christianity as acquiescence to injustice, specifically as reconciliation with the suffering and death of children.[26] This is indeed how characters such as Sonia and Zosima understand Christianity, but it exists in tension with another view in Dostoevsky's novels. The quest to define one's relationship to the terrible argument of the Crucifixion also leads to the rebellions of characters such as Raskolnikov, Stavrogin, Ippolit Terentiev, and Ivan Karamazov.

Dostoevsky's preparatory work in his notebooks reveals that these characters—who become very different in their final form, during the actual execution of the published novel—share a common genesis or origin in Dostoevsky's imagination. In the preparatory notebooks for his novels, Dostoevsky places almost identical words into the mouths of each of his major rebels. They express a desire for immediate change—social, spiritual, individual, communal—to be brought about by rejecting injustice and taking matters into their own hands. "I can't wait" for someone else to fix the injustices I see, the character becoming Stavrogin says (*Pss*, 11:168). "I don't want to wait," Raskolnikov says to Sonia in the notes for *Crime and Punishment*; "I want my human rights immediately" (*Pss*, 7:322). Raskolnikov's desire to help has a politicohistorical dimension, associating him with the upheaval accomplished by Peter the Great. "I want that everything that I see should be different . . . (Hollander Peter)," Dostoevsky writes in the notes for *Crime and Punishment* (*Pss*, 7:153).

This sentiment voiced by Stavrogin and preconversion Raskolnikov in the notebooks—the impossibility of waiting for someone else, such as God, to fix injustice—cannot be easily dismissed as a view repudiated in Dostoevsky's writings, for it is the basis of Russian Christianity in the *Diary*. These apparently un- or even anti-Christian characters, who rebel against the injunction to accept evil, are linked to Russia's defense of Christian principles—activism on behalf of the world's weak, even when this means rebellion against authorities that insist on reconciliation—in the *Diary*.

Dostoevsky, I believe, pours all the "authorial love" (as Emerson calls it) he felt for these ultimately ambiguous characters into his portrait of Russia in the *Diary*.[27] His impatience with injustice, with Providence, with the sense of despair experienced on the second day after the Crucifixion—these seek expression through the stories of figures such as Raskolnikov and Stavrogin but fail to achieve satisfying articulation. Dostoevsky finally found satisfaction in composing Russia's story. The deep connections linking Russia with characters such as Stavrogin and Ivan Karamazov are not surprising, for these figures share a genetic source in Dostoevsky's conception of what it means to be Russian.

Dostoevsky emphasizes the sympathy and affinity he feels for his great rebel hero Ivan Karamazov, asserting that Ivan's spiritual struggle arises from his spiritual profundity. "Ivan Fydorovich is deep, he's not a contemporary atheist, the kind whose unbelief simply shows the narrowness of his worldview and the dullness of his dull little abilities," Dostoevsky writes in his notebooks (*Pss,* 30.1:390, 27:48). Regarding Stavrogin, Dostoevsky likewise emphasizes the character's depth, Russianness, and the intimacy of his feelings for him. "This man," he writes of Stavrogin, "doesn't believe the faith of our believers but demands a belief that is full, complete, different" (*Pss,* 29.2:232). Stavrogin is "tragic," Dostoevsky insists, "a Russian and a tragic character." "I took him from my heart," Dostoevsky confides to Katkov in October 1870; "I've described this character through scenes, action, and not reasoning" (*Pss,* 29.1:142). Katkov and Liubimov put a great deal of pressure on Dostoevsky to revise the chapter "At Tikhon's," the scene of Stavrogin's confession. "I swear to you, I can't abandon the essence of the thing," Dostoevsky replies to Liubimov in 1872; Stavrogin is "our type, Russian, . . . depraved *from longing,*" but conscientiously trying "to renew himself and begin to believe again" (*Pss,* 29.1:232).

Ascertaining what position on the problem of theodicy receives greater textual weight or narrative endorsement has typically been approached as a matter of comparing characters: rebels versus Christians. We can better illuminate this question by expanding the investigation to include the character of Russia in the *Diary*. In the *Diary*, Dostoevsky presents Russia as the exclusive vessel of true Christianity in the world, so in trying to ascertain his views on theodicy, it is imperative to ask what stance toward injustice Russia adopts. The answer is, not that of the Christian characters in the novels.

Understanding what's at stake in the choice between Ivan and Zosima, or Raskolnikov and Sonia, is incomplete without taking the *Diary* into account. Rebellion and faith as they are portrayed in Dostoevsky's novels should be analyzed in light of Russia's moral development in the *Diary*. When he claims to speak in his own voice in the *Diary*, Dostoevsky endorses and ascribes to Christian Russia values held by his rebels. Characters such as Raskolnikov, Ippolit Terentiev, Stavrogin, and Ivan become more positive when their values and actions are analyzed within the intergeneric dialogue about redemption, whereas the faith of characters like Zosima and Tikhon acquires negative associations. The principles espoused by his positive Christian characters are similar to the Jewish idea as it is portrayed in the *Diary*.

The basis of Christian faith and redemption in the novels is the adoption of thought processes or logical operations the *Diary* labels "Jewish." Zosima urges people to reconcile themselves to the use of others' suffering as the basis of a higher good, their relationship with God. He presents salvation as something literally purchased with the coin of others' suffering. His Christian faith is similar to the Jewish idea portrayed in the *Diary*: it is based in utilitarian calculations and the principle of commensurability, which make it possible to think of the suffering of children as something that can be used in survivor narratives, as he understands the book of Job. To rebel against these principles in the *Diary* is to overcome the Jews, but in the novel it is tantamount to rebellion against God.

Association with Russia and her crusade against injustice and the Jews renders characters like Ivan more complex—Russia's story casts Ivan's in a more positive light. By the same token, however, association with Ivan casts Russia's story in a critical light. In the *Diary*, examples of innocent suffering are used to incite a Russian Christian rebellion against the Judaized West. In *The Brothers Karamazov*, the same examples are used to incite rebellion against God. In the *Diary*, Dostoevsky claims that Russia's mission against the Judaized West is based in the Christian principle of refusing to accept injustice. The *Diary*'s assertion that Russian Christianity commands intervention on behalf of the weak is problematized by its association with Ivan Karamazov. By the same token, Ivan's views acquire deeper, more positive connotations in light of their resemblance to the ideas about Russian Christianity Dostoevsky puts forth in the *Diary*.

Ivan's rebellion against God and Dostoevsky's rebellion against Europe in the *Diary* share a similar structure. Dostoevsky conceives of Western civilization as a higher order constructed through calculations of what can be purchased with innocent suffering; Ivan conceives of God's eternal harmony as a higher order constructed through calculations of what can be purchased with innocent suffering. Ivan ascribes to the Christian God, as the architect of harmony, the same qualities Dostoevsky in the *Diary* ascribes to Disraeli, the Jewish architect of the European order; Ivan and Dostoevsky use similar rhetoric, posing as the outraged voices of naive honesty condemning sophisticated calculation. What is valorized as a Russian and Christian protest against Jewish machinations in the *Diary* becomes un-Russian and un-Christian when it enters Ivan's spiritual narrative in the novel.

Affiliations and associations become very complicated in the intergeneric dialogue about redemption. In Dostoevsky's novels, it is Christianity, not Judaism, that is based in the use of sacrificial victims; Zosima and Tikhon espouse a logic associated with Jews in the *Diary*, whereas Raskolnikov, Stavrogin, and Ivan perform rebellions against this logic—rebellions analogous to that waged by the Russian people against Disraeli's "Judaized" West in the *Diary*.

When one reads the stories of Dostoevsky's rebels the way his original readers did—as embedded in an intergeneric dialogue among Dostoevsky's novels and journals—one sees that ideas ostensibly rejected or at least critiqued by Christian characters in the novels are corroborated, strengthened by their association with Dostoevsky himself in his journals. When Dostoevsky argues in the *Diary* that Christian Russia must intervene with military force in the Balkan War—must kill the Turkish aggressors to save innocent Orthodox Slavs—he is staking a position diametrically opposed to that of Sonia Marmeladova, who would not kill the wicked Peter Petrovich Luzhin even to save her little siblings. He is taking the side of preconversion Raskolnikov and his other rebels, advancing a definition of Christianity opposed to that held by the Christian figures of his novels.

Russia, as portrayed in Dostoevsky's essays from *Time* through the *Diary*, is one of Dostoevsky's great spiritual rebels against sacrificial or utilitarian exchange logic and the principle of moral immunity for higher authorities. As Dostoevsky's novels record his search for a type of redemption that is not purchased with blood sacrifice, antisemitism and Russian messianism develop into primary themes of his essays. The problem of what to do about innocent suffering and the role it seems to play in redemption remains open after composition of the *Diary* and *The Brothers Karamazov*; it continues to be a primary topic in a dialogue among different voices Dostoevsky continues composing after publishing these works.

Dostoevsky had many plans for future works during the last years of his life. On December 24, 1877, he entered into his notebooks: "Memento. For my whole life" and listed as projects "1. Write the Russian Candide.

2. Write a book about Jesus Christ. 3. Write my memoirs" (*Pss*, 15:409). He wrote *The Brothers Karamazov* as part of a projected two-volume project and built expectations of a continuation into the foreword, where the narrator says, "While I have just one biography, I have two novels. The main novel is the second one—about the activities of my hero in our time, that is, in our present, current moment" (*BK*, 3). Soloviev, who accompanied Dostoevsky to Optyna Pustyn' in June 1878 and with whom Dostoevsky discussed his evolving novel, recalls that it was to be the first in a "series of novels" (*Pss*, 15:412).

Neither the *Diary* nor *The Brothers Karamazov* represents a resolution or culmination in Dostoevsky's thinking. The novel and the *Diary* respond to each other in a dialogue that would have continued in unforeseen directions had Dostoevsky lived. Anna Grigorevna writes of her husband's intentions in her memoirs:

> Fyodor Mikhailovich planned to publish the *Diary of a Writer* for two years, and after that he dreamt of writing the second part of *The Brothers Karamazov*, where all the former heroes would appear, but after twenty years, almost in the present time, when they would have been able to do and experience much in their lives. (*Pss*, 15:489)

"He regarded the continuation of his *Diary* partly as a means to take up the fight about essential questions of Russian life," Alexei Sergeevich Suvorin wrote when Dostoevsky died. "Alyosha Karamazov was supposed to . . . be the hero, out of which he wanted to create a type of Russian socialist, not the current type, which we know and which grew up completely on European soil" (*Pss*, 15:485). The first novel, the existing *Brothers Karamazov*, treated Alyosha's life while at the monastery; the second would follow him out into the world. Suvorin recalls Dostoevsky saying about Alyosha, "He wanted to lead him through the monastery and make him a revolutionary. He would commit a political crime. He would be sentenced. He would seek the truth [*pravdu*], and in these searches, naturally, he would become a revolutionary" (*Pss*, 15:485).

The spirit of openness and exploration that characterizes Dostoevsky's thinking and writing leads him to create a dialogue among his journalistic and novelistic writing, a dialogue that circles around the problem of redemption. Inventing the Russian and Jewish ideas in the *Diary* as a means to evading participation in the merchant God's salvational economy is one station in this dialogue. Accepting an order built on the stone of a dead child—Alyosha's accomplishment at the end of *The Brothers Karamazov*—is another episode. Neither instance represents Dostoevsky's final conclusion or last words. Dostoevsky's relationship with the character of Stavrogin/the

Prince sketched in his notes for *Demons* is perhaps the most intimate of all his relations with his characters. In addition to voicing Dostoevsky's cherished convictions regarding Russia's sacred role in communal redemption, the Prince articulates his belief in the unfinalizability of human life: "We are, obviously, transitional beings, and our existence on earth is obviously the existence of a chrysalis, turning into a butterfly" (*Pss,* 11:184).

Disraeli and the Merchant God:
Victims and Villains, Jews and Europe

THE BIOGRAPHICAL BASES of Dostoevsky's concern with the problems of suffering children, bad fathers, and ultimately the Crucifixion reward investigation. The West became equivalent to the "Jewish idea," the epitome of everything Dostoevsky could not tolerate within his conception of Christianity, by a long process. Sensitivity to the possible coincidence of victim and perpetrator in one figure or action—one element of Dostoevsky's discomfort with the Crucifixion—may have a source in his European experience.

Over the second half of the 1860s, the West becomes for Dostoevsky a place where a child dies because a father fails. Dostoevsky is the father responsible for his child's death and a victim of the West himself. Life in the West confronted Dostoevsky with his own role as a bad father who contributed to the death of his child, and it convinced him that he himself was a victim of "Jewish" power—the triumph of money—that shackled him to the slave labor of a literary proletarian, ruined his health, and imprisoned him in Europe. This space where children die because of their fathers and where the dead child and the father who contributed to her death are linked as fellow victims of the West then becomes "Judaized" for Dostoevsky over the course of the 1870s.

The possible coincidence of victim and victimizer in one person was one of Dostoevsky's most significant personal psychological experiences, with immense consequence for the evolution of his heretical understanding of the Crucifixion. He bequeaths this experience to figures such as Raskolnikov. Understanding Dostoevsky's own struggles with the potential coincidence of victim and victimizer can illuminate the challenges facing such a character on the path to redemption.[1] Inspiring his characters' complexity is Dostoevsky's own biographical experience of and discomfort with the potential coincidence of self- and other-sacrifice, one basis of his anxieties about the Crucifixion.

The characters who express Dostoevsky's anxieties about Christianity share significant qualities with each other and with their author. Characters like Raskolnikov, Stavrogin, and Ivan Karamazov have trouble distinguishing victims from perpetrators. Raskolnikov, for example, thinks of himself as the victim of the pawnbroker, whom he mentally accuses several times of taking his life away. They struggle with the phenomenon of how easily identifying with or defending victims can turn into being oneself an agent of their suffering. Ivan Karamazov, for example, moves easily between championing children and encouraging their corruption, as in his relationship with Liza Khokhlakova.

Experiences in Europe played a catalytic role in the emergence of Dostoevsky's anxieties about the potential coincidence of victims and victimizers. He was first compelled to endure an extended sojourn in Europe as a kind of economic exile from Russia. During the second half of the 1860s, he endured what he experienced as a kind of forced exile in Western Europe necessitated by debts that made it impossible for him to remain in Russia.[2] The West becomes associated for him with the death of children; with his inadequacy as a father—his infant daughter Sonia dies, he believes, because his debts force them to live in Europe; and with his own victimization due to poor health and poverty. His first extended European exile thus establishes the West as a place that confronts Dostoevsky with the suffering of children, his own contributions as an inadequate father to that suffering, and the fact that the problematic father figure who contributes to the suffering of children is himself a victim as well—the distinctions between victim and perpetrator become blurred.

Over the course of the 1870s, Dostoevsky visited Europe as a kind of medical pilgrim seeking a cure for his emphysema at various German spas. During this period, the West becomes explicitly Judaized in his perception. During the last years of his life, as Europe becomes increasingly Jewish for Dostoevsky, it also becomes increasingly associated with the abuse of children and Dostoevsky's own sufferings. Problems of child abuse, Jews, and Dostoevsky's intense anxieties about money and his own health become more and more entangled. By the end of his life, Europe has become a place of financial or medical exile where unscrupulous Jews, "Judaized" Germans, and the spectacle of suffering children interfere with his ability to work, and where Russia and his own children merge as absent objects of longing and the source of his creativity.

The death of his first child in Geneva profoundly affected Dostoevsky's perception of the West as a malevolent power victimizing him *and* activated tormenting feelings of guilt about his own victimization of his dependents, his wife and child. He believed that Sonia died because of his own failings and the inadequacy of care she received from Swiss doctors; if they had been in Russia, he writes, she would still be alive. Writing to his brother Andrey in December 1868 about Sonia's brief life, Dostoevsky laments, "Towards spring God gave us a daughter, Sofia, and we praised God and were endlessly happy. But our joy didn't last long; we didn't know how to take care of the baby, who was healthy and strong" (*Pss*, 29.2:98). He confides to Apollon Maikov, "It would be better to return to Russia. Just think, Sonia would most likely be alive if we were in Russia!" (*Pss*, 28.2:324). Sonia dies in Geneva because of the debts that force Dostoevsky to evade his creditors. "Returning to Russia is unthinkable," he writes Maikov in October 1868. "There are no means. It would mean falling into debtors' prison as soon as we arrived," which would be a death sentence for Dostoevsky himself: "With my epilepsy I wouldn't survive prison" (*Pss*, 28.2:321). His survival entails Sonia's death.

Dostoevsky describes looking at Sonia's face, especially during what turned out to be the last moments of her life, with language that will be echoed in the visions Stavrogin has of Matresha. "There are minutes that are impossible to bear," Dostoevsky confesses to Maikov in June 1868, regarding his memory of Sonia's gaze. Dostoevsky, like Stavrogin, is transfixed by the memory of the girl's gaze, as if trying to decipher something contained in the look of a child on the brink of death, to which his own actions have contributed.

> On the day of her death, I left the house to read the newspapers, having no idea that she would die in two hours; she so followed and accompanied me with her little eyes, she looked at me so, so that to this time I see it more and more vividly. I will never forget and never stop being tormented! (*Pss*, 28.2:302)

"My Sonia died," Dostoevsky writes Sofia Ivanova in June 1868; he emphasizes the child's love for him, her gaze, and, like Stavrogin, claims that the intensity of her memory grows with time. "She knew me, smiled at me, already loved me, would follow me with her little eyes when I approached. Now a month has already passed since she is gone, and I not only haven't forgotten her; the further away, the stronger and brighter she is in my memory." The pain of this memory elicits the desire to die: "It is so hard and bitter for me, that it would be better to die" (*Pss*, 28.2:306).

As it is portrayed in the *Diary*, Russia takes on the Christ role of self-sacrificing martyr for others; it as though Dostoevsky cannot bear the many martyred children strewn throughout his novels and replaces them with a corporate body, the national community. The roots associating Russia with sacrificial children go deep in Dostoevsky's experience. Before Russia is associated with Christ's self-sacrifice, it is associated with victimized, absent, and longed-for children. There is an intriguing connection between the death of Sonia and the emergence of Russia as an object of longing and grief in his letters. Mourning for Sonia coincides with the appearance of homesickness for Russia in Dostoevsky's correspondence. Before Sonia's death, Dostoevsky reports that he and Anna Grigorevna are basically happy and content with their quiet lives abroad in each other's company. During the ensuing months of 1868, however, as the memory of their dead child grew stronger, he begins to complain about his difficult "moral condition" and *"grust' po rodine"* (melancholy for the homeland) (*Pss,* 28.2:319). "Anna Grigorevna is patient, but she longs for Russia, and we both cry about Sonia," he writes Maikov in the fall of 1868 (*Pss,* 28.2:321).

It is during this period of grief for the child victim of the West and guilt about his own failure as a father that Dostoevsky begins identifying Russia as the source of his creativity. "Unfamiliarity with Russia, the impossibility even of writing here without Russian impressions" emerges as a central complaint in his letters (to Sofia Ivanova, November 1868, *Pss,* 28.2:319). Hatred of the West and perception of himself as its victim as well are connected to Russia's emergence as the source of his creativity, and both of these phenomena are linked to the loss of his child. "I hate them [the Swiss] beyond all measure!" he exclaims in the same letter that tells of how they cry for Sonia; I work so hard here, he complains, that "my head is as if broken . . . I am becoming dull and stupid here" (*Pss,* 28.2:303).

While hating the West and accusing it of harming his health and creativity, however, Dostoevsky also blames himself for their misfortunes. He can't work, and Anna Grigorevna is suffering terribly, he laments. "It's all because of my sins. To this time I still can't at all get used to this unhappiness and get used to being without Sonia," he writes to his stepson Pasha Isaev in June 1868 (*Pss,* 28.2:201).

Russia and children become connected when grief for Sonia and Russia merge; the connection between children and Russia grows over the years. Like contact with his homeland, contact with children plays a special role in Dostoevsky's creative life. Separation from Russia and his family evoke similar feelings in him. "I need Russia, it is necessary for my *writings* [*pisanniia*] and work (I won't even speak about the rest of life), and how! I'm like a fish out of water; I lack strength and means," he writes Maikov in 1867 (*Pss,* 28.2:204). "Thank you for the details about the children," he writes Anna from Ems in June 1875, "they bring me back to life [*ozhivliaiut*]" (*Pss,* 30.1:36). "Every news about you and all of you," he tells her, "renews me here and brings me back to life, like medicine" (*Pss,* 29.2:106). "I look at their photographs often," he writes Anna of Liubov' and Fedor, their second daughter and first son (*Pss,* 30.1:115). Complaining of how difficult it is for him to write in Ems, he tells her, "Even though at home, in [Staraia] Russa, I sat alone, at least I knew that the children were in the next room, I could go to them sometimes, even get annoyed at their yelling—this gave me life and strength" (*Pss,* 29.2:43–44).

The possibility of harm coming to children torments Dostoevsky; he is acutely aware of the tenuousness of his children's lives. In March 1870, he writes Maikov about Liuba: "The child is healthy; you would marvel. But if it weren't for Anna Nikolaevna, Anna Grigorevna's mother, Liuba would die too" (*Pss,* 29.1:119). His dreams and fantasies torment him with violent visions. During a brief separation while he attended to business in St. Petersburg and Anna remained in Staraia Russa with the children, he writes that he dreamed Fedya fell from a fourth-floor window. "As he flew down, turning over and over, I covered my eyes with my hands and cried in despair: 'Goodbye, Fedya!' And woke up" (*Pss,* 29.1:282–83). He imagines how his children would suffer if they would ever be left alone with cruel caregivers. "What would they endure alone, without their mommy and daddy? How their little, offended souls would be depressed in melancholy" (*Pss,* 29.2:103). His children are present to him as phantoms while he is in Europe without his family. Writing to his wife in the summer of 1879 on the way to Ems, he recounts, "On the way I saw a little boy and a little girl (among the passengers), just like Lilia and Fedya, especially from behind, they were even dressed similarly!" (*Pss,* 30.1:82).

Reconstructing the complex associations that link children and Russia as victims of Western and paternal power illuminates Dostoevsky's "Russian idea" from a new angle. Championing Russia against the West in his essays is a way of championing children against their abusers. It is also a way to transform victimization into a decisive action, sacrifice by others into self-sacrifice, an individual victim into a corporate agent.

It is important to establish the final association of the West with bad fathers and Jews that takes place in Dostoevsky's imagination, for this explains why the Balkan War comes to function in his thoughts as a kind of alternative crucifixion. The web of associations among (dead) children, Russia, and Dostoevsky himself as victims of the West becomes even more complex during the 1870s, as Dostoevsky increasingly perceives the West as Jewish.

Dostoevsky pays very little attention to Jews or Jewish issues before the 1870s. During the 1860s, the things he identifies as moral errors—utilitarianism, greed, and so on—are not yet definitively associated with Jewishness for him. Peter Petrovich Luzhin and Alyona Ivanovna, two of the most unappealing characters of *Crime and Punishment,* are explicitly linked to "Yids" because of their greed and usury. But *Winter Notes on Summer Impressions* discusses Western depravity as a feature of French bourgeois culture and British imperial arrogance, without any references to Jews; and it is Catholicism that embodies the anti-Christian spirit for Myshkin in *The Idiot.*

In the 1860s, the Jews have not yet come to embody the principles Dostoevsky abhors. His letters and notes from this period, like *Winter Notes on Summer Impressions,* discuss greed and moneylending, phenomena he later defines as essentially "Jewish," as European qualities. How base the Germans are, he complains in an 1867 letter to Maikov, contending that "they are all to the last man usurers, scoundrels!" (*Pss*, 28.2:207–8). "The Frenchman is quiet, honest, polite, but false and money is everything to him," he writes Nikolai Strakhov from Europe in 1862. "There is no ideal. Don't bother to look for thinking, let alone convictions" (*Pss*, 28.2:27). "All glory, honor, worship, and so on" go exclusively to money in France, he asserts in *Winter Notes* (*WN*, 74).

For many years Dostoevsky identified socialism as the antithesis of Christianity. His 1864–65 notebooks contain a section entitled "Socialism and Christianity." The socialist, he writes here, cannot understand giving without expectation of return.

> But for a certain known reward—that is possible, that is moral. But the whole thing, the whole endless superiority of Christianity over socialism consists in the fact that the Christian (the ideal one), giving everything away, doesn't demand anything for himself. Even more: he is even hostile to the idea of reward, of an honorarium. (*Pss*, 20:193)

Here Dostoevsky proclaims socialism to be the source of an anti-Christian mentality that is incapable of understanding the gift. In the *Diary*, socialism will recede as an epiphenomenon of the Jewish idea, the utilitarian principle of using some for the advancement of the self or others.

It is interesting to note that Dostoevsky begins to make self-sacrifice essentially "Russian"—he begins to hint that a capacity for self-sacrifice is a racial characteristic, something in Russian blood—well before he pays any attention to the Jews. *Winter Notes* articulates a critique of Western modernity that is free of antisemitism, but it introduces a racial basis to the capacity for self-sacrifice. An instinct for brotherhood is either present in a people or not, Dostoevsky asserts, and the Russians have it and Europeans don't. The ideal of "completely conscious self-sacrifice," he writes in *Winter Notes*, the goal of "sacrifice of the self for the sake of all," is something found in "the flesh and blood" of a people, it must be part of what he calls a racial unconscious, "unconsciously a part of the nature of the whole race" (*WN*, 49). "And in general, all Russian moral understanding and goals are higher than the European world. We have more immediate and noble belief in the good and in Christianity, and not in the bourgeois resolution of questions in comfort," he boasts to Maikov in 1868 (*Pss*, 28.2:260).

In the writings of his later years, "Jewishness" becomes a partially flexible, detachable quality that can describe phenomena as diverse as socialism, Europeans in general, and all those involved in commercial activities. Something is "Jewish" for Dostoevsky in the last years of his life when it is concerned only with itself, with its own most narrowly conceived self-interest. "Petty, Yiddifying, third-rate" thinking is exhibited by Russians who fail to understand Russia's mission, such as the allegedly Orthodox Christian "stock exchange gamblers" and "all those Russians generally who have no concern in Russia other than their own pockets," he writes in the *Diary* (*WD*, January 1877, 995, 812, 816).

Dostoevsky expressed dislike of many groups. At various times he identifies Poland, Catholicism, socialism, and the European bourgeoisie (among others) as Russia's mortal enemies. Yet this multiplicity was showing signs of contraction and consolidation at the end of his life. Over the course of the 1870s, Dostoevsky gradually identifies the Jews as the root source of Western depravity. Catholicism, socialism, France, Protestantism—all these opponents were being gradually demoted from sources of moral error themselves into victims or pawns of the Jews. "Dostoevsky," Morson writes, "hesitated whether the Antichrist was the Pope or Disraeli."[3] During the last years of his life, Dostoevsky was in the process of settling on Disraeli and the Jews.

The role they come to play in Dostoevsky's imagination as the primary carriers of utilitarianism, materialism, and particularism, opposed to the ethnic genius of the Russian people, explains why Dostoevsky's hatred of the Jews stands out as something special among his prejudices. The writings of his last years show that he was coming to blame the Jews for the sins committed by the other entities he had previously identified as Russia's opponents; behind Catholicism, socialism, and the bourgeoisie, he espies the Jew lurking.

In the notebooks for the 1881 *Diary*, Dostoevsky reminds himself to address "the Yids as a world fact. Catholicism, yielding to the Yids" (*Pss*, 27:48). "The basic idea of the bourgeoisie," he writes in the March 1877 *Diary*, is "the idea of Jewry"—"trade in human labor" (*WD*, March 1877, 914). Socialism becomes a front for advancing Jewish rather than Catholic interests. "When will they realize how many Yids and possibly Polacks are operating in this band?" he impatiently asks, regarding the socialists. The Jews, he insists, are behind the student uprisings in Kazan Square and Odessa. In an August 1878 letter to V. P. Putsykovich, who was trying to launch an émigré journal from Dresden with Dostoevsky's encouragement, Dostoevsky argues that socialism manifests an essentially Jewish interest in social disruption.

Odessa, city of Yids, turns out to be the center of our belligerent socialism. In Europe it's the same thing: the Yids are terribly involved in socialism, and I won't even speak about the Lassals and Karl Marxes. And it's understandable: the Yid profits from every radical tremor and revolution in the state. (*Pss*, 30.1:43)

52

The emergence of the Jews as primary in Dostoevsky's imagination did not mean that he ceased speaking about the threat posed by Catholicism, socialism, France, and the like. They remained on his radar screen but were being gradually eclipsed by the Jews.

The Europeans were evolving from foes into fellow victims of the Jews in Dostoevsky's late writings. Dostoevsky was coming to believe that the Europeans, like the Russian people, needed protection from "the Yid . . . the monster of materialism, in the form of the bag of gold" (*WD*, October 1876, 672). It is the Jewish idea that is determining allegedly "European" policy, he argues there. Europe's alliance with the Turks against the Balkan Slavs, for example, is a Jewish maneuver. "Were the Jewish idea not so powerful in the world, that same 'Slavic' question (last year's question) might have been resolved in favor of the Slavs, not the Turks," he writes of events in the Balkans (*WD*, March 1877, 904–5). Europe, he maintains, finds itself in the grip of the Jews, "as the top level of Jews gains a stronger and surer hold over humanity and strives to mold the world to its image and essence" (*WD*, March 1877, 915). "One cannot fail to note [in Europe] the effective triumph of Jewry which has replaced many of the old ideas with its own," specifically "the idea of the Yids, which is creeping over the whole world in place of 'unsuccessful' Christianity" (*WD*, March 1877, 915).

One of the first references to Jews in Dostoevsky's correspondence appears to be a comment in an 1871 letter to Sofia Ivanova. The Dostoevskys finally escaped European exile, only to return home to problems with Jews. Complaining to Sofia about the difficulties he and Anna Grigorevna encountered on returning to St. Petersburg, he refers to the "nasty Yid landlords" they had to deal with while looking for an apartment (*Pss*, 29.1:218). The trips Dostoevsky makes to German spas in the 1870s seem to intensify his animus. Complaints about Jews and their pernicious influence on Europe are one of the primary themes of his letters to Anna. Dostoevsky identifies a general weakening of moral-intellectual culture and increasing materialism affecting society. Passing through Germany on the way to Ems, he wonders at the shallowness of the conversations around him. One hears "only about *gescheft* and percentages, about prices for goods, about wares, about the gay material life with camellias and officers—and that's all," he relays to Anna. "No education, no kind of higher interests—nothing!" This is spreading to Russia, he contends, and threatens him as an author, for can such people be an audience for his *Diary*? "I definitely do not understand, who now can read anything, and why does the *Diary* have a few thousand subscribers?" he asks her (June 1876, *Pss*, 29.2:90).

His "persecution" by Jews begins almost as soon as Dostoevsky's train leaves Russia. Approaching Eidkunen, he recounts for Anna, "One Yid attached himself to me, he got on in Vilnius, one of the higher Yids, so to speak, rich. . . . He spit terribly and uninterruptedly in the wagon and spit whole lakes . . . he began to expound for me a long story about how he was going to Karlsbad for a hemorrhoid cure . . . and I had to listen to all this out of politeness, and there wasn't any possibility to get away, and so he tortured me for four hours" (*Pss*, 29.2:90).

He experiences Jews as a kind of plague sent by God while he's in European exile. While in Ems, he feels persecuted by Jews; as his neighbors, fellow guests, and part of the local population, they take advantage of him and interfere with his cure and writing, making his time there comparable to a stay in prison camp. "My neighbor is a Russian Yid," he complains to Anna in 1879, "and many of the local Yids come to visit him, and it's all *gescheft* and a whole kahal—that's the kind of neighbor God sent me" (*Pss*, 29.2:56). "It's unbearably difficult and nasty for me here, Anna, almost not easier and nastier than in the *katorga* [camp], which I suffered. I speak without *exaggeration*," he laments to her in an August 1879 letter. "Alone, not a single familiar face, for example, all such nasty Yid mugs [*takie gadkie zhidovskie rozhi*]" (*Pss*, 30.1:97). "Life for me is nasty, unbearable," he confides to his wife in a letter from June 1875 (*Pss*, 29.2:47).

He came West to improve his health and concentrate on writing, but the Jews around him interfere with reaching these goals. The enormous expense of a spa cure weighed on the Dostoevskys terribly, and his letters are full of complaints about how little he is actually getting for their money, primarily due to unscrupulous Jews. "Things are terribly expensive here, it's impossible to buy anything, it's all Yids. . . . Even in the public that comes here it's almost a third rich Yids from all ends of the earth," he writes his wife in July 1879 (*Pss*, 30.1:89). He finds himself surrounded by "Yids" and what the *Diary* disparagingly calls "'Christians' who practice the Yiddish trade" in Ems (*WD*, April 1877, 933). "I bought a guest list," he writes Anna soon after arriving, but there is no one we know; only "Russian Yids and German bankers and lenders" (*Pss*, 29.2:95).

A significant amount of his correspondence with his wife details his perceived persecution by Jews, whose "Yid screeching" keeps him up at night. Two "rich Yids, a mother and her son, a 25-year-old little Yid [*zhidenok*]," occupy the next room "and are poisoning my life," he complains, adding that "they squeal, like in the kahal" (*Pss*, 30.1:89, 93). One evening,

> since it was already ten o'clock and time to sleep, I yelled, *as I lay down in bed:* "Ach, these damned Yids, when will they let me sleep!" The next day the landlady comes to me, Madame Bach, and says that her Yids called her and declared that they were very insulted that I called them Yids, and that they would leave the apartment. I answered the landlady that I myself wanted to

leave, because her Yids torment me so: you can't read, write, or think about anything. The landlady was terribly frightened by my threat and said that she would rather drive out the Yids. (*Pss*, 30.1:93)

These are more than the troubling sentiments of a private citizen; Dostoevsky impresses these views on Pobedonostsev as well. "Everything is alien, everything is completely alien—it's unbearable," Dostoevsky writes him. "And please note: it's literally half Yids. . . . Germany, Berlin at least, is becoming terribly Yiddified [*uzhasno zhidovitsia*]" (*Pss*, 30.1:104).

"Yiddified" Germany becomes associated with seeking a cure for what would turn out to be his fatal emphysema, sacrificing a great deal of their always meager resources for this, and being disappointed. "It's all Yids, everything has been taken over by Yids and they swindle beyond all limits, literally swindle," he writes Anna. "There were never such swindler-sellers in Russia as there are now in Germany" (*Pss*, 30.1:113). Jewish swindling, Dostoevsky believes, is at least partly responsible for the only modest results of his time spent in Ems.

Dostoevsky perceives the West as a place where the desire to advance oneself materially produces the willingness to sacrifice children; witnessing the neglect of children coincides with Dostoevsky's inability to write and his longing for his own children. The "Yiddified" Germans allow their little children to suffer painful diseases of the eyes—associated in his writings with sacrificial victims such as horses, Sonia, and Lizaveta—in order to save a few pfennigs. "Lizaveta! Sonia! Poor gentle things, with gentle eyes," Raskolnikov thinks, "their eyes are soft and gentle" (*CP*, 276). In a letter to Anna written just after he had sent off book 6 of *The Brothers Karamazov*, "The Russian Monk," Dostoevsky says, "My whole entertainment is to look at children, of which there are many here, and talk with them." He continues, "And there are vile things":

> Today I met a child, walking to school, in a crowd of others, five years old, he goes along covering his eyes with his hands and crying. I ask what's wrong with him, and find out from the passing Germans that he has an inflammation of the eyes (terrible torment) for a month already, but his cobbler father *doesn't want* to take him to the doctor, so as not to spend a few pfennigs on medicine. This upset me terribly, and in general my nerves are going, and I am very gloomy. (*Pss*, 30.1:106)

Dostoevsky's complex status as a victim of the Judaized West and one who is likewise the cause of a child's death in the West—it's his fault that they had to be in Europe and that Sonia died—is a biographical enactment of the same kind of tangled web of victims and abusers found in his novels.

Rahv points out that the abused horse with the gentle eyes symbolizes both his victims and Raskolnikov himself:

> The pitiful little mare, whipped across the eyes and butchered by Mikolka and a crowd of rowdy peasants, stands for all such victims of life's insensate cruelty, in particular such victims as Sonya and Lizaveta whose appeal to Raskolnikov is that of "poor gentle things . . . whose eyes are soft and gentle." Also, the mare stands above all for Raskolnikov himself, and in embracing her bleeding head in a frenzy of compassion it is himself that he is embracing, bewailing, consoling. He is present in the dream not only as the little boy witnessing an act of intolerable brutality but as at once its perpetrator and victim too.[4]

Children and Dostoevsky are victims of the Judaized West on multiple levels: the West takes his money and doesn't give enough back in return; it also makes him physically ill and emotionally distraught. To Anna he writes,

> I'm thinking about describing Ems in the *Diary*, but I'm still just putting the *Diary* together, and haven't begun yet, and it worries me terribly. When I go for walks, I always stop for children and watch them with pleasure or talk to them. I also stop for small year-old children—in each of them I imagine Lesha, who probably doesn't remember me. . . . The money goes quickly, even though I am carefully economizing. (*Pss*, 29.2:104)

The West actively opposes his creativity and success, he complains. "I went away in order to work," he writes of his decision to leave Russia. "And the idea of the *Idiot* almost failed" (*Pss*, 28.2:321). In a February 1872 letter to S. D. Ianovsky, he writes,

> This trip abroad was from my side a great miscalculation: I thought I'd go off to live abroad a couple of years, write a novel, accumulate money, pay my debts (they remained from the journal), and return a free man, even having improved my health. And what happened? The debts simply grew, my health (that is my epilepsy) quieted down a bit compared to before, but wasn't radically cured. (*Pss*, 29.1:228)

"Many thoughts are tormenting me, literally torment me terribly. The main thing is that I have to write the *Diary*, but I don't have any ideas," he writes to Anna in June 1876. Time spent in "Yiddified" Germany robs him of language—he is losing the ability to speak, write, and communicate, he fears. "I have totally forgotten how to speak, I even talk to myself, like a madman," he writes to Anna (*Pss*, 30.1:110). "I find myself here in such a wretched condition of the soul, that I am almost incapable of writing," he complains to Maikov in December 1870 from Dresden. The specific agents of his suffering in Europe in the 1870s are Jews. His neighbors make a racket, he complains, "and I have to work, read, write—how can it be done?" (*Pss,* 29.2:94). He would write himself out of this corner by predicting the triumph of the "Russian idea" over "the Kingdom of the Yids" (*WD,* March 1877, 902).

A Synagogue Mistaken for a Church:
Dostoevsky's Demon and the Jews

> "Give me your blessing, father," she begged
> him. "Take good care of everything! You will
> have to give me an account of it all some day,"
> he said, his last words proving that Christianity
> is the religion for misers, after all.
> —Balzac

> The true *gageure,* the wager which all works of
> art must be . . .
> —Baudelaire

THE WEST IS A PLACE where Dostoevsky experiences
the contrast between two kinds of spiritual economies, an experience that reflects his anxieties about Christianity and contributes to his eventual articulation of the "Russian" and "Jewish" ideas. Throughout his life, Dostoevsky was
intensely aware of the difference between a type of calculating approach to
wealth accumulation and the desire for a sudden windfall, for transformation
through risk taking. His own words and behavior, and the observations of those
who knew him, testify that Dostoevsky had a personal economy of risk, wager,
and largesse; for much of his life, he suffered from a gambling addiction.[1]

The emergence of Dostoevsky's antisemitism is linked to the moment
when he overcame his gambling addiction. Dostoevsky's faith in money/
gambling as a vehicle of redemption—his need for salvation through risk
taking—did not disappear. When he gave up gambling, Dostoevsky began
to invent the Jews as the embodiment of the faith in money's transformative power that had been at the root of his addiction; and the need for risk
taking that no longer expressed itself through gambling began to be acted
out through faith in the Russian people. Dostoevsky identifies the Russian
people—maligned and discounted by Europe—as the greatest wager; championing their mission in the Balkans enables him to take part in a kind of
holy folly and experience the thrill of betting against the odds.

For much of his life, Dostoevsky attests, he was plagued by a "demon":

the desire for redemption through money, specifically a gambling windfall that would enable him to redeem the many debts, financial and personal, that tormented him.[2] Dostoevsky spent much of his life feeling trapped in cycles of debt and redemption. In addition to his patient wife Anna Grigorevna and their children, Dostoevsky bore responsibility for numerous other dependents, some of whom accused him of failing them. When his beloved brother Mikhail died in 1864, Dostoevsky assumed his considerable financial obligations, including responsibility for Mikhail's widow and children. This turned into a terrible moral burden. Mikhail's widow, Emilia Fyodorovna, blamed Dostoevsky for her husband's death and her family's penury. "O, *golubchik,* it is hard, it was too much to take on myself this haughty thought, three years ago, that I could pay all these debts . . . ! Where am I supposed to get the health and energy for this!" he exclaims to Maikov in a letter from August 1867 (*Pss,* 28.2:213).

His first wife, Maria Dmitrevna, entrusted Dostoevsky with the care of her son, Pasha, on her deathbed, and Dostoevsky took his role as stepfather seriously. He frequently tormented himself with the belief that he failed to take proper care of all these dependents. "What will become of my Petersburgers [*Chto zhe budet s moimi peterburgskimi*], Emilia Fedorovna and Pasha and the others?" he asks. He needs "money, money, but there isn't any!" (*Pss,* 28.2:207).

He often experienced himself as a failed husband and father, and feelings of guilt and inadequacy drove him to roulette as a way of saving himself. My wife is expecting, he writes Maikov in late 1867 of Anna's pregnancy with Sonia; we need to spend the winter somewhere with a good climate and where we speak the same language as the doctors, we need to move, "but there's no money" (*Pss,* 28.2:207). I can't stop worrying about "what will happen to those who depend on my help," he confides. "All these thoughts are killing me" (*Pss,* 28.2:212). "How necessary accursed money is for me!" he exclaims (*Pss,* 28.2:292).

Desire to redeem himself from these oppressive obligations drove him to roulette. I was tormented by the seductive thought of sacrificing the little money I had at play so as to turn it into more, and so help everyone all at once, he confesses. "A seductive thought tortured me: sacrifice 10 *Louis d'or* and perhaps I will win 2000 francs, and that's enough to live on for four months, for everything, for all my Petersburgers," he relates to Maikov in August 1867 from Geneva (*Pss,* 28.2:207). "The demon immediately played a trick on me," he laments; I won 4,000 francs "with unusual ease" (*Pss,* 28.2:207).

I wasn't able to withstand winning. If at first I had lost 10 Louis d'or, as I assumed, then I would have given up everything immediately and left. But winning 4,000 francs ruined me! There was no possibility of withstanding the temptation of winning more (when this turned out to be so easy) and all at once escape from all these penalties, take care of myself and all of mine: Emilia Fyodorovna, Pasha and so on. (*Pss,* 28.2:212)

Anna Grigorevna begged me to stop when I'd won 4,000, he tells Maikov, but he couldn't withstand "this easy and possible possibility of fixing everything!" (*Pss,* 28.2:207–8).

It isn't only the desire to free himself from his guilt and obligations that drives him to gamble, however. There is also a certain spiritual thrill, independent of any desire for gain, something inherent in the game itself that draws him in. He explains to Maikov,

> Now I'll describe for you how this all appeared to me: on the one hand, this easy win—from *one hundred* francs I made four thousand in three days. On the other hand, debts, penalties, spiritual alarm, the impossibility of returning to Russia. Finally, the third and most important thing—the game itself. You know how this can draw one in. No, I swear to you, it isn't just about profit [*tut ne odna koryst'*]. (*Pss,* 28.2:207–8)

This demon can possess him, he admits to Anna. In November 1867, he left her in Geneva to investigate Vevey and Montreux as places for Anna to give birth, and he could not resist stopping to visit the roulette wheels of Saxon-le-Bain. "Ach, *golubchik,* don't let me near roulette! As soon as I touch it— my heart stops, my arms and legs shake and turn cold" (*Pss,* 28.2:234).

The gambling demon that periodically takes possession of him makes him unworthy as a husband and father. He sends Anna, who is in Geneva, a distraught letter in the spring of 1868 from Wiesbaden; regarding Sonia, "(whom I'm not worthy of)," he insists, "what kind of father am I?" (*Pss,* 28.2:285). The urge to gamble represents his failure as an authority figure, a husband and father. He cannot let his young wife down, he writes, because of the faith she puts in him. In Baden I was with a young creature "who believes in me completely, whose defender and protector I am, and therefore I can't ruin her and risk everything" (*Pss,* 28.2:208).

In addition to these many tormenting obligations, the nature of his profession contributed to his experience of life as a series of debts and redemptions. Lacking a regular income, he lived from publication advance to advance. Penury often compelled him to take advances on projects he had barely begun, and his letters are replete with anxiety about the extent of his debt to publishers like Katkov. "Our meager means trouble me," he confides to Maikov from Geneva in August 1867. "We came with extremely modest means and having borrowed THREE (!) thousand from Katkov *in advance*" (*Pss,* 28.2:205).

Advances on novels periodically redeem him from the need to gamble, but they represent yet another form of debt from which he in turn must redeem himself through writing. "I wrote Katkov again, again asked for 500 rubles (not saying anything about the circumstances, but the letter was from Baden, so he must have understood something). Well, he sent it! He sent it! And now there are four thousand taken in advance from *Russian Messenger,*" he laments (*Pss,* 28.2:208).

Dostoevsky's entrapment in cycles of debt and redemption began when he resigned from the army in order to pursue a career as a professional writer. Frank provides an eloquent description of the system Dostoevsky came to resent as something inimical to the creative process.[3] The editor A. A. Kraevsky, "notorious for his ability to exploit literary talent" through his "obliging willingness to advance funds to impecunious authors," in effect setting "a trap baited with honey," lent Dostoevsky five hundred rubles in the wake of *Poor Folk,* which had raised his credit. "Soon finding himself totally dependent on the editor for his sustenance, Dostoevsky was forced to turn out copy against his will to pay his debts," Frank writes.[4] Dostoevsky writes Mikhail in October 1846: "The system of eternal debt, which Kraevsky tries to extend to everybody, is the system of my slavery and literary vassalage."[5] "It's awful to work like a day laborer," he complains to Mikhail. "You ruin everything, your talent and youth and hope, you loathe your work, and you finally become a sloppy scribbler and not a writer."[6]

Existing as this kind of proletarian writer, like being in the West, harms Dostoevsky's creativity. Writing to Mikhail in September 1858 that the story he has to finish for Katkov has become repellent to him, he complains that he can't just throw it out as he would like to: "There's already a lot written, it's not possible to throw it out in order to begin something else, because the debt has to be paid. And all my life I will write for money!" (*Pss,* 28.1:316). "I don't want to write on order [*ne khochu pisat' na zakaz*]," he complains to Mikhail in December 1858 from Semipalatinsk:

> I want to leave at least one impeccable composition after me. But what's to be done? You can't write what you want to, instead it's write that which, if you didn't need money, you wouldn't even think about. And for money I must *intentionally think up* stories. But that is so hard! It's a nasty trade being a poor literary man. (*Pss,* 28.1:319)

Dostoevsky deeply resents having to subject his writing to commercial considerations. "If experience has shown anything, it's that there can only be success under one condition," he writes Maikov in 1868. "Only if each of my compositions is so well done, that it awakens sufficiently powerful attention in the public; otherwise—everything is destroyed. But is this really possible, can this really be made into an arithmetical calculation!" (*Pss,* 28.2:213). In

1868, he writes his niece Sofia Ivanova of his doubts regarding *The Idiot:* "The idea is one of those that succeed through its essence, not effects. This essence is good in its conception, but how did it turn out in execution? And even if it was successfully executed, an effective novel is still more profitable [*effektnyi roman vse-taki vygodnee*]. It can be sold for more money" (*Pss,* 28.2:292).

Dostoevsky invests hope for deliverance from his debts and obligations in two things: writing and gambling.[7] He proposes the idea of a literary journal to Mikhail as a kind of desperate gamble, a vehicle for escaping from poverty and social marginalization. In November 1859, he writes Mikhail from Tver':

> We turned out to be accursed somehow. You look at others—no talent, no abilities—but the man moves in society, accumulates capital. But we struggle, struggle. . . . I am convinced, for example, that you and I have much more ingenuity and ability and knowledge of the business, than Kraevsky or Nekrasov. They are peasants in literature. And meanwhile they get rich, while we run aground. . . . No, brother, we have to think, and seriously; we have to take a risk and undertake some kind of literary undertaking—a journal for example. (*Pss,* 28.1:376)

When he has the peace of mind necessary for work—when creditors do not torment him—he can write and redeem his debts. In an August 1867 letter from Geneva, he explains to Maikov that in 1865, "I convinced the creditors to wait just a little, focused in myself, and got to work [on *Crime and Punishment*]. I succeeded, and the creditors were paid" (*Pss,* 28.2:212). Now things will get better, he tells Maikov during composition of *The Idiot,* "under ONE EXCLUSIVE condition, namely: THAT THE NOVEL TURNS OUT WELL" (*Pss,* 28.2:213). "This Geneva is cursed, and what will become of us? I don't understand! Meanwhile the novel is the only salvation [*edinst-vennaia spasenie*]," he writes Maikov in October 1867 (*Pss,* 28.2:227).

Writing represents a means of escape from places he doesn't want to be. He is desperate to get out of Semipalatinsk, where his epilepsy has worsened; he feels deadened by what he calls the "provincial stupor" that makes it difficult for him to write, and he longs to get back to European Russia but needs money for the trip. If he doesn't get the money, "then there will be absolutely no way to get myself out of here," he laments to Mikhail in December 1858 (*Pss,* 28.1:319).

Dostoevsky perceives gambling, like writing, as a form of *spasenie* (salvation). At lucid moments, he hopes for deliverance from his gambling demon and understands that his desire for salvation through a gambling windfall is opposed to the principle of working off debt through writings.

He experiences a tension between the pull of the roulette table and the writing desk. "Ania, dear, my priceless one, I lost everything, everything, everything!" he exclaims after a bout of gambling in 1867.

> O, my angel, don't be sad and don't worry! Be sure that now will finally come the time when I will become worthy of you and will no longer steal from you, like a nasty [*skverny*], vile thief! Now the novel, only the novel will save us, and if only you knew how I put my hopes in it! (*Pss*, 28.2:235)

Things were bad like this back in 1865 during work on *Crime and Punishment*, he reminds her. "It would be harder to be any closer to ruin, but work carried me through. With love and hope I will get to work and you'll see what will be two years from now" (*Pss*, 28.2:235). This sensible attitude is frequently overpowered by the gambling demon during the late 1860s, however.

The importance of gambling in Dostoevsky's spiritual evolution is difficult to overestimate. It is the gambling demon, not a religious or philosophical dilemma, that provokes Dostoevsky's famous observation about himself: "Worst of all is that my nature is base and too passionate: everywhere and in everything I go to the final limit, my whole life I've gone past the boundary" (*Pss*, 28.2:207). Dostoevsky makes this comment about himself in the August 1867 letter to Maikov, while describing the seduction of winning at roulette. This urge to transgress limits distinguishes him from others. Ivan Goncharov, also gambling in Baden, reproaches him: "When I lost everything down to the bone (and he had seen lots of gold in my hands) he gave me, at my request, a loan of 60 francs. He judged me very harshly: 'why did I lose everything, and not just half, like him?'" (*Pss*, 28.2:210) "I began to play my *last* things, irritated to a fever—lost . . . ," he writes in self-recrimination; "Anna Grigorevna pledged *everything* of hers, to the last little things (what an angel!)" (*Pss*, 28.2:207–8).

Deliverance from his gambling addiction comes as an experience that opens his eyes to the distinction between Russians and Jews. By the late 1860s, Dostoevsky experiences gambling as a kind of hell from which he needs deliverance. "Finally it was time to save ourselves, to leave Baden," he recalls for Maikov; "we spent seven weeks tortured in this hell in Baden" (*Pss*, 28.2:208, 207). Dostoevsky leaves Anna in Dresden in the spring of 1871 to chase his "accursed dream" of fixing everything—helping his dependents and himself (the language he uses is similar to that of Raskolnikov describing the murder)—at the roulette tables in Wiesbaden. Struggling with his tormented relationship to money, with his belief that he can relieve himself from guilty feelings toward his dependents through a miraculous windfall at the roulette table, he again loses everything, unleashing a torrent of some of the most self-lacerating passages in all his correspondence. "Oh,

Anna, why did I come!" he exclaims. "I *stole* from you" (*Pss,* 29.1:197, 198). "I'm afraid," he writes her; "what will become of you!" He laments, "I know that you'll die if I lose again!" (*Pss,* 29.1:198). "And Liuba, Liuba, o, how base I was!" he exclaims, regarding his unworthiness of his little daughter (*Pss,* 29.1:199).

Despite these fears, he assures Anna that something new has happened this time, something that is worth much more than it has cost: an event has occurred that banishes the demon once and for all. "For the sake of our whole future do not worry," he writes; read the letter through, he instructs her, and you'll see that "the problem does not warrant much despair, but, on the contrary, there is something that is acquired that will be worth much more than what was paid for it! [*beda ne stoit takogo otchaianiia, a, naprotiv, est' nechto, chto priobretetsia i budet gorazdo dorozhe stoit, chem za nego zaplacheno!*]" (*Pss,* 29.1:196).

Seeking to confess to another in person as well as on paper to Anna, Dostoevsky explains, he had gone out looking for a priest. In the unfamiliar darkness of Wiesbaden, he mistook a Jewish synagogue for a Russian Orthodox church.

> Running to him in the darkness through unknown streets, I thought: he is God's pastor, I'll speak to him not as with a private person, but as in confession. But I got lost in the city, and when I got to what I thought was the Russian church, they told me in the store that it was Jewish, not Russian. It was like cold water poured over me. (*Pss,* 29.1:198)

Mistaking Jews for Russians creates the sensation of cold water pouring over him in a kind of strange baptism. This moment marks his spiritual transformation, Dostoevsky asserts. "It's as though I was totally reborn morally (I'm telling you and God)," he confides to his wife (*Pss,* 29.1:199). The demon has been banished. "O, now I've been released from this dream and I would thank God that everything turned out this way, even with such trouble, if only there weren't such fear for you at this minute" (*Pss,* 29.1:198). "A great deed has been accomplished over me, the vile fantasy that *tortured* me for ten years has disappeared," he declares, "now this fantasy is over forever" (*Pss,* 29.1:198). He relinquishes the desire to gamble in favor of zeal for writing. "Now I'm going to work for you and Liubochka, not sparing my health, you'll see, you'll see, you'll see, my life, and I WILL REACH MY GOAL! I will take care of you both" (*Pss,* 29.1:198). "My hands have been untied; I was bound to the game, but now I will think about work and not dream for whole nights about the game, as used to happen" (*Pss,* 29.1:198–99). Apprehending the danger of confusing Russians and Jews has worked a spiritual upheaval in him.

Dostoevsky thinks of this moment—the disgust he feels at confusing

Russians and Jews—as a resurrection. "Now that I am so renewed—we will go together, and I will do so that you'll be happy!" he persuades his wife (*Pss,* 29.1:199). "Ania, believe that our resurrection has begun, and believe that I will now reach the goal—I'll give you happiness!" (*Pss,* 29.1:199). Mistaking Judaism for Orthodoxy in the darkness produces mortal revulsion; Dostoevsky draws a parallel between his experience of transformative disgust with Judaism and Christ's death on the cross. He tells Anna, "I will be reborn in three days and begin a new life" (*Pss,* 29.1:200). Anna Grigorevna ascribed similar importance to this event. He had promised her many times before to stop playing roulette and never fulfilled his promise, "but his happiness became real, and this was in fact the last time that he played roulette. . . . It seems that this 'fantasy' of Fyodor Mikhailovich of playing roulette was some kind of delusion or sickness, from which he was suddenly and forever cured" (*Pss,* 29.1:467).

Why does the possibility of any confusion between Christianity and Judaism disturb him so much? What, exactly, is it about Judaism that he so fears, that he doesn't want to admit within himself or Christianity? Belief in the redemptive quality of money, which held such power over Dostoevsky for so long, will be banished from Russianness and Christianity and made the essence of the "Jewish idea."

The need to take risks that Dostoevsky expressed through gambling will be gradually transferred to the Russian people. Before this event, Anna Grigorevna writes, her husband would periodically grow despondent and speak despairingly of the "demise of his talent." In order to banish the gloomy thoughts preventing him from concentrating on his work, she writes, she would bring the conversation around to the possibility of playing roulette. I had no illusions about the fact the money would be lost, she writes, "but I knew from previous experiences of his trips to the roulette wheel that, having experienced new burning impressions, having satisfied his need for risk, for the game, Fyodor Mikhailovich would return peaceful" (*Pss,* 29.1:466–67). In the *Diary,* Dostoevsky will write about the Russian people making a grand wager for the sake of humanity in the Balkans, risking their lives to save oppressed Slavs specifically and Christian civilization in general.

PART II

"I Have the Heart of a Lamb": Roots of the Russian and Jewish Ideas and the Problem of the Crucifixion in *Poor Folk*

THE CONCEPTS of Jewishness and Russianness that organize Dostoevsky's moral and historical consciousness in the late 1870s begin evolving in *Poor Folk*. This brief (barely 142 pages in English translation) epistolary novel brought Dostoevsky overnight acclaim when it appeared in Nekrasov's *Petersburg Anthology* in 1846.[1] *Poor Folk* disappoints hopes in a benevolent, or at least just, God and earthly authorities and dramatizes different ways of responding to that disappointment. Varvara Alekseevna displays a nascent form of what later Dostoevsky calls a Jewish mentality of limited empathy and willingness to accept the suffering of others as the price of one's own advancement. Her behavior differs sharply from that of Makar Devushkin, who exhibits a form of what Dostoevsky later claims is the distinctively Russian practice of total empathy with others. Devushkin progresses from justifying injustice on the grounds of God's inscrutability to expressing dissatisfaction with the world as he finds it. He is the prototypical Dostoevskian rebel, responding to injustice by questioning God's order and displaying the first hesitant gestures toward appropriating the right to make changes himself.[2]

It's worth examining the origins of the Russian and Jewish ideas in *Poor Folk*, for these beginnings shed light on later developments. The characters who perform ambiguous interventions against injustice in Dostoevsky's mature works—Raskolnikov, Stavrogin, Ivan Karamazov, and Russia in the *Diary*—become even more complex when we recognize Devushkin as their common ancestor. In the *Diary*, Dostoevsky will claim that total empathy and active intervention against injustice are Russian and Christian; his fictional rebels against injustice demonstrate the ambiguity of this claim, however. Their stories dramatize connections between empathy, a desire to intervene against injustice, and dissatisfaction with God. These connections first become apparent in the figure of Devushkin, whose hesitant impulse toward appropriating the right to save others is linked to an incipient rebellion against God.

Characters like Devushkin reveal that the relationship between the

Russian idea and Christian faith is not as straightforward as the *Diary* would have readers believe. Examining the interactions of Devushkin and Varvara Alekseevna shows that the moral ambiguity of the desire to correct injustice derives partly from a complex web of associations among victims and victimizers, or characters associated with what Dostoevsky later calls Russian and Jewish ways of thinking. Dostoevsky begins spinning this web of connections in *Poor Folk*.

Devushkin and Varvara Alekseevna are among the most pathetic characters Dostoevsky ever creates. Orphaned by impoverished parents as a young girl on the cusp of adolescence, Varvara fell into the hands of a procuress who posed as a benefactor only to arrange her seduction and abandonment by an older man. "I am afraid to look backwards," she tells Devushkin; "The past is full of such misery that my heart breaks at the mere memory of it."[3] Finding herself without guardians or means of support, she looks to Devushkin, a distant relation, as her only connection. Yet even she, who has suffered so much, expresses astonishment at the bleakness of his existence. "Have you really lived your whole life like that, alone, joyless, without a friendly word of greeting, renting out corners in other people's houses?" she asks him (*PF*, 21–22).

They find themselves in comparable situations as the novel begins: they are both poor and alone but hopeful. Despite the hardships they have endured, Devushkin and Varvara Alekseevna believe that their worst sufferings are over. "We shall see better days, my sweet!" he assures her (*PF*, 32). "Our misfortunes are now finally at an end. Let us offer our thanks to heaven!" he exclaims (*PF*, 31). They base their hopes for a happier chapter in their lives on God's goodness, believing that a just, reliable God can be counted on to look after them now. When they are subjected to increasing misfortunes, however, they respond to the escalating pressure of injustice differently. She degenerates, whereas he undergoes a transformation from reconciliation to the beginnings of rebellion.[4] "I'm not grumbling, I'm quite content," Devushkin says initially, but the injustices he witnesses eventually impel him to say he "looks at the world differently" (*PF*, 20, 89).

Devushkin's initial response to his own suffering is self-effacing accommodation. "I've always acted as if I didn't exist," he explains to Varvara (*PF*, 120). Tormented by his coworkers because he is so meek, he responds by trying to make himself even smaller and quieter (*PF*, 120). Assuring himself and her that all things good and bad are God's will and should be humbly accepted as such, he explains, "who is able to do what is arranged by God himself"; and "a man's condition, whatever it may be, is determined by the Lord according to his lot. One might be meant to wear a general's epaulets, another to be a titular councilor, one to give orders and another meekly and fearfully to obey them" (*PF*, 80). He bases his accommodation with his fate on the grounds that he is getting what he deserves. "I'm not from a line of counts!" he exclaims (*PF*, 24).

Devushkin initially believes that a just God and his own good behavior—his humble acceptance of his lowly station—will protect him from extreme misfortune or persecution. His modest hope is to "live my life in peace in my little corner . . . without interfering with anyone, fearing God and fearing lest someone should start interfering with me" (*PF*, 80). "I shall pray for you always, and if God in heaven hears my prayers you will be blessed," Varvara Alekseevna writes him, but her prayers either fail to reach their addressee or God disregards them, for the kind, gentle Devushkin is destroyed, calling on her, him, and us to decide what we will do about it (*PF*, 26).

Poor Folk shows the possibility of a range of responses to injustice. People can lose the ability to smell the odor of corruption. "There's a bad smell," Devushkin writes of his dingy tenement house populated by backbiting, cruel people who hound the unfortunate, "a slightly rotten, bitter-sweet odor," but it doesn't matter, for "it only takes a couple of minutes for that to pass, and you're not even aware of it happening because you take on the same bad smell yourself" (*PF*, 27). Vulnerability to corruption, the capacity to not just tolerate moral rot but to stink oneself, distinguishes people from animals. "Finches can't live in it," he writes Varvara; "in this air they just die and that's all there is to it" (*PF*, 27).

Children are located somewhere on the moral spectrum between the absolute sinlessness of animals, with whom they are often associated in Dostoevsky's writings, and the utter moral flexibility of adults. "I call them little birds," Myshkin says of children, "because there is nothing better than a bird in the world" (*I*, 90). Devushkin muses about the future of a little beggar boy he encounters on the street; the child may become hardened under the influence of adult cruelty, he realizes, but for now he is like a trembling little bird: "The child's heart becomes hardened, and the poor frightened little boy trembles in the cold, like a little bird fallen from its broken nest" (*Pss*, 1:87).

"You get used to it," Devushkin says of the stench that is metaphoric as well, but he never does; instead he begins to lose his ability to tolerate injustice. From the beginning of his epistolary relationship with Varvara Alekseevna, Devushkin shows signs of divided consciousness. Evidence of the work he has to do to silence his awareness that all is *not* right exists alongside his justifications from the start. "What a slum I've ended up in, Varvara Alekseyevna!" he exclaims amid his protestations that he doesn't mind his wretched quarters (*PF*, 19). "All the same, if the truth be known, my old apartment was incomparably better in every way," he admits, although he quickly adds, "I have no objection to it, although I still miss the old one" (*PF*, 24; *Pss*, 1:20).

His own misfortunes do not stir much dissatisfaction in him, however; on their own, they would probably never lead him into rebellion. The catalysts in his development toward rebellion are his encounters with other victims of injustice such as the Gorshkov family and Varvara; the contrast between the wealth he sees on display on Gorokhovaia Street and the misery of the lives of Petersburg's poor; and his engagement with the Russian literary heritage.

It is the suffering of other people, not his own, that triggers Devushkin's moral development. "I am not grieving for myself, it's not for myself that I'm suffering," he writes Varvara; I don't care if I go about in the cold without a coat and boots, for "What am I [. . .]? Nothing" (*PF,* 99, 65). The thought of her deprivations, however, gives him no peace. "Why are you so unhappy, Varenka?" he asks. "Why is your lot so wretched?" he wonders. "When I think of you, my heart is anguished" (*PF,* 112).

The sufferings of the Gorshkovs, an impoverished family living in his tenement house, make Devushkin restless. I'm pathetic, he writes Varvara, but Gorshkov is worse. "He's so pitiful and sickly," Devushkin laments, living with his "puny" children and "pitiful" wife all in one room (*PF,* 29). One night he overhears sobbing in their room, "but so quiet it was and so pitiful that it broke my heart, and for the rest of the night I kept thinking about these poor people so that I couldn't sleep properly" (*PF,* 29). He regrets his inability to help them. "How distressing it is, really, to see them like that, with a child suffering, still a baby, too, and not even be able to help," he writes (*PF,* 64).

Dissatisfaction with the suffering of the Gorshkovs and Varvara spurs Devushkin to reevaluate his own self-conception and relationship to God and authority.[5] "He's so shy and fearful of everyone, that he sidles rather than walks," he says of Gorshkov; "I can be timid sometimes myself, but he's much worse" (*PF,* 29). Impatience with *their* lot briefly inspires him to question his own humility. "Why have these misfortunes befallen me, then, may God forgive me?" he asks. "What am I being punished for? What ill have I ever done anyone?" (*PF,* 60). I rank myself so low, he realizes, just because "I'm frightened and hounded" (*PF,* 115). Instead of responding to abuse by making himself smaller, there are a few moments when he dares to question his mistreatment: "If I am just a copyist, what of it? Is it a sin to be a copyist?" (*PF,* 61).

Dissatisfaction with the injustice of Varvara's fate slides into dissatisfaction with the world in general. Impressions created by the glaring contrast between the opulence of Gorokhovaia Street and the lives of St. Petersburg's poor elicit the incipient social critique of his September 5 letter to Varvara. This letter is remarkable for its powerful combination of moral indignation and social commentary, and for what it contains for the future; years later

Dostoevsky will borrow from Devushkin in some *Diary* passages that blur the distinction between the voice of the *Diary* and this fictional character.

"It's joyless walking on the Fontanka!" Devushkin exclaims; he encounters "such frightful, depressing faces," "drunken peasants," "a haggard, puny man with his face bathed in sooty grease," and "such dirty damp women" "selling soggy cakes and rotten apples" (*PF*, 111). Then he turns onto Gorokhovaia Street, where "everything shines and glows, there are lights on everywhere"; he is dazzled by "sumptuous shops and stores," amazed by "flowers under glass," and impressed by carriages with "velvet and silk" (*PF*, 112).

Such discrepancies provoke new thoughts, he confesses—new "thoughts crawled into my head" (*Pss*, 1:87). The sight of rich ladies driving by in carriages provokes him to say, "When I think of you, my heart is anguished. Why are you so unhappy, Varvara? . . . Why is your lot so wretched? . . . I know, dearest, I know it's not right to think like that, that it's free thinking, but in all candor, in real truth, why is it that while yet in his mother's womb the raven of fate bodes good fortune to one man while another greets the world in a foundling hospital?" (*PF*, 112).

Reading Gogol's "Overcoat" is another turning point in Devushkin's development. "The Overcoat" frustrates his desire for justice and provokes him to rewrite it. Although he never explicitly demands justice for himself, he rejects his fate obliquely, by identifying with Akaky Akakievich and rejecting the story's unhappy ending. He would rewrite the story "so that it would work out like this: evil would be punished and virtue would triumph," Akaky Akakievich would find his coat and get a nice promotion (*PF*, 82). In his desire to rewrite his literary heritage according to justice, Devushkin will be linked to Nelli in *The Insulted and Injured*, who wants to rewrite *Poor Folk* so that Devushkin has a happy ending. Dostoevsky's first sacrificial child and first rebel are linked. Dostoevsky's later rebels who protest in the name of the oppressed will themselves abuse or contribute to the suffering of others and suffer intensely. In Devushkin, Dostoevsky's first experiment in articulating social and theological critique, we see the proximity of rebel and victim that will be so important in his mature novels.

The reader is linked to this first sacrificial child and first rebel as well. Nelli and Devushkin are not the only ones who want to rewrite Russian literature; Dostoevsky invites our dissatisfaction with his work as well. There are moments when Devushkin feels the futility of counting on God. "Oh, Varenka, how it torments me to hear someone begging alms for Christ's sake, and to walk past and say: 'God will take care of you,'" he confides (*PF*, 115). "May the Lord watch over you," he occasionally tells Varvara, but at times he loses confidence in God's ability or willingness to do so (*PF*, 103). We also witness him trying to retain his faith in God's wisdom in the face of mounting contradictory evidence. Gorshkov and his little child die, and Varvara leaves Devushkin brokenhearted and alone to marry Bykov, her former seducer. "There's something not quite right about it all," Devushkin muses (*PF*, 133).

He tries to convince himself that things are as they should be. "Of course, God's will will be done in all things. It must be so in this case, too, I mean, this must be God's will, also. The divine creator's providence is of course good and inscrutable, as is fate's, which is one and the same thing," he mutters, but we are not persuaded (*PF*, 133). The contrast between Devushkin's acquiescence and God's indifference prompts the desire to rewrite Dostoevsky, as Nelli will seek to; Dostoevsky invites his own correction.

"For every kindness God will bless you," Devushkin tries to convince Varvara and himself. "Kind deeds do not go without their reward, and virtue will always be crowned by God's justice, sooner or later," he writes, but *Poor Folk* shows him to be wrong (*PF*, 138). God's world is deeply flawed, for the good are punished, the bad are rewarded, and there are no benefits to suffering—it has not elevated but rather degraded Varvara's character.

Her response to his suffering begins as limited empathy but degenerates into the willingness to sacrifice him when it becomes advantageous for her to marry Bykov. Putting faith in God, Varvara's story shows, can be linked to a willingness to see others suffer, an ability to tolerate their pain. "Rely on God," she tells him. "He will make everything work out for the best" (*PF*, 105).

She articulates a sensible and sinister philosophy of limited empathy. "Everyone will of course say you have a kind heart, but what I say is that it is too kind," she admonishes. "Let me give you some friendly advice, Makar Alekseevich. I am grateful to you, very grateful, for everything you have done for me"; I see that "you now only live for me and my life—my joys, my woes, my heart." this empathy is problematical, she warns, for, "If you take other people's affairs so much to heart and sympathize so strongly with everything, then truly there is reason to be miserable" (*PF*, 98). "You must be more sensible," she advises. "Otherwise, life will be such a burden for you, feeling eternally melancholy and suffering for the sorrows of others" (*PF*, 99). In the *Diary*, the Jewish spider ruling Europe—Disraeli, "Viscount Tarantula"—will offer just this advice to Europe: Dostoevsky will identify him as the source of the view that Russia and Europe should put strict limits on their empathy and in fact write off the Balkan Slavs, abandon them to their Turkish oppressors.

Devushkin is not an entirely sympathetic character, however. He is complex in ways that are significant for understanding Dostoevsky's later rebels and the "character" of Russia in Dostoevsky's journalism. Devushkin's total empathy with the suffering of others is highly problematic, although not for the reasons Varvara identifies.[6] On the one hand, he shows a special regard for children that links him to Dostoevsky. For Devushkin, how people treat a child, especially an orphan, is a measure of their moral worth. People think they can abuse you, he tells Varvara, "because you're an orphan, because you're defenseless" (*PF*, 113). In his opinion, willingness to abuse children excludes someone from humanity. People who would insult an orphan, he claims, are "just scum, not people, simply scum" (*PF*, 86). When the proper adult-child relationship is violated—she supports him rather than the other way around—he plunges into despair. "My heart broke looking at your little orphan coins," he writes of the money she sends him (*Pss*, 1:82). "To torture your heart, my precious, one would have to be no more and no less than a bloodthirsty tiger, while I have the heart of a lamb" (*PF*, 106); "*u menia serdtse ovech'e*" (*Pss*, 1:81).

Devushkin's self-affiliation with the lamb—his total empathy with Varvara's suffering and desire to help her—is morally ambiguous. Characters such as Russia, Raskolnikov, Stavrogin, and Ivan Karamazov will also seek to take on the suffering of others and do something about it; why this is problematic becomes clearer by examining Devushkin. Devushkin's empathy is permeated by taboo erotic desires and the desire to gain a sense of self—the desire for self-assertion or identity—through performing sacrifices for others who may experience these gifts as aggressive and unwanted.[7] "When I think of you, my pet, it's like medicine to my sick soul, and although I suffer for you, suffering for you is easy," he writes Varvara, but she does not find his self-beneficial suffering on her account easy to bear (*PF*, 119).

As a relationship between a father figure and his "child" that is based on aggressive, exorbitant gifts that the recipient finds difficult to accept and that seem to benefit the giver most of all, the relationship between Devushkin and Varvara invites comparison to how Dostoevsky experiences the relationship between humanity and the God of the Crucifixion. Those who are saved by God's outrageous gift of his son may experience this excessive gift as entailing unbearable obligations. The Devushkin-Varvara relationship also parallels that between Russia and Europe as portrayed in Dostoevsky's essays. In *Time*, Russia likewise acquires a sense of self through self-sacrificial giving to another, the Europeans who, by Dostoevsky's own admission, don't even realize they need saving.

Varvara protests against Devushkin's gifts because she understands their self-sacrificial nature and cannot or does not want to reciprocate on the same level; she resists becoming the victim of his potlatch. Her first letter begins, "I am actually finding your gifts rather difficult to accept. I know what they cost you, the deprivations and self-denial in things you badly need. How many times have I told you that it is beyond me to repay even those kindnesses you have showered upon me up to now" (*PF,* 21). She pleads with him to stop spending money on her and accuses him of betraying their friendship through his inordinate sacrifices on her behalf. She also perceives an erotic undercurrent to his giving, a betrayal of the fatherly status he claims. "You took my outpourings quite amiss," he assures her; "I was animated by paternal affection, nothing but pure paternal affection, Varvara Alekseevna, for the place I occupy in your life is that of your own father, since you are an unfortunate orphan," he protests (*PF,* 23).

Devushkin gives because he gains a sense of self through sacrificing himself; his giving may be more about him than her. If I stopped giving to you, he asks, "What would happen to me . . . ?" (*PF,* 72). "What will happen to me? I'll go to the river and that will be the end of it all," he replies (*PF,* 76). Giving to her sustains him: "What will there be left for me to do without you? It's obvious that what you want to happen is for me to be put in a dray and carted off to the Volkovo cemetery" (*PF,* 76). She is obligated to accept the gifts that sustain his life, he quite explicitly tells her.

He gives beyond his means as a way to gain entrance into human community, to acquire an identity, which he lacked before. His life had previously consisted of self-effacement and feeling "ashamed in front of others" (*PF,* 17). At work, "They didn't stop at turning my name into a kind of byword, indeed almost a swear word—they started to find fault with me over my boots, my clothes, my hair, my appearance, none of it was to their liking, all of it had to be changed!" (*PF,* 60). Serving her elevates him. "I know my debt to you, my pet. Once I had got to know you, I began, first of all, to know myself better and to love you. Before I knew you, my angel, I was lonely and spent my life asleep, as it were," he confesses (*PF,* 107).

The progress toward identity and pride Devushkin makes by giving to Varvara has a curious parallel in the similar progress Russia will make through giving to Europe in *Time* and the *Diary*. In some of the first writings he published after returning to St. Petersburg from Siberian exile, Dostoevsky describes the relationship between Russia and Europe in language that recalls the relationship between Devushkin and his tormentors. Russians, Dostoevsky writes in his essays in *Time,* suffer from an inferiority complex—they mistakenly believe that they are insignificant and humble themselves before Europe. But Russia actually possesses a priceless gift that will save Europe, Dostoevsky argues.

The Europeans may not realize it yet, but they need the Russians, who will bring their gift of "pan-humanness" to the West; through this gift giving, Russians will simultaneously exalt and humble themselves. "How we cursed ourselves because we couldn't become contemporary Europeans," Dostoevsky writes in *Time*. "We used to accuse ourselves of being unable to be European," he writes of Russian self-hatred.[8] "Now we think differently," because we know what we have to give.[9] Because we understand our gift, "We have finally become convinced that we too are a separate nationality, original in the highest degree" (*Pss*, 18:36). The moral ambiguity of the spectacular gift of self-sacrifice Russia makes in the *Diary* begins with Devushkin's potlatch with Varvara.

Another intriguing parallel to the relationship between Devushkin and Varvara is the relationship between God and humanity as it takes shape around the potlatch of the Crucifixion. By giving his only son, God has made an extraordinary sacrifice for humanity, one that exceeds humanity's ability to repay and so may evoke ambivalence. "Is it some kind of joke, the amount you've been spending on me?" Varvara asks Devushkin. "The amount of money horrifies me! . . . I feel uncomfortable about accepting them from you, I know what they cost you," she complains regarding his gifts (*PF*, 62). "Everything which you intended to give me pleasure has made me sorrowful," she reprimands him (*PF*, 83). The relationship that forms around this strange gift giving serves to keep the father figure alive at the expense of the child's happiness. Giving to her, Devushkin protests, is what keeps him alive. "If I can't help you it would be as good as death to me, Varenka, pure death," he admonishes her (*PF*, 96).

Poor Folk reveals Dostoevsky's suspicion that an excessive gift like the Crucifixion may be a means to salvation for the giver, not the recipient, who actually tries to evade the ministrations of the aggressive giver. It's the strange father figure Devushkin who needs resurrection from shame and sleep into life, which he accomplishes by placing onerous burdens on an orphaned child.

"God Sent Her to Us as a Reward for Our
Sufferings": The Origins of Dostoevsky's
Preoccupation with Child Sacrifice
in the Dialogue Between *Time* and
The Insulted and Injured

THE PROBLEM of redemption preoccupied Dostoevsky in
the early 1860s, after his return to St. Petersburg from Siberian exile. There
were good reasons why this should be so. The sensation of awaiting what he
thought would be his execution by firing squad, only to receive a last-minute
reprieve, was seared in his consciousness. This traumatic, near-death experience was followed by what he experienced as the living death of prison.
"I consider those four years a time when I was *buried alive and closed in a
coffin*," he later wrote his brother Andrey (*Pss*, 28.1:181). After the living
death of prison, Dostoevsky spent several years languishing in what he called
the "provincial stagnation" of Semipalatinsk, where he did compulsory military duty. The 1850s was a decade of anguished existential marginalization;
Dostoevsky experienced his return to the intellectual life of the capital in
December 1859 as a kind of resurrection back into life.

On arriving back in St. Petersburg ten years after his departure in
convict's chains, Dostoevsky immediately began writing again. He under-
took an ambitious publishing venture with his brother Mikhail, launching
the monthly journal *Time* in 1860. His writings from this period—*The
Insulted and Injured, Notes from the House of the Dead,* and the essays
written for *Time*—place the need for individual and communal redemption at the center of attention. They assess several potential vehicles of
redemption and come to different conclusions about their efficacy. The
dialogue about redemption carried throughout Dostoevsky's novels and
journal essays starts here, in the early 1860s. Through this early multi-
perspectival conversation about different ways to salvation, Dostoevsky
embarks on the paths of inquiry that eventually lead to his mature
antisemitism.

Each of these works begins with the premise that a fallen state exists, argues the need for redemption, and considers various possible catalysts or vehicles of change. They conceive of this fallen state in similar ways, as social or familial conflict—the estrangement of nations, classes, and family members from one another. In *Time,* Dostoevsky argues that redemption can be found through art; *The Insulted and Injured* and *Notes from the House of the Dead* rescind this hope. They counter *Time*'s optimistic predictions of immanent rebirth through the experience of beauty with stories of how art fails to revive those who place their hopes in it.

These fictional writings go a step further. In addition to disappointing hope for redemption through aesthetic experience, they address the possibility of resurrection through vehicles associated with Christianity. *The Insulted and Injured,* published serially in *Time* throughout 1861, contrasts the failure of art to the success of child sacrifice; little Nelli's ambivalent self-sacrifice succeeds where the semiautobiographical narrator's ministrations through art and caritas fail.

"Mr. –bov and the Question of Art," published in 1861 in *Time,* is one of Dostoevsky's most important critical essays. He makes grand claims for art in this essay, arguing that we can experience morally transformative impressions when reading works like *The Iliad* or Pushkin's poetry or looking at a statue like the *Apollo Belvedere.* Such individual moral transformations, he maintains, will contribute to the resurrection of society as a whole. The beauty of the *Apollo Belvedere* "impresses itself on the soul," he writes; "such impressions last a whole life" and can influence one's actions many years later. Imagine that a young man gazes at the statue for a few moments, Dostoevsky suggests; "some kind of inner change happens in the person, some kind of rearrangement of parts," he believes, "in one moment making what's there not what was there before" (*Pss,* 18:78). Russians have access to their national idea, "panhumanism" or reconciliation, through works of art like Fet's poetry. The spirit of panhumanism [*obshchechelovechnost'*] expressed in art "will soon renew our social life," Dostoevsky declares.[1]

In contrast to this optimism, *The Insulted and Injured* dramatizes the failure of literature to make anyone better or solve any problems. The novel, subtitled "From the Notes of an Unsuccessful Literary Man," goes a step further and makes this failure personal: the narrator is a semiautobiographical figure, resembling Dostoevsky himself, and the literature that fails is a text meant to suggest Dostoevsky's own *Poor Folk.* Because a Dostoevsky figure and his art fail to deliver the promises made for literature in essays like "Mr. –bov," a different vehicle of redemption becomes necessary, a child sacrifice. Nelli's reluctant self-sacrifice accomplishes what the writer and his work failed to do. *The Insulted and Injured* tells the story of how an unhappy orphaned child reluctantly offers herself up to save others when a Dostoevsky stand-in and his story fail.

Similar problems move the plots of these early writings. In the case of *Time,* the estrangement of classes and nations must be overcome; in *The Insulted and Injured,* parents and children need reconciliation. When Dostoevsky examines societies, he assesses them in terms of spiritual unity; multiplicity of values suggests cultural degeneracy and danger to him. His historical visions are structured by the opposition between the ideals of reconciliation [*primirenie*] and synthesis, on the one hand, and the danger of disintegration [*raspad*], on the other. He identifies Western culture as the source of harmful multiplicity and contention and perceives Western ideas abetting the disintegration of Russian society. "There is no general opinion; all opinions are allowed, one thing lives alongside something else; there is no common opinion, no common belief," he writes with concern to Ivan Turgenev in 1865 (*Pss,* 28.2:113). One of the questions that most preoccupies me, he tells his correspondent Christina Danilovna Alchevskaia in 1876, is: "What do we have in common, what are the points around which we could all, despite our different orientations, join together?" (*Pss,* 29.2:79).

Russian society suffers from the "moral division of the people from the higher stratum" that began with Peter's reforms; the most urgent national task, he insists, is "unity no matter what," for "both parts of society suffer terribly from this splitting of the people in two."[2] Dostoevsky placed great hopes in the reforms implemented by Alexander II; the emancipation of the serfs, he believed, could signal the beginning of a new era for Russia. He discerns "signs of that great revolution" [*togo ogromnogo perevorota*], evidence that the Russian people are about to "say their new word."[3] Despite the hopes he placed in it, however, Dostoevsky believed that the emancipation would be ineffective unless the legal changes it introduced were accompanied by moral changes in society, which could only be accomplished through art. "Man changes not for external reasons but for no other reason than from moral change," he writes in his 1863 notebooks (*Pss,* 20:171).

The Westernized elite and the common people must overcome their mutual alienation, even antagonism, and be reconciled, he argues, for Russia to be reborn. He's optimistic that it can happen. "Can it really be that we are so suffocating, so frozen, that there is no hope for our revival?" he asks in the 1862 *Time* essay "Two Camps of Theoreticians" (*Pss,* 20:22). The elite and common people depend on one another for their own rejuvenation and that of Russia as a whole. "Without unification with the people, the higher classes will never succeed at their attempts to improve the social life of the nation" (*Pss,* 20:19). "Even if life has frozen within us, it is still alive within the untouched native soil . . . this is our sacred conviction," he tells his educated readers (*Pss,* 20:22). The common people are equally incapable of extricating themselves from the fallen state they find themselves in without help. "Left to his own devices," Dostoevsky writes of the common man,

> he stagnates in ignorance, totally deprived of any participation in those general human products of European civilization . . . by himself he finds it extremely difficult to escape from the unenviable position into which historical circumstances have placed him. Rarely, rarely does he find for himself a leader who shows him new paths, gathers together his scattered strength and powerfully moves them toward a single goal. (*Pss,* 20:18)

The people need the elite to guide them out of ignorance and toward certain aspects of Western civilization, such as "the gift of science" and the "magnificent, golden fruits" borne by "the tree of civilization."[4]

Passages like this problematize the belief that Dostoevsky's convictions were definitively transformed in Siberia. In the 1870s, Dostoevsky himself will claim that he experienced an epiphany while in prison; he will write that the Russian people need no other culture besides their Orthodox faith and that the educated elite should humbly accept guidance from them. Passages like this from *Time,* however, show that he acquired such views gradually during the years after exile, for here, in 1862, he writes of the ignorance of the Russian people, their need for secular Western culture, and the elite's leadership role.[5]

Just as Russia suffers from debilitating internal fissures, so do the people of Europe suffer the effects of harmful antagonisms. The great nations of Europe have degenerated into hostile camps and are separated from Russia by ignorant mistrust, *Time* warns. "For Europe, Russia is one of the riddles of the Sphinx," Dostoevsky opines.[6] "They cease to understand each other," he writes of the leading European nations, continuing that "they more and more stubbornly separate themselves from each other with their different rules, morality, and view of God's world."[7] "Some kind of unusual thickness of mind falls on those same people who invented gunpowder and counted the stars in the sky" when the subject turns to Russia, Dostoevsky complains.[8]

He enumerates the vehicles usually identified as capable of healing these rifts, only to reject them. Christianity has failed as a cohesive social force in Europe, he maintains. "They are all separating from each other according to their native interests, they are hostile toward each other to the point of irreconcilability, and more and more move apart along different paths, away from the general road," *Time* declares. "The Christian connection, which until now has united them, is losing strength with each day," he pronounces in his "Series of Essays on Russian Literature: Introduction" (*Pss,* 18:54). He also strikes at one of the most fervent hopes held by his progressive contemporaries, the belief that science could serve as a new unifying principle. "Even science," he argues in this essay, can't solve these problems.

The disintegration under way in Europe will not end peacefully, Dostoevsky predicts here. The Europeans are incapable of countering centrifugal forces on their own due to their inherent cultural weakness: their civilization is "so powerless, that up to this time it has not been able to overcome these hatreds" (*Pss,* 18:54). The roots of their hatreds lie too deep for self-help to be effective; their disease of contentious individualism exists in "the soil itself, and not in mere accidents [*v sluchainostiakh*], in the blood, in the whole spirit" (*Pss,* 18:54).

The cure, Dostoevsky claims in the 1863 essay "Answer from the Editors of *Time* to the Attack by *The Moscow News*," lies in a special Russian gift, the power to reconcile and synthesize. "And what have we been proclaiming for three whole years in our journal?" *Time* asks readers. "That the Russian land will say its new word, and this new word, perhaps, will be the new word of common human civilization [*obshchechelovecheskoi tsivilizatsii*]" (*Pss,* 20:98). Russians cast a reconciling glance "on the other [*na chuzhoe*]," he asserts in the brief essay "Subscription Announcement for the Journal 'Time' for 1861" (*Pss,* 18:37). "The Russian idea, perhaps, will be the synthesis of all those ideas which Europe has developed with such stubbornness and courage in its different nationalities," he maintains there. "Perhaps everything hostile in those ideas will find its reconciliation and further development in Russian nationality [*v russkoi narodnosti*]" (*Pss,* 18:37).

The quest for new life through reconciliation that animates the essays in *Time* is at the heart of *The Insulted and Injured* as well. The novel increases the stakes by adding a familial dimension to the problem of national-historical disintegration: the corrosive class division antagonizing the Valkonskys and Ikhmenevs is accompanied by the tragic estrangement of fathers and children. Here, however, the functions performed by art and Russia in the essays are performed by a semiautobiographical character. Through the figure of Ivan Petrovich, Dostoevsky himself tries to perform the reconciling, redemptive role played by Russia and art in his essays, shows himself failing, and stages the heart-wrenching death of a child as the consequence of his failure.

Dostoevsky endows Ivan Petrovich with elements of his own biography that were familiar to the Russian reading public. Like Dostoevsky, the narrator is an ambitious young man of proud but impoverished background, seeking fame and fortune in Petersburg through literature. Ivan Petrovich voices Dostoevsky's frustration about the need to make a living through writing. Like his creator, Ivan Petrovich complains about the pressures of a "proletarian" literary existence and resents the advantages enjoyed by independently wealthy writers. "They are provided for and don't write for deadlines, but I am an old post-horse!" Ivan Petrovich objects regarding the unfair advantages enjoyed by his well-off literary competitors (*Pss*, 3:426). The Russian public was well acquainted with the vicissitudes of Dostoevsky's tense relations with the wealthy Turgenev.

The story of how Dostoevsky became an overnight sensation when the literary critic Vissarion Belinsky acclaimed *Poor Folk* as the work of a new Russian master was common knowledge; Dostoevsky endows Ivan Petrovich with a similar story. "B. rejoiced like a child when he read my manuscript," the character recounts (*Pss*, 3:186). Dostoevsky tried to rehabilitate the poor man through his moving portrait of Devushkin; Ivan Petrovich tries to heal the deep division separating the rich from the poor through his writing as well. Belinsky (and progressive Russia following him) had been so delighted with *Poor Folk* partly because it tried to rehabilitate the poor and downtrodden, to establish their equality with their social betters: humble Devushkin overcomes his sense of inferiority and declares himself a man. Like *Poor Folk,* the story that makes Ivan Petrovich famous tries to create solidarity by revealing the common humanity beneath social differences. After he reads the story aloud to the Ikhmenev family, Ikhmenev exclaims, "You recognize that the most downtrodden, lowliest man is also a man and is my brother!" (*Pss,* 3:189).

Dostoevsky even reopens some of the most painful experiences of his life by making them part of Ivan Petrovich's story. The initial sensation around *Poor Folk* eventually subsided; Dostoevsky's next publication, *The Double,* received a cool reception from Belinsky and the public. A very public reassessment of Dostoevsky's talent followed, colored by the schadenfreude of those who had resented his meteoric rise to fame. You may be talented, Ikhmenev concedes to Ivan Petrovich, "well, but you're not a genius, the way they initially shouted about you, but just talented" (*Pss,* 3:191).

Ivan Petrovich's story temporarily moves the Ikhmenevs to tears, but it fails to accomplish its goal of making the poor equal to the rich. They have raised Ivan Petrovich, an orphan, like a son. Now he and their daughter Natasha are in love, but despite their affection for him, her parents reject him as a suitor because he is poor. They have succumbed to the attitude described by Alyosha Valkonsky, the man with whom Natasha eventually runs away. Money is more important than birth now, Alyosha observes: "Nowadays the most important prince is Rothschild" (*Pss,* 3:238). When he becomes aware of their feelings for each other, Natasha's father tells Ivan Petrovich that talent is worth less than money: "You may be talented, even remarkably talented. . . . But look: talent isn't money in the bank, and you're both poor. Just wait . . . if things go well, you establish yourself on your path—Natasha will be yours!" (*Pss,* 3:191). The Ikhmenevs weep over his story, but it doesn't effect their actions; they reject the penniless literary man, opening the way for Natasha to fall in love with Alyosha, abandon her parents, and thus create a parent-child rift that eventually requires Nelli's self-sacrifice as its solution.

After Natasha has abandoned her family and Ivan Petrovich, who was her first love, he tries to reconcile Ikhmenev with his wayward daughter. Outraged that his daughter has left home without his consent to live with Alyosha, Ikhmenev implacably resists any attempt to appease his anger. "Will this terrible discord never stop?!" Ivan Petrovich exclaims in despair (*Pss,* 3:230). Ivan Petrovich is described in terms that clearly suggest the sociopolitical agenda Dostoevsky was articulating in *Time.* The editors of Dostoevsky's collected works perceive a connection between Ivan Petrovich and *Time*'s humanist goals. "In the figure of Ivan Petrovich," they write, "Dostoevsky embodied his own humanist program that he was developing in the journal *Time*" (*Pss,* 3:525).

Ivan Petrovich manifests Christian caritas. He is linked to later characters like Myshkin and Alyosha Karamazov: he is so free of self-interest and loves others so deeply that he simply doesn't perceive any insult to himself.[9] "Ivan Petrovich's behavior . . . is that of the purest, most consistent altruism and brotherly love for all the humiliated and unhappy," Dostoevsky's editors write (*Pss,* 3:525). Natasha has abandoned him for Alyosha, and herself exclaims, "My God, how guilty I am before you!" but he serves her and her new lover with unconditional love. He thinks only of how her actions hurt her and her parents—"You will kill them and ruin yourself!"—so that she marvels, "And not a word about yourself! I abandoned you first, but you forgave everything, and think only of my happiness" (*Pss,* 3:197). "You'll never stop loving me," Natasha admires. He eagerly volunteers for the humiliating job of carrying their letters to each other. "I'll take care of everything for you both," he tells Natasha. "Everything, your meetings, everything. . . . I'll take your letters to each other; why shouldn't I carry your letters?" (*Pss,* 3:197).

When Ikhmenev makes a wounding remark about the narrator's waning literary fortunes, pointing out that his muse is going hungry, Ivan Petrovich expresses no resentment, reacting only to the pain he perceives motivating Ikhmenev's words. "The old man was not himself," he thinks. "If he didn't have his wound in his heart, he wouldn't have spoken to me about my hungry muse" (*Pss,* 3:193).

The service she especially needs him to perform is to reconcile her father to her, to mediate for her with her parents. A significant gulf has arisen between father and child, described in terms that evoke the gulf separating the people from the elite described in the essays in *Time.* Ivan Petrovich urges Natasha to "make the first step" in the belief that her father "will forgive you unconditionally" (*Pss*, 3:229), but she perceives significant obstacles. Her story is described in terms similar to that of the Russian people in *Time*. "It would be impossible to turn one's back on the old shore more, impossible to burn one's boats more boldly, than our people did on setting out on these new roads," Dostoevsky writes there (*Pss*, 18:36).

Her father will never accept the woman she has become, the ways she changed during the period of their estrangement, she retorts. "He loved a little girl, a big child," she explains. "He knew and loved a little girl and didn't want to even think about the fact that someday I too would become a woman" (*Pss*, 3:230). "So he has to get to know you and love you again. Most importantly: get to know," Ivan Petrovich says (*Pss*, 3:230). Like Ikhmenev, who hasn't participated in the development of his estranged child, the Russian elite may have difficulty accepting how the people have changed during the years of their independent development. "The people renounced their reformers and went off on their own road," Dostoevsky writes in *Time* in "Two Camps of Theoreticians" (*Pss*, 20:15). "History opened an abyss between us and them" (*Pss*, 20:17). The common man likewise "doesn't understand us well"; "he avoids us," with the result that now the people are "an unknown country" (*Pss*, 20:17, 20:5).

Natasha asks Ivan Petrovich to use his words for reconciliation, to narrate her story so that her father will forgive her. "Tell them everything, everything, *with your own words* from the heart; find the right words," she entreats him (*Pss*, 3:202). Ivan Petrovich's words fail to reconcile the angry father Ikhmenev with his erring child, however. Frustrated by Ikhmenev's implacability, Ivan Petrovich asks Natasha when the time for reconciliation will finally arrive. She answers, "We have to somehow achieve our future happiness through suffering; buy it with some new torments. Suffering cleanses everything [*Nado kak-nibud' vystradat' vnov' nashe budushchee schast'e; kupit' ego kakimi-nibud' novymi mukami. Stradaniem vsë ochishchaetsia*]" (*Pss*, 3:230). The suffering that cleanses everything and buys her happiness, however, is not her own but Nelli's.

Nelli is one of Dostoevsky's oddest creations. Orphaned on the streets of Petersburg, she crosses paths with Ivan Petrovich when he moves into the rooms her dead grandfather used to occupy. She behaves self-destructively, initially resisting his attempts to help her. "It's not necessary; it doesn't matter. . . . I don't have a name," she replies evasively when he tries to get to know her (*Pss*, 3:255). When he points out that she wears no socks on a cold day, she replies, "Let me die"; when he tries to prevent her from returning to the place she works as a servant, she replies, "Let them beat me! Let them ruin me, let them torture me. . . . I'm not the first" (*Pss*, 3:282).

This strange child is linked to Dostoevsky through her critical engagement with the Russian literary heritage and through her epilepsy. In a scene similar to the horse-beating scene in Raskolnikov's nightmare, Ivan Petrovich witnesses how Bubnova, her employer, beats Nelli in a scene of theatrical violence, with the other residents of the building watching from their windows. "She beat her victim on the face, on the head; but Elena remained stubbornly silent, and didn't utter one sound, not one cry, not one complaint, even under the blows" (*Pss,* 3:259). The violent assault brings on an epileptic attack. "Elena, standing as though senseless, suddenly fell to the ground with a terrible, unnatural cry and was wracked with terrible convulsions. Her face distorted. She had an attack of the falling sickness," Ivan Petrovich recounts (*Pss,* 3:260).

Dostoevsky, Devushkin, and Nelli are linked through their dissatisfaction with the treatment the little people receive in Russian literature. Dostoevsky rewrites Gogol's "Overcoat" with *Poor Folk,* which accords Devushkin greater dignity and complexity than Gogol's Akaky Akakievich. Devushkin wants to rewrite Gogol so that Akaky triumphs over his abusers; and Nelli wants to rewrite Dostoevsky himself. She reads Ivan Petrovich's story and demands to know why one of the minor characters of *Poor Folk,* a pitiful student named Pokrovsky, had to die young. "Why, why did he die?" she demands from Ivan Petrovich, who defends his plot. "What's to be done, that's how it had to be, Nelli," he explains. "It's not at all necessary," she objects, and she inquires whether Varvara and Devushkin will get to live happily ever after. "The girl and the old man," she asks, "well, will they live together? And won't be poor anymore?" "No, Nelli, she goes far away," he explains, marries a rich man, and leaves the old man all alone (*Pss,* 3:324). *Poor Folk* and *The Insulted and Injured* associate literary and social impulses known to be Dostoevsky's own with the sacrificial victims *and* with those who are at least partly responsible for their suffering.

The Insulted and Injured introduces elements of the biblical Job story into the plot of reconciliation and redemption. Finding themselves bereft of a child, Natasha's parents contemplate various possible responses to their loss. Ikhmenev displays characteristics of the Job who can be happy with other children; he wants to replace Natasha with a new daughter, Nelli. "He seriously thought about taking her into his home in place of his daughter," Ivan Petrovich writes (*Pss,* 3:26). This response—accepting the substitution of one child with another—is later validated by Zosima as the basis of Christian faith. Here, however, it is unfavorably contrasted to the behavior of Natasha's mother and is criticized by the very child who would serve as the substitute. Anna Andreevna loves her daughter enough to forgive her, and this love inspires her to refuse the kind of substitution Ikhmenev wants to perform. "I don't want any orphan!" she exclaims; "I don't want anyone but Natasha. There was one daughter and will always be one daughter" (*Pss,* 3:219). Here, willingness to accept substitutions seems based on insufficient love for the lost child.

Nelli criticizes the type of exchange Ikhmenev wants. The novel allows her, the child identified by the father as a potential substitute and the eventual child-sacrifice to his implacability, to confront him and comment on his desire to substitute a new child for the old one. "I had a daughter," Ikhmenev tells Nelli, "I loved her more than myself . . . but she's not with me anymore. She died. Would you like to take her place in my home and . . . in my heart?" (*Pss*, 3:383). Nelli wants no part of it and accuses him of being evil because he wants to forget his original child and love a new one. "You want to forget her completely and take in a new child, but is it really possible to forget one's own child [*rodnoe ditia*]?" she asks him (*Pss*, 3:383). Nelli hates him for refusing to forgive his child, resists being given to him as a substitute, and says, "He's a bad old man [*durnoi starik*]. . . . He doesn't want to forgive his daughter" (*Pss*, 3:295).

Ivan Petrovich is initially on what seems to be the correct side of these issues. Unlike the others who witness Nelli's beating, who defend their inaction by demurring, "It's not our business," or, "What is it to us, we're bystanders [*postoronnie*]," he stands up to Nelli's abuser and removes her from harm's way (*Pss*, 3:260, 3:261). "How dare you treat a poor orphan that way!" he scolds Bubnova (*Pss*, 3:259). He begins as someone who refuses the type of substitution Ikhmenev wants to perform. "I will never give you up," he assures Nelli (*Pss*, 3:282). He articulates an ethics of the gift, lecturing to Nelli, who has difficulty understanding his generous efforts on her behalf, about the importance of doing good for its own sake. "Good people don't wait until others give to them first, Nelli. They love to help those in need without getting anything first" (*Pss*, 3:376).

> I am acting with you the way my heart commands. You are now alone, without relatives, unhappy. I want to help you. That's how you would help me, if things were hard for me. But you don't want to think that way, and so it is difficult for you to accept the simplest gift from me. You immediately want to pay, to work for it, as if I were Bubnova and resented you. If that's the way it is, then it's shameful, Nelli. (*Pss*, 3:286)

He betrays his promises to her, however, and calls in the debts she has reluctantly incurred through his gifts. As the alienation of Ikhmenev from his child drags on, Ivan Petrovich comes to believe that Nelli's narration of her story might succeed even though his words and *Poor Folk* have failed. Nelli, he thinks, "could perhaps touch the old man and move him to magnanimous thoughts through the sad, tragic tale of her earlier life and the death of her mother" (*Pss*, 3:393). The ground was prepared. "Now it needed just a push, the final event, and this fortuitous event might be Nelli" (*Pss*, 3:393).

"'Nelli, angel!' I said, 'do you want to be our salvation? Do you want to save all of us?'" You can save us, he tells her, by offering up your life story. "Tell them, Nelli, everything, the way you told me. Tell everything, everything, holding nothing back" (*Pss*, 3:406). She agrees, but looks at him strangely as she does so, and "something like reproach was in that glance" (*Pss*, 3:407). Together with Anna Andreevna, who agrees that Nelli's story might soften Ikhmenev toward Natasha, Ivan Petrovich orchestrates the spectacle of Nelli's self-narration.

"I've brought you my Nelli," he tells Natasha's parents, advising them to "take her and love her" (*Pss*, 3:407). When he urged Nelli to speak, he later recalls, she looked "as though calling on me for help. She was breathing somehow unevenly and heavily" (*Pss*, 3:408). "She got up in great agitation and wanted to go to the door," but they call her back (*Pss*, 3:409). "Nelli looked at me questioningly as though in bewilderment and fear"; her lips quivered; "getting hold of herself with torment [*s mucheniem peresilivaia sebia*]," she begins her story (*Pss*, 3:419). When she describes how her grandfather arrived too late—her mother was already dead—Anna Andreevna cries, "I, I will be your mother now, Nelli, and you my child!" and even Ikhmenev rushes to embrace the poor child (*Pss*, 3:420). But Natasha rushes in at that moment, and they forget all about Nelli. They remember the child only later, after they have calmed down. "We left her alone so!" Anna Andreevna exclaims. Nelli has regressed to infancy; they find her alone in another room saying, "Where, where is my mama?" and she soon suffers an epileptic attack (*Pss*, 3:422).

Her self-sacrificial self-narration has two consequences for Nelli, the epileptic child sacrificed to an angry father. On the one hand, she is worshipped by the Ikhmenevs, in whose house she lives like an idol—"Nelli is now the idol of the whole house," Ivan Petrovich writes after that fateful day (*Pss*, 3:425). On the other hand, it has precipitated a fatal illness. "She fell sick on that very day when we took her to the old people, on the day of their reconciliation [*primirenie*] with Natasha," Ivan Petrovich admits (*Pss*, 3:429). "I, Natasha, and the Ikhmenevs felt and acknowledged all our guilt before her, on that day when she, trembling and tormented, *had* to tell us her story" (*Pss*, 3:430). Ikhmenev does not seem to share Ivan Petrovich's sense of guilt, however; he accepts Nelli's loss as his gain, saying, "God sent her to us as a reward for our sufferings" (*Pss*, 3:429).

The connections between Nelli, the sacrificial child offered up to assuage the angry father, and Dostoevsky/Ivan Petrovich deepen in their shared status as epileptics and victims. Ivan Petrovich is not only the agent of Nelli's demise; in addition to encouraging her to sacrifice herself for Natasha and her parents, he too becomes their victim. When *The Insulted and Injured* opens, he is lying sick and abandoned in a hospital bed, narrating the stories of Ikhmenev, Natasha, and Nelli while he waits to die. When the actions I'm going to tell you about began, he tells the reader, spring was approaching, and I hoped for a fresh start. I wanted "to refresh my mind and begin again with new strength. Back then I still dreamed of this and hoped for resurrection [*nadeialsia na voskresenie*]" (*Pss*, 3:207). "There was thirst for life and belief in it!" he remembers (*Pss*, 3:207). He still hoped for a successful literary career as well as resurrection. "I was still contributing to journals, wrote essays and firmly believed that I would succeed at writing something big and good. I was working then on a big novel; but things nevertheless ended so that I'm now in the hospital and, it seems, will die soon" (*Pss*, 3:177). "My inspiration fizzled out," he admits (*Pss*, 3:231). Now, he writes, "I'm lying in my sick bed alone, abandoned by all whom I loved so much and so strongly" (*Pss*, 3:371).

Nelli and Ivan Petrovich are agents of reconciliation who die in the process of restoring life to others. They re-create the Ikhmenev family but are themselves excluded from it; Ikhmenev had called Ivan Petrovich his son, and Anna Andreevna said she would be Nelli's mother, but they accept the death of the former and abandon the latter to die as the consequences of their own happy ending. Nelli's death is especially disturbing. Her loss helps others but is unredeemed for her; her suffering and death are like a remainder, a residual left over after others are taken care of, that will haunt Dostoevsky and his later characters.

Poor Folk questions Christianity and Russia's mission to Europe by rendering problematic relationships based on inordinate gifts that may harbor elements of self-interest and (taboo erotic) aggression. *The Insulted and Injured* continues this questioning by staging the disturbing self-sacrifice of a child. Each of these works focuses on how much the resurrection of a lucky few costs in terms of suffering for others. Devushkin is left alone, presumably to be carted off to the cemetery as he predicted, and Nelli and Ivan Petrovich die. Their losses represent gains for others. *Notes from the House of the Dead* will question the belief that some can be aided through the sacrifice of others by showing the possibility of absolute, utter loss that benefits no one. Akulka's death, for example, recapitulates the Easter Passion, but nothing good comes of it for anyone.

The pain of this situation portrayed in Dostoevsky's early works finds a solution of sorts. The absolute loss of unwilling or ambivalent sacrificial victims like Devushkin, Nelli, and Akulka evolves into the Russian people's more self-determined act in the Balkans; the passive sacrificial victim becomes a willing agent of resurrection for others, as Christ and individuals like Nelli and Akulka are replaced by a messiah people.

Sources of Dostoevsky's Antisemitism in *Notes from the House of the Dead*: The Problem of Redemption and the Resemblance of Christians and Jews

"NOW, IT SEEMS, we are entering a new life," Dostoevsky proclaims in *Time* (*Pss*, 18:37), but *Notes from the House of the Dead* disappoints this hope for resurrection. *Notes from the House of the Dead* (alternately translated as *Memoirs from the House of the Dead*) began appearing in serial installments in the journal *Russian World* in September 1860. Dostoevsky halted its publication in that journal after January 1861 so that he could publish it in *Time*, where it began appearing in April 1861. *Notes* undermines *Time*'s faith in immanent resurrection in two primary ways: by questioning the possibility of reconciliation between the Russian people and the elite, which *Time* insists is a necessary precondition for salvation; and by raising concerns about the efficacy of the Crucifixion as a vehicle of redemption. The dead house, and all of Russia behind it, is a world to which redemption has not yet come, despite Christ's death on the cross.

Dostoevsky subjects the Crucifixion to critical scrutiny in several ways in *Notes*. He stages spectacles of suffering and death that have the potential to redeem those who witness them but fail to do so. The Christian premise that time has been transformed through Christ's appearance on earth—the belief that his birth inaugurated a new era—is undermined by the persistence of empty time; the caesura of the Crucifixion was supposed to put an end to the kind of meaningless sequentiality in which the inhabitants of the dead house remain trapped. Christ's life and death are further robbed of meaning through the disappointment of hopes placed in Christmas and Easter.

In addition to interrogating the possibility of rebirth through Christ, *Notes* undermines *Time*'s optimism about resurrection through its ambivalent portrait of the Russian people. *Time* rallies its educated readers around confident assertions that union with the people and resurrection into a new life are just around the corner; *Notes* portrays serious moral obstacles to such a union. *Time* impresses on readers how difficult such reconciliation will be but believes that it will happen nevertheless. "Even our best 'experts' on the people's life have failed to understand how *wide* and deep the gulf separating us from the people is," Dostoevsky concedes in *Time,* "for the simple reason that they have never lived with the people."[1] The common man, Dostoevsky informs his educated readers, "will never think of you as one of his own"; "he will never think of you as his brother, . . . And he will never, never trust you" (*Pss,* 19:7). A difficult task faces the elite, he warns: "The trust of the people has to be earned now; we have to love them. . . . Do we know how to do this?" (*Pss,* 19:7).

We do, Dostoevsky asserts. Despite the significant admissions about the deep gulf separating the elite and the people in *Time,* an assertive voice overrides any doubts that have been awakened. "We are optimists, we believe," Dostoevsky proclaims (*Pss,* 19:7). "Now the division is ending," he states in the "Subscription Announcement for the Journal 'Time' for 1861" (*Pss,* 18:36). Reconciliation with the people will be accomplished through education, love, and mutual respect, *Time* confidently advises. "In all of our classes there are many more points of unity than difference, and this is the main thing."[2]

Notes from the House of the Dead strikes a more hesitant note, however. It is as though the difficulties that are acknowledged but glossed over in *Time* receive real faces and voices in the characters of *Notes.* The narrator, a member of the educated elite, personally experiences the negative consequences of the gulf separating the classes. Members of the educated elite, he writes, "are separated from the people by the most immense abyss" (*Pss,* 4:198). "The prisoners in general regarded former members of the nobility with resentment and ill will," he writes. "They watched our sufferings, which we tried not to show them, with delight."[3] "There is nothing harder than to gain the confidence of the people," he warns (*MHD,* 32). Alexander Petrovich Gorianchikov never achieves the kind of union with the people hoped for in *Time,* casting the possibility of a new life for Russia in doubt. "You may associate all your life with the people," he tells readers near the end of his story, but

> you will never know the essence of them. It will be an optical illusion, no more. I know, of course, that everybody, absolutely everybody, who reads this remark of mine will say I exaggerate. But I am convinced that it is true. My conviction was reached not through books, not theoretically, but through reality, and I had quite enough time to verify my conviction. Perhaps in the future everyone will learn to what degree it is correct. (*MHD,* 309)

Gorianchikov's warning about the impossibility of true union with the people harmonizes with a general tone of caution and hesitancy sounded in *Notes* that distinguishes it from many of Dostoevsky's other works.[4]

Time claims that exceptional spiritual gifts—"the highest and most noble gifts of nature"—indicate Russia's election for a redemptive mission to Europe.[5] "Yes, we believe that the Russian nation is an unusual phenomenon in the history of humanity," Dostoevsky proclaims in *Time*.[6] One historical period is ending, Dostoevsky asserts there, and a new Russian era is beginning. Who knows, he addresses the Europeans, our "older brothers, beloved and dear," as he calls them, "perhaps Russia was destined to wait until you finished" (*Pss*, 18:54, 18:56).

The situation in *Notes* looks very different. Far from being a vehicle of transformation for others, here the Russian people represent a spiritual nadir; it is unclear how they themselves will be saved, let alone save others. In Dostoevsky's later works, images of the people frequently do bear the burden of transformation: Myshkin believes that the face of a peasant mother he encounters manifests true Christian faith; one catalyst of Zosima's spiritual regeneration is the face of his servant, a simple man of the people. Here in *Notes*, however, the Russian people are not yet a messiah people; they are not even truly Christian.[7]

The contrast between *Time*'s optimism and the hesitancy of *Notes* is striking. One of the most startling ways *Notes from the House of the Dead* questions the possibility of salvation through Christ is by implying the moral equivalence of Orthodox Russians and Jews. The moral flaws of the Russian prisoners—lack of conscience, vanity, and formalism, or adherence to the law in place of dynamic spirituality—link them to the Jewish prisoner Bumstein. The true Christians in this work, the people who grasp and live the truth of Christ's message, are the Muslim prisoners Gorianchikov gets to know. Some of the most important convictions we associate with later Dostoevsky, such as belief in Russian Orthodox exceptionality and superiority, are definitively *not* in place in the early 1860s.

Dostoevsky's later insistence on sharp distinctions between Russians and Jews appears different in light of *Notes*. Unlike the *Diary*, *Notes* doesn't use the figure or idea of the Jew to highlight the moral superiority of Orthodox Russians; on the contrary, it hints at a similarity of Russians and Jews in order to illustrate the failure of Christ's mission and underscore the continuing difficulty of resurrection. The antisemitism of Dostoevsky's later years, a close reading of *Notes* implies, may have arisen less from confident faith in Russia or Christianity and more from the perception of an impermissible likeness between the self and an "other."

Notes differs from Dostoevsky's other works so profoundly that its uniqueness has frequently eluded appreciation. The central convictions of Dostoevsky's contemporaneous journalism and later works that *Notes* refutes include belief in the possibility of union with the people and belief in spiritual resurrection through union with the people or Christian faith. These convictions are undermined by the negative moral portrait of Russians—their association with the Jew—and the irresolvable status of the semiauto-biographical narrator's fate as well.

"I remember that nothing but passionate longing for resurrection, re-newal, a new life, gave me the strength to wait and hope," Gorianchikov says, and the last words of the text are his thoughts on gaining release from prison (*MHD*, 342). "Freedom, a new life, resurrection from the dead . . . What a glorious moment!"—these ecstatic thoughts are the closing words of the book (*MHD*, 361). The reader knows, however, that Gorianchikov's textually final moment of "resurrection from the dead" was followed by a biographically final period of disappointed hopes, an existence dragged out in embittered isolation. "But it is painful for me now to recall my spiritual condition at that time," the postrelease Gorianchikov admits.[8]

Notes juxtaposes a drama of communal redemption to stories of individuals in need of resurrection. The starting point for the narrator and other prisoners is hell. "This was Hell, the nethermost pit and the outer darkness," Gorianchikov says of the prison, characterized by "corruption and terrible perversity" (*MHD*, 12). "It is difficult to conceive to what extent human nature may be perverted," Gorianchikov writes, raising the question how people this fallen could be raised up (*MHD*, 241). *Notes* asks what the vehicles of salvation from this Hell could be and leaves the question unanswered.

Like the narrator of *The Insulted and Injured,* the narrator of *Notes from the House of the Dead* is semiautobiographical. Alexander Petrovich finds himself in even greater need of redemption than Ivan Petrovich, who was hoping for "resurrection" (*voskresenie*) before the events of *The Insulted and Injured* unfolded. Gorianchikov seeks but fails to find conclusive reconciliation with the people, and he never accomplishes spiritual resurrection after his sin of murder. He seems to derive little benefit from his sojourn in the dead house; his passage through "this life outside life" lacks redemptive value, for no good seems to come of it for him or anyone else (*MHD*, 14). The sterility of his suffering and passage from life into death and back into life again on his release from prison casts the value of such experience as a redemptive vehicle into question.[9]

Notes from the House of the Dead is a work of disappointed expectations; it casts a skeptical glance at the enthusiasms of Dostoevsky's contemporaneous essays, undermining the claims for national election and spiritual regeneration he makes there. The relationship between *Notes* and Dostoevsky's later works is one of critical skepticism as well. Perhaps no other work by Dostoevsky has been made to bear so much responsibility by scholars. *Notes* supposedly documents the transformations that would determine the future course of Dostoevsky's creative life; it is typically interpreted as a decisive turning point in his development.[10] Later Dostoevsky himself makes claims about his experiences in prison that have influenced how readers interpret *Notes*. But this text simply does not conform to the anachronistic expectations created by the spiritual autobiography Dostoevsky composes for himself in the 1870s or suggested by the later literary works. The people portrayed in *Notes* fail according to the expectations created by Dostoevsky's later writings.

Biographical material from the period when *Notes from the House of the Dead* was composed shows that the ambivalence expressed there characterizes Dostoevsky's personal experience as well. His statements about his spiritual life from this period have a cautious tone that contrasts to the decisive quality of his later reminiscences. The complexity of his Siberian experience was still vivid in the early 1860s, and Dostoevsky's ideological positions were more complicated as well. *Time* finds much more praise for Westernizers and Peter the Great than for Slavophiles, whom Dostoevsky accuses of having "the remarkable ability to not understand anything about contemporary life."[11]

In *Time*, Dostoevsky accuses Ivan Aksakov's Slavophile journal *Day* of being staffed by "domestic despots" who want to terrorize those who think differently. "Yes, this almost smells of bonfires and tortures," he writes of what he calls *Day*'s ideological terrorism (*Pss,* 19:59). "The Slavophiles have the rare ability not to recognize their own and to understand nothing in contemporary activity," he alleges (*Pss,* 19:59). He mocks their "dark [*smutny*] and indefinite ideal: an abstract, bookish love of the fatherland, a panoramic view of Moscow, and Karamzin's Marfa Posadnitsa" (*Pss,* 19:60). It is Westernism, he writes, that has progressed further and has native principles on its side; "through self-awareness it returned to the native soil and acknowledged unification with the popular basis and salvation in the soil" (*Pss,* 19:61). In comparison, "In the current almost universal return to the soil," Dostoevsky asserts, "the influence of the Slavophiles has participated very little and perhaps didn't contribute at all" (*Pss,* 19:61).

The Dostoevsky who publishes "The Peasant Marey" in the 1876 *Diary* confidently recommends himself as one who can mediate redemption through the people, but Dostoevsky in the early 1860s emphasizes the difficulty of communicating his experiences of prison and liberation. These experiences defy transmission even to his brother Mikhail, the person to whom he's closest at the time. "Well how should I convey to you my mind, understanding, everything that I experienced . . . such a task is definitely impossible," he writes Mikhail (*Pss,* 28.1:167). "Even if I wrote you one hundred pages, even then you wouldn't have any idea about my life then. It's necessary at the very least to see it oneself—I won't even say to experience it" (*Pss,* 28.1:181).

Letters written to Mikhail from Omsk in 1854, immediately after his release from prison, show little indication of mystical union with or admiration for the people. "This is a crude, irritated and angry people. Their hatred for the nobility exceeds all bounds, and so they met us with hostility and evil joy over our sorrow. They would have eaten us if they could have" (*Pss*, 28.1:169). Any rapprochement between himself and the people he describes to Mikhail exists only in the people's gloating perception that now the nobleman has fallen to their level. "Before you were a master, tormented the people, but now you're worse than the last of us, have become our brother," Dostoevsky paraphrases the people's thoughts; "one hundred and fifty enemies couldn't stop persecuting us, it was their delight, entertainment, and occupation" (*Pss*, 28.1:169). Dostoevsky clung to awareness of his superiority. "The only thing that saved us from despair was the indifference, moral superiority, which they couldn't help understanding and respecting, our not succumbing to their will. They always recognized that we were higher than them."[12]

Notes lacks the faith in the Russian people that Dostoevsky acquires later; any kind of regeneration with them or for them seems unlikely due to their depravity. Evidence that the people are so fallen that even Christ's intervention is ineffectual is preponderant in several ways. Most obviously, there is much more of it, and it is delivered as detailed, concrete observation, whereas the few positive statements Gorianchikov makes about the people come in the form of abstract assertions uncorroborated by any observations. What he says should be given less weight than what he chronicles as an observer. The few abstract positive assertions about the people remain unsubstantiated by action or dialogue; this is especially noteworthy in light of the narrator's critique of abstraction. There are many things in life, he writes, "which can't be understood except in reality" (*Pss*, 4:197). Fear of censorship cannot be cited as a reason why Dostoevsky did not portray the prisoners in a more positive light; if he could allow Gorianchikov to make a few positive assertions about the people, he certainly could let Gorianchikov provide examples as well.

Careful examination shows the few statements about the people's positive qualities to be unreliable. "A high and most characteristic trait of our common people is their feeling for justice and their thirst for it," Gorianchikov says, but he gives few examples of the prisoners desiring a form of justice that would be recognizable to his educated readers and instead provides many examples of their bizarre, objectionable sense of right and wrong (*MHD*, 184). "One need only remove the outer husk and scrutinize the grain within attentively, closely and without prejudice, to see things in the people of which he had never even dreamed," he says; but when he actually removes the husk, he exposes depravity and horror (*MHD*, 184). When Gorianchikov makes positive statements about the people, one of the qualities he cites most frequently in their favor is their strength. There were "strong characters among them, men who all their lives had been used to rule and domineer, tough and fearless men," he asserts (*MHD*, 14). "How much great strength perished here in vain!" Gorianchikov exclaims. "Truly this was an unusual people. Truly this, perhaps, is the most gifted, the strongest of all our people" (*Pss*, 4:321).

Yet strength and intelligence are not Christian or desirable values or qualities in themselves. The individuals who manifest strength and intelligence in the dead house place their abilities in the service of evil. Orlov, Gorianchikov writes, is the spiritually strongest man he has ever known, and also one of the most depraved. Orlov is "a man of terrifying strength of will"; he is "an evil-doer such as rarely occurs, a cold-blooded murderer of old men and children" (*MHD*, 65). He exhibits extraordinary "inner, mental energy," Gorianchikov observes; "I have never met a man of stronger, more rock-like character" (*MHD*, 66). He witnesses Orlov transcending the power of the flesh in order to do evil. Even after extremely harsh corporal punishment, "Orlov quickly recovered. Obviously, his inner, spiritual energy powerfully helped nature" (*Pss*, 4:153). Orlov combines exceptional strength and intelligence with utter lack of conscience. When Gorianchikov tries to draw out some remorse about his crimes, Orlov "looked at me with such arrogant contempt as though I had suddenly become in his eyes a stupid little boy with whom it was impossible to talk reasonably, as with a grown-up" (*MHD*, 67). Along with Orlov, Gazin is one of the most remarkable individuals Gorianchikov encounters, and also one of the most depraved. Like Orlov, Gazin is strikingly intelligent and strong: "His eyes showed that he was far from stupid, indeed extremely shrewd" (*MHD*, 56).

Gorianchikov makes some allusions to a change in his attitude toward the prisoners' moral qualities. This goes only so far as realizing that some prisoners may be "*no worse* than other men," however (*MHD*, 81). The prisoner who opens his eyes to this possibility is Sushilov, who trades his relatively mild punishment for a more severe one because he is tricked with "a red shirt and a ruble in silver" (*MHD*, 84). Although Gorianchikov holds Sushilov up as an example of a prisoner who is "no worse" than men on the outside, this claim is undermined. The "meekness" behind Sushilov's cooperation with his swindling is not positive; it is one of many examples of the lack of a sense of personal dignity or individual worth that Gorianchikov observes interfering with the development of Christian moral conscience among the prisoners. The mentality that makes Sushilov meekly accept his fate is the basis of a terrifying moral indifference Gorianchikov observes among them. The principles behind corporal punishment—abuse of authority, lack of respect for the individual, degradation in general—are self-evident to the prisoners but elicit astonishment from Gorianchikov:

I was always astonished at the extraordinary good nature and lack of malice with which men who had been flogged spoke of their beatings and of those who had inflicted them. Very often it was impossible to detect the slightest shade of resentment or hatred in narratives which sometimes made my heart rise into my throat and begin to thump heavily and violently. (*MHD*, 224)

Like the nobleman Gorianchikov, the Polish political prisoner Miretsky suffers from "some internal pain" and "indignation" at the memory of his corporal punishment (*MHD*, 225). The Russian people lack the values, shared by the Russian and Polish noblemen, that could make Christian moral conscience possible.

The people lack any concept of moral accountability. At one point the prison horse, used for tasks like drawing water, falls down dead, but "it never entered anybody's head, not even the major's, to blame Roman [*the driver*] in any way; it was the will of God, that was all, and Roman was a good driver" (*MHD*, 293). Gorianchikov never gets used to the moral vacuum that is the world of the common people. He wonders at how serious offenses against each other seem to have no consequences. The Lomovs, father and sons, are in prison for murders they did not commit; the real murderer is in the same prison for other crimes. "Although the Lomovs knew that Gavrilka was the criminal, and although they were in prison because of what he had done, they did not quarrel with him"; one of the Lomovs does eventually stab Gavrilka, but "over a most repulsive wench," not the crime committed by Gavrilka for which they are unjustly suffering (*MHD*, 285). Gorianchikov is astonished by the lack of recrimination against those who do not take part in the communal grievance:

They were not in the least angry, either, with those who had refused to associate themselves with the grievance and remained behind in the kitchen, or with those who had been the first to shout out that they were satisfied with everything. Nobody, in fact, even referred to this. I found this last particularly difficult to understand. (*MHD*, 322–23)

The conviction that actions have consequences separates the educated man from the people to the end.

Later works such as "The Peasant Marey" and *Crime and Punishment* established Dostoevsky's reputation as an artist skilled in the representation of transformative moments, flashes of redemptive insight. *Notes from the House of the Dead* raises but disappoints desire for such moments. In "The Peasant Marey," Dostoevsky claims to have experienced an epiphany that revealed the moral goodness of the prisoners to him while he was in prison. Gorianchikov, on the other hand, addresses our expectation of significant moments in order to disappoint it, insisting that he never experienced any decisive turning points while in prison. "I have said before that I finally did grow accustomed to my situation in prison. But this 'finally' was reached with great pain and anguish, and by too small degrees" (*MHD*, 303). He likewise addresses expectations that he experienced moments of revelatory insight regarding the other prisoners. "It sometimes happened in prison," Gorianchikov writes, "that you knew a man several years, thought of him as a brute and not a man at all, and despised him. Then suddenly a chance moment would reveal his soul in an involuntary convulsion and you saw such wealth, such feeling and heart . . . that your eyes would be opened" (*MHD*, 307).

The examples of revelatory chance moments Gorianchikov provides do not describe the exposure of moral beauty in the people, however; on the contrary, they reveal horror at glimpsing depravity deeper than he had suspected or dismay at the abyss separating him from them. "With such people," he writes of the prisoner Petrov, "it sometimes happens that they stand out large and clear in their true colors at the moment of some general movement or upheaval and thus attain their full activity at one bound" (*MHD*, 127). His stunning realization about Petrov is that this man would stick a knife in someone for the sake of vodka if he suddenly felt the urge for drink. "I do not believe that Petrov will come to a good end; he will perish all in a moment" (*MHD*, 127).

The moment that comes closest to the kind of epiphany described in "The Peasant Marey" is in fact the kind of Dostoevskian transformative moment familiar from his later writings, but it is a moment of negative insight. Change is accomplished by the effect of one face gazing at another, as when Raskolnikov experiences a flash of total insight looking at Sonia. Gorianchikov describes a structurally similar revelatory moment with Petrov. Suspecting the people may be angry at the noble prisoners for not taking part in the kitchen grievance, he tells Petrov he regrets that they, the nobles, did not join in "out of comradeship." "But . . . but how can you be our comrades?" Petrov replies. "I glanced at him quickly," Gorianchikov recalls; "he definitely did not know what I was driving at. I, on the other hand, in that moment understood him completely [*ia poskoree vzglianul na nego i ponial ego v eto mnogvenie sovershenno*]" (*MHD*, 322; *Pss*, 4:207). What Gorianchikov suddenly understands is that the people will never accept him; what is revealed is Petrov's inability to conceive the possibility of union between the gentry and people.

Now for the first time a certain idea, which had been obscurely stirring in me and haunting me for a long time, became finally clear to me and I suddenly understood what I had until then only vaguely divined. I understood that I should never be received into their company, even though I was a prisoner, even if it were for forever and a day, even if I were in the Special Class. (*MHD*, 322)

The real evidence of the people's moral state Gorianchikov provides through observation casts any possibility of their resurrection in serious doubt. They have the wrong experience of time. The "favorite occupation" of one convict "was to count the pales of the stockade" (*MHD*, 8). Mere counting corresponds to an experience of time as meaningless sequentiality, in which experience has no positive significance. Their sufferings in the dead house bring no redemption; instead they merely repeat their errors in freedom and return to prison. "Many of them came back to prison almost at once, for second, serious offenses, and no longer for short terms, but for twenty years" (*MHD*, 10).

Once I saw a convict saying goodbye to his friends when after twenty years in prison, he had at last achieved his freedom. There were people who could remember him as he was when he entered the prison for the first time, young, careless, unconcerned about either his crime or its punishment. He emerged a gray-haired old man, with sad and sullen face. (*MHD*, 8)

Ethical responsibility and remorse—necessary preconditions for resurrection—are impossible when the prisoners deny their own past, even their families, in order to evade the consequences of their actions. One tramp explains of tramps in general: "He can never remember anything and even if you was to hit him over the head with a club, he's forgotten everything, he doesn't know a thing" (*MHD*, 250). This individual recounts the following exchange between one of his accomplices and the authorities: "'But surely you had a father and mother? . . . You remember them, at least?' 'I suppose I must have had, your worship, but I disremember. Perhaps I had, your worship'" (*MHD*, 251). Listening to the other prisoners whisper and groan at night, Gorianchikov says, you would feel "that nothing of all he spoke about would ever return to him, and that the speaker himself had floated away from it all like a piece of driftwood" (*MHD*, 253). They are disconnected from the present and future as well. Petrov "was always in a hurry" on his way to nowhere; "he lived in utter idleness" and his life seemed spent "merely in passing" (*MHD*, 121).

The prisoners write the wrong stories for themselves. Instead of composing meaningful redemption narratives, "each had his own story, as hazy and disturbing as the fumes of yesterday's drunkenness" (*MHD*, 11). Their free time in the evenings is dedicated to "games of chance," indicative of their experience of the world as ruled by fate, not determined by their own ethical behavior (*MHD*, 68). Their idea of a goal or purpose to their lives is to parade around in new clothes for a few hours of drunken stupor before selling them "for a mere trifle" (*MHD*, 46). The prisoner is "so irresponsible and undisciplined," Gorianchikov marvels, that he wants just "one noisy revel and so to forget his anguish if only for a fleeting moment" (*MHD*, 46). A day of drunkenness represents their highest goal. "A prisoner who has worked for several months like a black and saved up his few kopecks simply in order to squander them all in drink on a certain day fixed beforehand" appears before the vodka dealer, Gorianchikov explains. "The poor toiler has been dreaming of this day long before it comes, both in sleep and in happy reveries over his work, and his spirits have been sustained through the dreary course of prison days by the thought of its enchantments. At last the first glow of that bright day appears in the east," and he drinks.

> When everything has been drunk down to the very last rag, the drunkard goes to bed; next morning, waking with the inevitable thick head, he pleads in vain for even a mouthful of vodka to clear it. Sadly he bears his troubles, and the very same day sets to work once more and again labors for several months without straightening his back, dreaming of his day of happy indulgence, now receding irrecoverably into the past, and then little by little he begins to cheer up and look forward to another day like it, still far off, which will nevertheless come in due course. (*MHD*, 50–51)

"It was quite strange," Gorianchikov comments, to see them toil for months in order to squander all they earn in one day, "and then once more plod away at work for months, until the next outbreak" (*MHD*, 46).

The difficulty of redemption is underscored by the fact that these moral flaws are not caused by the environment or social status—at least not primarily by them.[13] The flaws Gorianchikov observes in the prisoners are not caused by their experience in prison. They characterized these individuals in freedom as well; indeed, they are the flaws that brought them to prison initially.

Dostoevsky insists on moral accountability, and *Notes* is no exception. These moral flaws are not explicable as what happens to men who experience the unique hardships of peasant life in Russia, for they characterize prisoners from the upper class as well. A shared lack of conscience seems to unite Gorianchikov and the other nobles with the people. There is no indication that Gorianchikov engages in any soul-searching or self-examination; he shows no signs of remorse. Soon after his arrival in the prison, Gorianchikov observes another prisoner from the nobility "wasting away in prison like a candle—'No,' thought I, as I looked at him, I want to live, and I will live" (*MHD*, 116). He identifies survival, not moral expiation, as his goal. He appreciates certain forms of work, like summer bricklaying, that increase his physical strength. I was pleased to see that "the work was visibly developing my strength," he writes (*MHD*, 275). The wife murderer emphasizes the need for physical stamina in prison but evades moral exercise.

The prisoners are likewise characterized by a lack of conscience. "The majority of them believed themselves to have done nothing wrong," he writes of the prisoners; "I never once saw among these men the slightest sign of remorse, the least gnawing of conscience" (*MHD*, 16). Conceding the limitations of an outside observer—"Who could say that he had penetrated into the depths of those lost souls and read in them what was hidden from all the world?"—he nevertheless objects, "But surely it must have been possible, in so many years, to discern something, at any rate, in those souls, seize some hint, however fleeting, which bore witness to inward anguish or suffering. But there was nothing, nothing at all" (*MHD*, 16). "I saw no evidence of remorse, even when the crime had been against one of their own class. Crimes against the ruling class were not even worth mentioning" (*MHD*, 225).

Any rehabilitation of people this fallen would be difficult; union between them seems equally unlikely. *Notes* does provide two examples of reconciliation between the elite and the people, but these are examples of union in depravity. Akim Akimovich "was at home among them from the first moment" because he too lacks conscience; like them, "he seemed genuinely incapable of understanding of his guilt" (*MHD*, 33, 34). The informer Aristov, who "sold the lives of ten men to ensure the gratitude of his insatiable thirst for the coarsest and vilest pleasures," entered the camp "without the least distress or even repugnance, suffered no moral disturbance and feared nothing in it" (*MHD*, 89, 90). This "monster, a moral Quasimodo," is to the people's liking, Gorianchikov observes, noting that "they were all very friendly with Aristov and behaved incomparably more amicably with him than with us" (*MHD*, 90, 91).

In the *Diary*, Dostoevsky claims that he experienced a singular, miraculous moment of revelation in prison, an epiphany that revealed the common people's innate human dignity and even spiritual superiority. "It was the second day of Easter Week," he writes; the drunkenness, quarrels, and violence of the camp "had worn me out to the point of illness."

At last, anger welled up in my heart. I ran across the Pole M-cki, a political prisoner; he gave me a gloomy look, his eyes glittering and his lips trembling: "Je hais ces brigands!" he muttered, gritting his teeth, and passed me by. I returned to the barrack despite the fact that a quarter-hour before I had fled it half demented when six healthy peasants had thrown themselves, as one man, on the drunken Tartar Gazin and had begun beating him to make him settle down. (*WD*, February 1876, 351)

I lay down and tried to sleep, Dostoevsky recalls, "But dream did not come to me; my heart beat restlessly, and M-cki's words kept echoing in my ears: 'Je hais ces brigands!' ['I hate these bandits!']" (*WD*, February 1876, 352). Losing himself in reverie, he "sank into memories of the past" and suddenly remembers his childhood encounter with Marey. "This memory came to me all at once—I don't know why. . . . Suddenly I roused myself and sat on the bunk" (*WD*, February 1876, 354). "I suddenly felt I could regard these unfortunates in an entirely different way and that suddenly, through some sort of miracle, the former hatred and anger in my heart had vanished" (*WD*, February 1876, 355).

Notes lacks any such sudden redemptive moment. In *Notes*, what serves as the catalytic statement of "The Peasant Marey"—Miretsky's statement "Je hais ces brigands"—occurs repeatedly, as opposed to being a singular event. Here, these words are repeated several times as part of a continuing, unresolved dialogue between Gorianchikov and Miretsky. "'Je hais ces brigands,' he repeated often to me, looking with hatred at the prisoners, whom I had already learned to understand more closely, and no evidence of mine in their favor had any effect on him" (*Pss*, 4:216). Gorianchikov claims that he has already learned to recognize the prisoners differently when he hears Miretsky's repetitive "Je hais ces brigands"; this phrase/interaction doesn't function as the catalytic event it is in "The Peasant Marey."

Notes can be read as the tragedy of an absent union with the people. Even after the better recognition Gorianchikov claims to have achieved, he continues to experience bewilderment and estrangement with the prisoners. *Notes* ends with hatred and empathy in coexistence; no pure state of reconciliation is ever accomplished. Some of the prisoners, understanding that he was returning "to the masters," took leave of him on his release "politely," yet "not as with a comrade, but as if with a *barin* [gentleman]. Some turned away and sternly didn't answer my good-bye, some even looked with some kind of hatred" (*Pss*, 4:231). But some others, removing his fetters, said good-bye "as though with some kind of satisfaction in their voices" (*Pss*, 4:232). The qualifications and continuing coexistence of opposing tendencies is striking in comparison to the absolutes of "The Peasant Marey."[14]

Can Christ save these people? This is a world in which people convert to Christianity—accept Christ's suffering on their behalf—as a way to lessen their own physical suffering. Alexander the Kalmuck takes Christ into his soul when he's sentenced to four thousand blows because he hopes the authorities will go easier on a Christian. Alexander's story is similar to that Akulka and some of the animals described: they are abused for no discernible reason, and no one, least of all they themselves, derives any discernible benefits from their torments. Suffering has not brought Alexander the

Kalmuck any insight or spiritual growth but has perhaps enabled him to survive physical hardship. He survived his four thousand blows, he explains to Gorianchikov, because he'd been beaten all his life and was used to it. Like Akulka, he seems to have been a kind of scapegoat in his community. When he spoke of the abuse he'd received, Gorianchikov recounts,

> He almost blessed his upbringing under the whip. "I was beaten for everything, Alexander Petrovich," he told me once, sitting on my bed one afternoon before the lights were lit, "for anything and everything, everything that ever happened; I was beaten for fifteen years, from the very first day I can remember; everybody used to beat me who felt like it; and so in the end I got quite used to it." (*MHD*, 222)

The physical suffering of scapegoats like Alexander the Kalmuck lacks any spiritual dimension. The way he seeks protection from Christ shows that in a world this fallen, even Christ's sacrifice is misused.

Dostoevsky's later obsession with Holbein's painting *The Body of the Dead Christ in the Tomb* is prefigured here, as Gorianchikov questions whether there is any spiritual dimension to the human being that transcends the body. He seems to doubt it. Describing his observations of men right before their corporal punishment, he writes, "At this point there descends on the condemned man an agonizing and purely physical terror, involuntary and irresistible, which completely overwhelms his moral nature" (*MHD*, 234). While in the hospital, he observes men awaiting the second part of their punishment. They "were extremely dismal, sullen, and silent. There was to be observed in them a kind of stupor of the mind, an unnatural vacancy" (*MHD*, 234). The cross is too great a burden for those suffering physical pain. Watching a young man die in the hospital, he observes, "Nothing at all remained on his body but a wooden cross and a reliquary and his fetters, through which he could by now have pulled his wasted leg" (*MHD*, 214). "Finally, with his aimless, nerveless hand he groped for the reliquary on his breast and tried to tear it away, as though even it were too great a burden. Some ten minutes later he died" (*MHD*, 215).

The contrast between the moral vacuity of the inmates' hopes and the promises of religion is thrown into high relief. Everyone is "unsettled and full of longing to be gone" in prison; it's a place of "eternal restlessness, expressed plainly though silently," a place of "strange fever and fret," hopes that are "so utterly without foundation as to seem like delirium" that nevertheless manage to survive "in men of apparently the most realistic common sense" (*MHD*, 304).

As Christmas draws near, "the prisoners looked forward to it with heightened feelings and, watching them, I also began to expect something out of the ordinary" (*MHD*, 136). The day before Christmas, "everybody seemed to be expecting the next day to bring some sort of change, something out of the ordinary run of things" (*MHD*, 156). The night before, no one plays cards, everyone goes to sleep early, "waiting for the morning" (*MHD*, 160). After the brief visit by the priest Christmas morning, however, the day degenerates. "Although I cannot explain how it happened, . . . an unusually large number of drunken men appeared; and yet five minutes before they had all been almost completely sober" (*MHD*, 164). There are quarrels, and "Gazin was in his glory" (*MHD*, 165).

"Melancholy, nostalgia, stupefaction, began to loom up through the drunken merriment"; those who had been laughing an hour before were now sobbing (*MHD*, 167). "All these poor creatures had wanted to enjoy themselves and spend the great festival in rejoicing—and Lord! How heavy and dreary the day had been for almost every one of them. Each had passed it as though hope had cheated him" (*MHD*, 168). "Up to the very last hour," Gorianchikov writes of Petrov, "he was still waiting for something which must inevitably happen, something extraordinary, festive and joyous. . . . But nothing special happened or came under his eyes except drunkenness and senseless brawling and heads aching with fumes of drink" (*MHD*, 168). "Little by little the barracks became disgusting and unbearable. . . . I felt full of sadness and pity for all of them, and oppressed and stifled among them," Gorianchikov remembers (*MHD*, 168).

The birth of the lamb is marked by a performance of idiotic violence between a butcher and a pig. Gorianchikov observes two men, "one tall, corpulent, fleshy, a real butcher to look at," together with his friend, a "feeble, wizened" man with "little pig's eyes" (*MHD*, 170). After telling the pig, "You are the only person left to me on earth now" but receiving only "pompous" and "dogmatically" delivered remonstrance in return, the drunken butcher suddenly knocks his little friend unconscious (*MHD*, 171, 170).

The feast of Christ's birth witnesses the prisoners evading moral accountability by finding fault with one another rather than engaging in critical self-reflection. The prisoner Varlamov, "negligently" strumming a balalaika and strolling the barracks, is followed by Bulkin, who "was following him in a state of dreadful agitation, waving his arms, beating his fist against the walls and planks" (*MHD*, 171). "'He keeps on lying, he's lying again!' cried Bulkin, banging the boards with his hands in a kind of despair" (*MHD*, 172). "He followed him like a shadow, caviled at every word he spoke, wrung his hands . . . and suffered, visibly suffered, from his conviction that Varlamov 'kept on lying!'" Gorianchikov observes; "It was just as though he had taken on himself the duty of being responsible for Varlamov's actions, as though all Varlamov's shortcomings lay heavy on his conscience" (*MHD*, 173). *Notes from the House of the Dead* itself represents a form of scrutinizing the flaws of others as a means of evading one's own conscience—not once in the extensive descriptions of the prisoners' moral shortcomings does Gorianchikov express any remorse about his own past.

The absence of any signs of self-reflection in Gorianchikov undermines his belief in a moral distinction between the elite and the people. "Here, for example, is an educated man, who has an active conscience, a mature mind, and a feeling heart," he writes.

> The pain in his own heart is alone enough to kill him with its agonies before any punishment begins. He condemns his own crime more harshly, more pitilessly, than the cruellest of laws. Here beside him is another who has not once so much as thought of the murder he committed during the whole of sentence; he does not even think he has done wrong. (*MHD*, 59–60)

Neither Gorianchikov nor the other elite prisoners display remorse. Class distinctions are blurred in *Notes* not through any attribution of moral rectitude to the common people but by questioning the elite's possession of conscience.

The significance of Christ's birth is deflated by situating the holy day as one of a series of days characterized by similar depravity. "But why describe this inferno?" Gorianchikov concludes his holiday report. "At last the heavy day comes to an end. The prisoners fall asleep on their plank beds. They talk and wander in their sleep even more than on other nights. . . . The long-awaited holiday is over. Tomorrow is another weekday, we must work again" (*MHD*, 175).

The status of the Crucifixion as an allegedly onetime, decisive event is further deflated through a seemingly endless parade of meaningless suffering and death the reader witnesses. The horror of meaningless sacrifice reaches a low point with the chapter "Akulka's Husband," which comes just before Easter. "Akulka's Husband" and the rest of *Notes* expose the ineffectuality of things that seem to hold out hope—Easter and spring—when confronted with the depth of the characters' spiritual fall.[15]

"Akulka's Husband" begins with Gorianchikov, a wife murderer who never speaks of his wife or his crime against her, lying in the hospital unable to sleep, overhearing another wife murderer tell his tale to another prisoner. The other wife killer is an "empty, silly creature," "cowardly and unstable" (*Pss*, 4:166). His bunkmate is "morose and completely indifferent" to the story being told, occasionally mumbling something "more out of politeness than from any real interest"; this individual is "a soulless rationalist and a conceited idiot" (*MHD*, 255). Shishkov, the killer, tells of how Akulka survives mental and physical abuse from him, her family, and the entire town when she is falsely accused of adultery, only to be finally butchered in a cart.

"I grabs her by the hair," he recounts; "her plaits were so thick and long and I twisted them round my hand and I squeezed her between my knees from behind and I took out my knife and bent her head back and I cut her throat like a calf" (*MHD*, 266).

The meaning of the story is entirely lost on those who hear it. Akulka represents sheer victimization; she has done nothing wrong, but she absorbs the community's evil. The listener's only response, however, reveals that he has entirely missed the point of the story, which is that communities seem to need sacrificial victims, but not for the purpose of their regeneration.[16] Akulka was innocent, but Shishkov's listener simply remarks, "Of course, no good comes of it if you don't beat them" (*MHD*, 267).

No one changes as a result of Akulka's death. The community in which she served as a sacrificial victim derives no benefit from the spectacle of her victimization; her killer shows no sign of remorse; the person to whom he tells his story shows no sign of understanding it; and the other killer in the room, Gorianchikov, gives no indication that any pangs of conscience have been awakened in him. There is no resurrection over Akulka's dead body. Her brutalized life and horrific murder are the meaningless desecration of innocence that precedes the celebration of the Easter Passion.

The desecration of a sheer victim like Akulka leads to nothing; the story of her death does not signal any kind of meaningful turning point, even though it is followed by Easter and spring. Akulka's story does awaken hopes for a turning point—it seems as though nothing could be worse than her loss—but these hopes are disappointed, and we are shown that things can get even worse. Following Akulka, *Notes* confronts the reader with increasingly distressing vignettes of suffering and abuse.

Up to this point in the narrative, *Notes* has concerned itself mostly with accounts of violence done by men to one another. After Akulka, however, the category of victims becomes broader and more troubling: an entire chapter is dedicated to the subject of animals. More troubling than simply the litany of how animals can be abused is the fact that even among the animals, who are helpless victims of human beings, there emerge victims and abusers, and seemingly meaningless, gratuitous acts of violence take place—the dog Belka is torn apart by a pack of other dogs; the dog Sharik torments the captive eagle the prisoners nurse back to health.

Gorianchikov observes a similar phenomenon among the prisoners; the very category of victims acquires disturbing complexity. Some of those who initially elicit our sympathy because they seem to be innocent victims are revealed to harbor cruelty themselves. We pity Ustyantsev, who is dying of consumption, when another prisoner tells him he should just lie down and die; but then we witness him occupying the role of tormenter himself. Ustyantsev, we are later told, "meddled in everything"; from his hospital bed "he would first gaze steadily and solemnly at his victim and then in a calm, assured tone of voice begin to read him a lecture" (*MHD*, 248). "Why should he yell over a lancet?" Ustyantsev objects, regarding another prisoner's pain. "He must learn to take the rough with the smooth and put up with things" (*MHD*, 249). The persistence of sadism and cruelty down into what would seem to be the depths of victimization is one of the most challenging aspects of *Notes from the House of the Dead*.

The story of Akulka's murder is immediately followed by the arrival of Easter and spring, but the promises of renewal held out by religion and nature do not correspond to anything in the dead house. Instead, the re-birth celebrated in the natural world and the church exists in sharp contrast to the absence of resurrection among the inmates. The chapter "Akulka's Husband" is immediately followed by the chapter "Summer Time," which begins with the promises of nature and Christianity: "But now it was the beginning of April and Holy Week was drawing near" (*MHD*, 267). Spring and Holy Week, however, are not rejuvenating; instead they are portrayed as embedded within cyclic, repetitive processes. The descriptions of Easter and spring emphasize that they just bring more of the same.[17]

Now Easter came. Each of us received from the authorities an egg and a slice of wheaten bread made with milk, butter, and eggs. *Once again* the townspeople heaped gifts upon the prison. *Once again* there was a visit from the priest with his cross, *once again* a visit from the Governor, *once again* our cabbage soup was made with meat, *once again* men got drunk and staggered about the prison—all was exactly as it had been at Christmas, with this differ-ence, that now it was possible to walk in the courtyard and warm oneself in the sun. . . . There seemed to be more light and space than in the winter, but also more sadness. The long endless summer days seemed especially unbear-able on holidays. (*MHD*, 273–74, my emphases)

Easter shows Gorianchikov degenerating toward the prisoners' abdi-cation of moral responsibility. In church, he recalls, "We were fettered and stigmatized as criminals; everybody drew aside from us and even seemed afraid of us; we always had alms bestowed on us and I remember that this somehow even pleased me, and there was a peculiar subtlety in that strange feeling of satisfaction. 'If it must be so, so be it!' I thought" (*MHD*, 273). The wife murderer's "strange feeling of satisfaction" with his branded status, like the lack of conscience he perceives in the other prisoners, interferes with moral regeneration.

The story of Akulka's death, which effects no change in its listeners, is followed by chapters that show how Christ's death has effected no change in the Russian common people, who try to change their lives by killing and stealing rather than imitating Christ's self-sacrifice. Christ's attempt to change humanity's fate through his self-sacrificial gift is juxtaposed with the Russians' attempts to change their lot through sacrificing others, or what they call "changing one's lot." Gorianchikov explains, *"Changing one's lot* is a technical term" (*MHD,* 271). The tramp dreams of "going no matter where, so long as it is not back to the old place which has grown so tiresome to him, not back to his former prison," and he is willing to kill to do it (*MHD,* 271). Tramps are ready to "steal and loot and even kill" to get what they want. "'An exile is the same as a baby: whatever he sees he wants,' they say in Siberia of convict-settlers" (*MHD,* 269). They are spiritually dead: one tramp had "a singularly calm, almost blank, expression, indeed to the point of idiocy. . . . His features had a wooden look. . . . His attitude toward everything was one of complete calm" (*MHD,* 270).

Gorianchikov provides many examples of people sacrificing others in order to help themselves or change their lot. Sirotkin is so unhappy in the army that he wants to go anywhere else, even the grave through suicide or wherever a crime might take him. After his attempt to shoot himself fails, he says, "I made up my mind what I was going to do; they could do what they liked with me so long as I got out!" and then bayonets his captain in the stomach (*MHD,* 54). For Sirotkin, killing himself or killing someone else are equivalent means to changing his situation. Men condemned to corporal punishment had recourse to "terrible expedients in order to postpone the moment of punishment": they would stick a knife in someone, anyone, thus using a new crime, requiring another trial, to postpone their punishment. "It mattered little to them that in two months time the punishment would be twice or three times as severe, if only they could put off the fatal minute for a few days, at whatever cost" to themselves or someone else (*MHD,* 220).

The prisoner awaiting corporal punishment "is capable of flinging himself on the chance bystander for no reason at all, simply because, for example, he must face a flogging on the morrow, and if a new accusation is brought against him, it means the postponement of his punishment. This is the cause and aim of his attack, to 'change his lot' at any cost and as soon as possible" (*MHD,* 62). One of these, Dutov, "a most pitiable coward," attacked an officer with a knife the day before he was to run the gauntlet for robbery (*MHD,* 63). "Needless to say, he understood very well that such an action would immeasurably increase his sentence and the term of his penal servitude. But his calculations were directed simply to the postponement, if only for a few days, or even a few hours, of the terrible moment of punishment" (*MHD,* 63).

The possibility of redemption, supposedly guaranteed by the Crucifixion, is also questioned through the very structure of the narrative, which permits two opposite interpretations of Gorianchikov's fate. Dostoevsky builds an unanswerable question into the structure of *Notes*. Gorianchikov has two endings: his chronological/biological ending, which is hopelessness, futility, and death; and his textual ending, which is hope for new life. The reader knows that the man who hoped for resurrection from the dead ends his days in unregenerate despair. One of the residents of the small Siberian town where Gorianchikov settles after his release describes him as "a puny little man, extremely pale and thin . . . a terrible misanthrope who shunned everybody" who "had resolutely broken off all connection" with the world and was "mistrustful to an insane degree" (*MHD*, 3). Gorianchikov existed outside all community, this character explains; he never spoke to anyone, and when you tried to speak to him, it was so "awkward" that you were "glad when at last the conversation ended" (*MHD*, 3). The text is constructed in a way that gives the reader freedom of choice between the textually final state-ment of hope and chronologically final despair.

Dostoevsky preserved this frame, with all the discrepancies between his biography and *Notes* it introduces, when he republished the originally se-rialized novel in book form. There is a great deal of additional evidence that the disjunction between art and biography was intentional. Dostoevsky him-self maintained that Gorianchikov was not simply a stand-in for the author. "I wrote my Letters from a Dead House fifteen years ago under the name of a fictitious person, a criminal who supposedly had murdered his wife," Dostoevsky recounts. "In passing, I may add, by way of detail, that since that time many people have been under the impression, and are even now as-serting, that I was exiled for the murder of my wife."[18] When we read *Notes* as the account of a murderer among murderers, rather than as a Dostoevsky stand-in, it is a much stranger, more troubling work of art. The disjunction between hope and tragedy created by the frame should be appreciated; at this point in his life Dostoevsky did not yet have the faith in redemption he acquired later, because the vehicles he comes to believe in—the Russian people and their Christianity—are missing here.

Most surprising in light of the anachronistic expectations readers bring to *Notes* is the way this text portrays Christian Russians, Muslims, and Jews. The most uplifting episodes of the book, which come closest to moments of brotherly reconciliation across cultural divides, involve the narrator and Muslim inmates. The community that does emerge in *Notes* is not one that encompasses the Russian elite and common people as envisioned in *Time*, but a new brotherhood that unites Gorianchikov, his beloved Aley, and Aley's brothers, in common appreciation of Jesus's message.

The Russian Christian prisoners are morally inferior to the Muslims. Among the Russians, Gorianchikov writes, "Backbiting and scandal-mongering went on ceaselessly," and "gossip, intrigue, cattiness, envy, squabbles, malice were always to the fore" (*MHD*, 14). The prison is a place of inexpressible cynicism and shameless laughter, relieved only by the moral goodness of the Dagestanian Tatars. Gorianchikov's description of the Tatars has the same curious blending of feminine and masculine qualities and almost erotic attraction that characterize the later description of Marey. *Notes* offers some of the first examples of iconic, transformative beauty Dostoevsky creates, and they are Muslim tribesmen.

Nurra is "built like a Hercules, very fair, with light blue eyes like a Finnish woman's"; he "produced a most comforting, a most pleasing impression on me from the very first," Gorianchikov confides.

> The other prisoners all liked him. He was always cheerful and friendly towards everybody, did his work without repining and was good-natured and placid, although he often showed his dislike of the filth and squalor of prison life and was roused to fury by every instance of theft, drunkenness, swindling and general knavery, and vice. . . . He himself never stole anything or did one wrong thing all the time he was in prison. (*MHD*, 71)

During Gorianchikov's first half hour in prison and over the next days, he recalls, Nurra "wanted to show me that he was friendly, and to cheer me up and assure me of his help. Good, simple Nurra!"; "it was impossible to miss his kind, sympathetic face among all the sullen, spiteful, jeering faces of the other prisoners" (*MHD*, 72).

Gorianchikov confesses an attraction to Aley's beauty as well. He is "as chaste as a pure young girl," and "his handsome, candid, intelligent and at the same time naively good-natured face attracted my heart to him at first sight" (*MHD*, 72). Gorianchikov is grateful that he sleeps next to Aley. "I was very glad that fate had sent me him, and not somebody else, as a neighbor" in the barrack, he writes. Aley's iconic beauty improves those who look at him. "His whole soul was reflected in his handsome—one might almost say beautiful—face. His smile was so trustful, so childishly artless, his big black eyes were so melting and tender, that I always felt particular satisfaction, even a lightening of my grief and longing, when I looked at him" (*MHD*, 72). Aley's face has a similar effect on his older brothers, who "always smiled when they looked at him"; when they talked with him, "their grim faces relaxed" (*MHD*, 73). "I think of Aley as no ordinary being and I remember my meeting with him as one of the most valuable in my life," Gorianchikov asserts (*MHD*, 73–74).

Among the depraved Russian prisoners, Aley "kept himself so strictly honest, so sincere, and so attractive, and never became hardened or corrupted. His personality, moreover, was strong and direct in spite of all his seeming gentleness" (*MHD*, 74).

Any evil, cynical, filthy, or unjust instance of violent conduct lit the fires of indignation in his fine eyes, making them even more beautiful. But he avoided disputes and strife, although he was not one of those who allow themselves to be insulted with impunity and was able to stand up for himself. But he had no quarrel with anybody; everybody liked him and was kind to him. (*MHD*, 74)

A brotherly community encompassing Gorianchikov and Aley's brothers arises around appreciation of Aley's beauty and the message of the Gospels. Gorianchikov gives Aley lessons in the Russian language and reading the New Testament, which the young Muslim "learned with zeal and enthusiasm."

Once we read through together the Sermon on the Mount. I noticed that he seemed to pronounce some parts of it with special feeling. I asked him whether he had liked what he read. He looked up quickly and his cheeks were flushed.

"Oh, yes!" he answered. "Yes, Jesus is a holy prophet. Jesus spoke the word of God. How wonderful!" (*MHD*, 76)

Seeing this special friendship between their younger brother and the Russian prisoner, Aley's brothers reach out to Gorianchikov. Aley and his brothers take pleasure in doing things for Gorianchikov. "It was plain that it gave him great pleasure to make things even a little easier and pleasanter for me," he writes of Aley. "In this endeavor there was not the slightest abasement or search for personal advantage, but only the warmth of his friendship for me, which he made no attempt to hide" (*MHD*, 75). A community based in spiritual love, not national, biological, or sectarian ties, emerges. Aley, Gorianchikov reflects, "loved me perhaps as much as he loved his brothers," who "vied with each other in helping me" (*MHD*, 77, 76). When Aley leaves prison, he kisses Gorianchikov and weeps, saying he has done more for him than his own father or mother would and telling him, "You have made me a man" (*MHD*, 77).

"Nurra is a lion," the prisoners say, but the Jewish prisoner Bumstein is a plucked chicken.[19] Gorianchikov recalls "his little figure: fiftyish, puny, wrinkled, with horrible brands on his cheeks and forehead, with a skinny, feeble, white body like a plucked chicken's" (*MHD*, 136). The physically beautiful Muslims stand out as beacons of moral rectitude among the degenerate Russians, but the ugly Jew is the butt of the prison's laughter. "Lord, how comical, how laughable, that man was!" Gorianchikov exclaims. All the prisoners liked the Jew, "although absolutely all of them, without exception, laughed at him" (*MHD*, 78). "Isaiah Fomich evidently served as an entertainment and a perpetual diversion for them" (*MHD*, 137). The prisoners tease him "exactly as one amuses oneself with a dog, a parrot, a trained animal, or something of that kind" (*MHD*, 139). Everyone laughed at him, Gorianchikov recalls, "and even now I cannot remember him without laughing" (*MHD*, 78).

Beneath his comic/grotesque characterization, however, the truth is that this branded Jew actually embodies the spiritual disfigurement of the Russians. Bumstein concentrates in himself all the moral flaws of the superficially Christian prisoners: formalism, vanity, and lack of true values and conscience. The shallowness of their Christianity is exposed through their association with the Jew.

The moral flaws tragically disfiguring the Russians are comic/grotesque in the Jew. Bumstein is "cunning and yet distinctly stupid," Gorianchikov observes, "impudent and insolent, and at the same time terribly cowardly" (*MHD*, 78). "There was in him a most comical mingling of naivete, stupidity, sharpness, impudence, artlessness, timidity, boastfulness, and effrontery," Gorianchikov explains (*MHD*, 137). "Generally speaking," he says of the Russians, they have "a certain peculiar personal dignity," observing that "the whole tribe . . . was sullen, envious, terribly conceited, boastful, touchy, and preoccupied in the highest degree with forms" (*MHD*, 13, 12). Bumstein is "innocently vain and conceited"; the Russian prisoners are "in the highest degree vain and frivolous" (*MHD*, 140, 184).

Bumstein and the Russians have no moral conscience; prison holds no shame for them. Bumstein "was always in excellent spirits. Prison life was easy for him"; he is a jeweler and busy with orders from town; he's the moneylender and pawnbroker (*MHD*, 78). "The expression of his face revealed unwavering, unshakeable self-satisfaction and even beatific happiness. He felt apparently not the slightest regret at having fallen into prison" (*MHD*, 136). He is wrinkled and branded; he is accused of murder; yet he nurses absurd hopes that are repulsive in him—about fifty years old, he plans on absolutely getting married when he's released, an intention that Gorianchikov relays with repugnance.

The Russians, including Gorianchikov, "did not like to talk, and evidently tried not to think, of the past" (*MHD*, 11). The prisoner on the bed next to him in the hospital is in for counterfeiting; he is "far from stupid, an extremely cheeky and confident young man, morbidly vain and quite seriously convinced that he was the most honest and upright person in the world, and even that he was completely innocent of all wrongdoing" (*MHD*, 202). Many of them "are even glad to have reached the prison at last (a new life is sometimes so great an attraction!) and are consequently disposed to settle down in peace and quiet" (*MHD*, 62). The situation is the same on both sides of the class line. The nobleman Aristov entered prison "without the least distress or even repugnance, suffered no moral disturbance and feared nothing in it" (*MHD*, 90). They act "as if the status of convict, or condemned man, constituted some kind of rank, and that an honorable one. Not a sign of shame or remorse!" (*MHD*, 13).

Nurra, Aley, and his brothers live the Sermon on the Mount even though they are not Christian; Christ's message continues to elude the Russian prisoners, on the other hand, because they are mired in a kind of formalism they share with the Jew. Bumstein and the Russians live by empty words, formalism, and the law instead of living conscience. "Preoccupied in the highest degree with forms," the prisoners frequently repeated "proverbs and sayings" such as "'You wouldn't heed your father and mother, now be ruled by the drum,' . . . but never seriously. They were only words. There was hardly one of the prisoners who in his heart acknowledged his own lawlessness" (*MHD*, 13). Akim Akimovich, who "had even settled himself in prison as though he were preparing to spend the rest of his life there," produced in Gorianchikov "immeasurable dejection" (*MHD*, 323). "I would be hungry sometimes for a living word of some kind," but instead Akim Akimovich would patter on "in a sedate, even tone, like water falling drop by drop" (*MHD*, 324).

Bumstein practices his Sabbath "with forced and pedantic solemnity"; everything he does is "prescribed by his ritual" (*MHD*, 140). The old believers have "fanatical literal belief in their religious books" (*MHD*, 79). "They were highly developed people, shrewd peasants, believing pedantically and un-critically in the literal truth of their old books, and very powerful dialecticians in their own way; a haughty, arrogant, crafty, and highly intolerant people" (*MHD*, 44). Akim Akimovich "was not particularly pious, because morality had apparently swallowed up all his human talents and particular qualities, all his passions and desires, both good and evil" (*MHD*, 157). "Generally speaking, he did not like to have to do much thinking. He never troubled his head, apparently, about the meaning of any act, but he fulfilled a principle, once it had been shown to him, with religious accuracy" (*MHD*, 158).

Akim Akimovich's preparations for Christmas, like Isaiah Fomich's for his Sabbath, emphasize form and ritual to the exclusion of living spirit. "Blindly devoted to ritual, he regarded even his Christmas suckling pig, which he had stuffed with kasha, and roasted . . . with a kind of anticipatory esteem, as though it were not an ordinary piglet, which might be bought and roasted at any time, but a special, Christmas one" (*MHD*, 158). "I am sure that if he had ever once failed to eat pork on that day he would have felt a certain pang of conscience all his life for the obligation unfulfilled" (*MHD*, 158). Sarcastically describing Akim Akimovich's attention to the details of the new clothes he has saved for Christmas, Gorianchikov writes, "Pious respect for a button, for a shoulder knot, a loop had been ineffably imprinted in his mind from his childhood as an incontestable obligation, and in his heart as the highest degree of beauty attainable by an honest man" (*MHD*,

159). He executed his obligations "with calm, methodical seemliness of conduct, just as much as was required for the performance of his obligations and the ceremonies laid down once and for all" (*MHD*, 158).

Gorianchikov critically describes how Bumstein delights in fulfilling the "ingenious provision of the Law" in his religious observances and observes Russians misusing the concept of the law (*MHD*, 141). Overseeing a flogging, Lieutenant Zherebyatnikov takes recourse to the law as a substitute for individual moral conscience.

> "My dear friend," says he, "what am I to do with you? The law punishes you, not I."
> "Your honor, everything depends on you. Be merciful!"
> "Do you not think I am sorry for you? Do you think it will be a pleasure for me to watch you being beaten? After all, I too, am a man! . . . I am quite well aware that I must, in all humanity, look with compassion and even indulgence on you, sinner though you are. . . . But this is a matter for the law, not for me!" (*MHD*, 227–28)

Russia has too many people who believe that "the relentless application of the letter of the law" is foremost in human affairs, Gorianchikov maintains (*MHD*, 176).

"These advocates of the application of the law definitely do not understand, and are incapable of understanding, that the mere literal fulfillment of the law, without reason or comprehension of its spirit, leads straight to disorder and has never led to anything else," Gorianchikov objects (*MHD*, 176). The prisoners, he critically observes, dispute "as an exercise in style." The formal qualities of argument eclipse content and critical thinking among them. "Not infrequently they got carried away and began to dispute with passionate heat and frenzy," he recounts, only to part company as though nothing had happened. "The man who could argue down or shout down his opponent was highly esteemed and all but applauded like an actor," Gorianchikov notes with disapproval (*MHD*, 31). Isaiah Fomich's arguing skills are highly regarded in the prison.

The Christmas theatricals do effect a temporary transformation in the prisoners. It is what happens in the audience—the spectacle enacted among the viewers—that has some regenerative power. "For me," Gorianchikov explains, "the greatest interest lay in the audience" (*MHD*, 189). "Aley's charming face shone with such beautiful child-like joy that I confess it made me immensely happy to look at him," Gorianchikov recalls (*MHD*, 188). Aley has a similar effect on other usually glum prisoners as well. Their joy momentarily transforms them into a brotherly community, with each man seeking to communicate his impressions to the others. They nudge one another, look around; one "would turn in an ecstasy of appreciation to the crowd, embrace them with a rapid glance as though exhorting them to laugh" (*MHD*, 189). After such experiences, "they all went to sleep, not as on any other night, but almost with a quiet spirit" as if "their moral nature was changed, even if only for a few minutes" (*MHD*, 198).

Several factors serve to render the theater's promise as a vehicle of moral redemption problematic, however. Gorianchikov's reflections on the *temporary* transformation accomplished in the prisoners are interrupted by the reality of how the "ugly dream" of their lives continues on as before (*MHD*, 198). Most important, however, is the contrast between the audience's joy and what is actually portrayed on stage.

"Kedril the Glutton," one of the pieces performed, is a strange, one-act fragment lacking a beginning and ending; like the prisoners' lives, it seems abortively disconnected. "There is not the slightest reason or logic in the whole thing" Gorianchikov observes (*MHD*, 191). Set in a provincial Russian inn, "something like Don Juan," it tells of a master and servant being dragged off to hell. The servant Kedril is in one sense a victim—his fate is tied to that of his master, who has sold his soul to the devil. But Kedril is not simply a victim; his own gluttony and moral immaturity, rather than oppression by a master, doom him. This fragment enacts the contrast between the moral irresponsibility of the people and the (alleged) acceptance of accountability in the elite. The master accepts the consequences of his crime—he displays volition and understanding of his sin and its repercussions—whereas Kedril is taken against his will because he lacks the strength to resist.[20]

As they are shown to their room, the innkeeper warns the gentleman and his servant Kedril, "a great glutton," that it is haunted (*MHD*, 191). The gentleman replies that he knows of the devils and orders Kedril to prepare supper; Kedril, "a coward and a glutton" (these qualities are emphasized several times), "turns pale and trembles like a leaf" (*MHD*, 191). Kedril has several opportunities for escape, but base emotions outweigh his desire to save himself. "He would run away, but he is very afraid of his master. Besides, he is very hungry. He is lustful, stupid, cunning in his own way, and cowardly" (*MHD*, 191). When the master explains to him that he once long ago sold his soul to the powers of darkness and that tonight they will come for him "in accordance with the bargain he made," Kedril "begins to grow terrified. His master, however, has not lost heart and bids him prepare supper" (*MHD*, 192). Kedril consumes almost an entire chicken while the gentleman paces; the master, "gloomily preoccupied and noticing nothing," pays no attention to the fact that only one chicken leg remains for him, a fact that sets the audience laughing (*MHD*, 193).

Kedril and his master react differently to the appearance of the devils.

"The gentleman turns sufficiently boldly to the devils and cries that he is ready for them to take him" (*MHD*, 193). Kedril, on the other hand, is torn between his fear of eternal damnation and his more powerful physical desires. Turning "timid as a hare," he hides under the table, "not forgetting, in spite of all his fright, to seize the bottle as he goes" (*MHD*, 193). He ignores his master's cry of "Kedril, save me!" and enjoys his meal after the devils have taken the gentleman away. Instead of escaping and saving himself, he stays to eat and drink. The devils pounce on him just as he pours himself a glass of wine; "he is too faint-hearted to dare turn around. Neither is he able to defend himself; in his hands are the bottle and glass, which he cannot find the strength to put down" (*MHD*, 194). He is dragged off to hell with a "comical expression of lily-livered terror," while "still holding the bottle" (*MHD*, 194).

Like Petrov and many of the other prisoners, Kedril seems to know nothing higher than his immediate, physical inclinations. This figure—joyfully acclaimed by the prison audience as one of their own—exemplifies the complex contributions even the victims make to their hopeless condition in the dead house. One of the most distressing obstacles to resurrection portrayed in *Notes from the House of the Dead* is surely this: that it is not even clear who the victims in need of saving are because the very category of victim seems to break down; and that when salvation is offered, the supposed victim himself seems incapable of accepting it.

"I Don't Want Your Sacrifice": The Morality
of the Son in *Crime and Punishment*

THE MENTALITIES Dostoevsky eventually labels "Russian" and "Jewish" and his problematic characterization of redemption through the Crucifixion continue to evolve in *Crime and Punishment.* The attitude that accepts the suffering of others as the price of one's own well-being was first expressed by Varvara Alekseevna in *Poor Folk,* where she accepts Devushkin's loss as her gain. This attitude toward others acquires new and surprising dimensions in *Crime and Punishment.* The novel explores the ramifications of this mental operation by showing how it can develop into the philosophy of utilitarianism, based on the presumption that some have the right to make cost-benefit calculations about human life. We expect negative or ambiguous characters such as Luzhin and Lebeziatnikov to espouse the legitimacy of utilitarian calculations, but we may be less prepared to discover that the mentality condoning this way of thinking isn't limited to those who are under the sway of fashionable Western ideologies.

Notes from the House of the Dead upsets expectations shaped by Dostoevsky's later writings and reveals surprising aspects to the origins of his antisemitism by portraying a (negative) spiritual affinity of Russians and Jews. *Crime and Punishment* defies our expectations by linking Christianity to what Dostoevsky, when writing in his personal notebooks or speaking in a more autobiographical voice in genres such as the speech (e.g., the Pushkin Speech), essay, or travel narrative, asserts is its irreconcilable opposite, allegedly Western and un-Christian utilitarianism. *Crime and Punishment* suggests that the basis of utilitarianism—the belief that some may be sacrificed for the good of others—may be the foundational principle of Russian society and Christianity as well. The novel associates contemporary Western utilitarianism with a kind of sacrificial exchange logic that Raskolnikov perceives to be the basis of the Crucifixion. Raskolnikov's perception of a shared emotional and philosophical logic linking the Crucifixion with Western utilitarianism is never fully repudiated. The pervasiveness of this logic in the novel is a primary obstacle blocking redemption that is not tainted by an exploitative relationship to the suffering of others.

Raskolnikov perceives sacrificial exchange logic, and the utilitarian calculations it supports, informing everything around him, from the behavior of his family to the structure of society to the Crucifixion as he understands it. He tries but fails to find a viable, morally superior alternative to this logic. *Crime and Punishment* suggests that everything is contained within this logic: the state of affairs Raskolnikov perceives around him, in which his mother is willing to sacrifice her daughter for the sake of her son and in which society tolerates the suffering of some for the benefit of others; the murder itself, which he justifies as the suffering of one for the good of others; and the Christian faith that allegedly redeems him in the epilogue, a redemption achieved over the corpses of several women (the pawnbroker, Lizaveta, and Raskolnikov's mother, whose death is precipitated by his crime).

The Christian faith Raskolnikov acquires at the end of the novel recapitulates his initial moral error, the thinking that led him to commit the murder. The epilogue defines Raskolnikov's resurrection as the realization that his bad deeds can be paid off by performing good ones. This belief that bad deeds can be paid off with good works was precisely the initial moral error, the thinking Raskolnikov used to justify the murder. The faces of Raskolnikov and Sonia "were bright with the dawn of a new future, of a full resurrection into a new life," the narrator proclaims; "he had risen again" (*CP*, 504). Thinking of Sonia, Raskolnikov "remembered how continually he had tormented her and wounded her heart. . . . But these recollections scarcely troubled him now; he knew with what infinite love he would now repay all her sufferings [*on znal, kakoiu beskonechnoiu liubov'iu iskupit on teper' vse eti stradaniie*]" (*CP*, 504; *Pss*, 6:422).

The new Christian life into which Raskolnikov is resurrected will be attained the same way he thought a new life would be attained after the murder. The same language of heroics, striving and suffering in atoning—literally purchasing—permeates how preconversion Raskolnikov thinks about his life after the murder and how the narrator describes his life after resurrection. "He did not know that the new life would not be given to him for nothing, that he would have to pay dearly for it, that it would cost him great striving, great suffering," the narrator explains [*on dazhe i ne znal togo, chto novaia zhizn' ne darom zhe emu dostaetsia, chto ee nado eshche dorogo kupit', zaplatit' za nee velikim, budushchim podvigom*] (*CP*, 505; *Pss*, 6:422).

Buying new lives at the price of old ones by performing a great deed was precisely how Raskolnikov justified the murder. Sonia, the model Christian, participates in this thinking as well. She urges him to confess. "Then God will send you life again," she explains, but he must earn this new life. "Suffer and expiate your sin by it," she tells him, "that's what you must do" (*CP*, 389). This is precisely the logic that Raskolnikov used to talk himself into the crime: the murder, he told himself, could be paid off with acts of penitential good works; committing the crime, he believed, was a form of taking penitential suffering on himself.

The novel concludes, in other words, with the narrative or plot itself practicing the very logic Raskolnikov has allegedly overcome. Raskolnikov's final conversion consists of accepting the logic he rejected when it was practiced by others (such as his mother and Russian society) and which he himself half-heartedly practiced through the murder. This acceptance seems to occur without any apparent awareness, on his part or the novel's, of the continuity.

The reduction of spiritual life to calculations of sacrificial exchange was the initial object of Raskolnikov's revulsion. He abhorred the way society permitted some—the poor, the young, the female—to suffer on the grounds that their suffering was part of a justifiable social structure. He thought of the murder as a form of protest against the logic used to defend blatant injustice. Yet this logic becomes what he affirms in the epilogue; his spiritual journey follows a path from rebellion against sacrificial exchange logic applied to human life, to the practice of it himself through the murder, to acceptance of it when it is performed by the authorities who allegedly have a right to it.

Raskolnikov believed that the murder represented a revolt against an old, bad thing—an "old harpy" and "a Jew," as Alyona Ivanovna is described (*CP*, 62, 61). She is linked to Bumstein, the most significant Jewish figure in Dostoevsky's writings to this point, in their mutual resemblance to chickens. "She was a diminutive, withered up old woman of sixty, with sharp malignant eyes and a sharp little nose. Her colorless, somewhat grizzled hair was thickly smeared with oil, and she wore no kerchief over it. Round her thin long neck, which looked like a hen's leg, was knotted some sort of flannel rag" (*CP*, 4).

His attempt to replace this old Jew with something new and better fails, however: the murder doesn't help anyone, and the Christian faith that is the ultimate positive outcome of the murder for Raskolnikov has a moral structure identical to the thinking behind the killing, which he superficially repudiates. Behind this failure to find something truly new and better lurks doubt about the relationship between Christianity and Judaism: *Crime and Punishment* questions Christianity's claim to be a New Covenant. *Notes from the House of the Dead* questions the efficacy of the Crucifixion as a vehicle of redemption; *Crime and Punishment* furthers this questioning by associating the "new word" allegedly brought by Christ with repudiated, Jewish-associated ways of thinking.[1]

Dostoevsky sympathized with the desire to intervene against the injustices perpetrated by an old Jew he ascribes to his impoverished young intellectual character. In a letter to Katkov describing his plans for the novel, he explains that Raskolnikov will kill the old woman because she is a usurer who "takes Yiddish percentages" (*Pss,* 7:310). *Crime and Punishment* poses the question: Is it a crime to kill an old "Yiddish" parent figure who consumes, indentures the young? The novel comes to no final conclusion.

Crime and Punishment introduces what will be a central conundrum in Dostoevsky's future writings: the reduction of spirit to the logic of sacrificial exchange revolts Raskolnikov, but he perceives that it informs all the options, both Christianity and the Western ideologies it allegedly opposes; his protest remains trapped within it, and his postconversion state is merely acceptance of what previously repulsed him. To be saved, Raskolnikov has to clarify his relationship to sacrificial exchange logic, and thereby to the Crucifixion, for to him, the Crucifixion is the paradigmatic instantiation of this logic. How one should act in light of a perceived combination of freely given self-sacrifice and use of a sacrificial victim to help others contained in the Crucifixion is one of the novel's major concerns, but it is never resolved.

Raskolnikov gives several explanations for the murder. The murder, as he understands it, exemplifies the complex coexistence of the desire for justice—the desire to save others and impatience with the existing state of affairs—and egotistical self-assertion that characterizes so many of the grand "gift events" portrayed in Dostoevsky's writings, from Devushkin and Varvara to Russia and Europe. It also exemplifies the coexistence of self- and other-sacrifice, helping others and using them as means to self-assertion, that perplexes and characterizes the actions of so many of Dostoevsky's most important figures, from Devushkin to Russia.

In Dostoevsky's notes for *Crime and Punishment,* Raskolnikov reflects on the murder in terms that reveal the depth of his self-affiliation with Christ, the parallels he perceives between the murder and the Crucifixion:

> "Don't I love, since I decided to take such horror on myself? So what if it is other blood, and not my own? Wouldn't I give my own blood? if necessary?" he thought. "Before God, who sees me, and before my conscience, speaking here with myself, I say: I would give it!" (*Pss,* 7:195)

He cannot disentangle the desire to help others from self-centered purposes. "For myself, for myself alone," he insists, regarding the murder; yet he also declaims, "I didn't want unfairness" (*Pss,* 7:154).

The murder, Raskolnikov explains, was an attempt to break through injustice on behalf of the weak and vulnerable. "I am not the kind of man who can allow a scoundrel to ruin defenseless weakness," Dostoevsky has him proclaim in the notes for *Crime and Punishment* (*Pss,* 7:165). Raskolnikov's desire for sudden transformation through the murder echoes Dostoevsky's desire for transformation through gambling. "I wanted to take care of myself and my mother. There wasn't time for the German route [*Nemetskim putem bylo nekogda*]," Raskolnikov proclaims (*Pss,* 7:166). Sounding very much like Dostoevsky lamenting his need for a gambling windfall in order to help his dependents, Raskolnikov mentally addresses *his* dependents: "Afterwards I will be your support, I will be honest, but money, money, before everything else money" (*Pss,* 7:83).

His attempt to intervene on behalf of the defenseless is also, however, an attempt to assert his own power. "Whether I was a benefactor of humanity or sucked the living juices out of it like a spider doesn't matter to me. I know that I want to rule [*vladychestvovat'*], and that's enough," he proclaims in the notes (*Pss,* 7:155). In Raskolnikov's imagination, Christ and political figures like Napoleon merge as "great men" bringing a "new word," benefiting humanity in general but exacting a high price from many individuals. The "new word" of the Gospels is associated with the "new word" of Napoleon as something that brings death and destruction to some while advancing others; the advent of Christ on earth—God's gift of his son—becomes increasingly ambiguous in *Crime and Punishment.*

The complexity of emotions motivating the murder as a kind of ambiguous gift is paralleled by the complexity of the categories of victim and perpetrator, sacrificial offering and redeemer. Both Raskolnikov and the novel itself have difficulty ascertaining who occupies these positions and distinguishing between sacrifice of the self as opposed to the use of others as sacrificial victims in utilitarian calculations. The need to disentangle these categories is not satisfied in *Crime and Punishment,* and lingering dissatisfaction with this confusion ultimately leads to the Russian people's pure self-sacrifice in the *Diary.*

Raskolnikov and the novel that revolves around him are preoccupied with Christ and the Crucifixion. Raskolnikov frequently associates himself with Christ, and the Crucifixion is the paradigmatic event against which he tries to understand the things happening around him. *Crime and Punishment* shares his perception that a kind of sacrificial exchange logic underlying the Crucifixion structures familial and social relations in contemporary Russia as well; one of the things this novel is about is the presence of sacrificial exchange logic and the drama of the Passion in everyday life.

Dounia, Raskolnikov believes, has seized an opportunity to play Christ and reenact the Crucifixion by sacrificing herself for her brother; he angrily rejects what he perceives to be her attempt to redeem him. "No, Dounia," he says to himself after reading the letter from his mother describing Dounia's experiences with the Svidrigailov family and her decision to marry Luzhin for her brother's sake; "I see it all and I know what you want to say to me; and I know too what you were thinking about, when you walked up and down all night, what your prayers were like before the Holy Mother of Kazan who stands in mother's bedroom. Bitter is the ascent to Golgotha" (*CP,* 39). A writer as Christ-obsessed as Dostoevsky was would not use a reference to "Golgotha" lightly. The many references to sacrifice in this passage, overshadowed by the image of the ascent to Golgotha, indicate the clear connections linking the actions of his mother and sister with the Passion in Raskolnikov's mind. "I won't have your sacrifice, Dounia, I won't have it, mother!" he angrily addresses them in his thoughts (*CP,* 43). "You are marrying Luzhin for *my* sake," he understands. "But I won't accept the sacrifice" (*CP,* 184).

His mother, Raskolnikov realizes, sanctions Dounia's desire to be his redeemer. "For such a son who would not sacrifice such a daughter!" he imagines his mother thinking (*CP,* 42). Dounia "is ready to put up with a great deal" for your sake, Praskovia Alexandrovna writes her son, because she, like Christ, loves others more than herself: "She loves you beyond everything, more than herself" (*CP,* 29, 32). Raskolnikov discerns maternal guilt mixed with his mother's admiration of Dounia: "Are pangs of conscience secretly torturing for agreeing to sacrifice her daughter for her son?" he wonders (*Pss,* 6:36). The guilt she feels sanctioning one child's self-sacrifice for the other prompts Praskovia Alexandrovna to instill guilt in the beneficiary. "Know how Dounia loves you and what a heart she has," she admonishes her son (*CP,* 29).

Like Varvara Alekseevna, Raskolnikov is the unwilling recipient of an excessive gift, the target of a complex will to self-assertion on the part of the giver. He understands how much marriage to Luzhin would cost his sister, and how the greater that cost, the greater the satisfaction rendered to a kind of desire for martyrdom will be. "She'd live on black bread and water, she would not sell her soul, she would not barter her moral freedom for comfort; she would not barter it for all Schleswig-Holstein, much less Mr. Luzhin's money," Raskolnikov understands about his sister (*CP,* 42). What she would not stoop to as a means to better her own situation, she will ascend to as a form of glorious self-degradation for her family's sake. The pain this benefaction causes Raskolnikov is clear. When his mother and sister enter his room, Zossimov "noticed in him no joy at the arrival of his mother and sister, but a sort of bitter, hidden determination to bear another hour or two of inevitable torture" (*CP,* 207).

Raskolnikov perceives Dounia's imitation of Christ as a kind of sale, a market transaction. "I know she would rather be a black on a plantation or a Lett with a German master than degrade her soul, and her moral dignity, by binding herself forever to a man whom she does not respect and with whom she has nothing in common—for her own advantage [*vygoda*]," Raskolnikov reflects (*CP,* 42). Why, then, is she doing it? Raskolnikov muses:

> It's clear enough: for herself, for her comfort, to save her life she would not sell herself, but for someone else she is doing it! For one she loves, for one

she adores, she will sell herself! That is what it all amounts to: for her brother, for her mother, she will sell herself! She will sell everything! In such cases, we "overcome our moral feeling if necessary," freedom, peace, conscience even, all are brought into the market. (*CP*, 42)

Raskolnikov's perception that Dounia's attempt to sacrifice herself—her imitation of Christ—is a kind of shameful sale is correct. Dounia herself later repudiates her initial desire to sacrifice herself in marriage to Luzhin. "I'm ashamed, Rodya," she admits (*CP*, 283). This marriage parallels the murder—it is Dounia's improper attempt to save others by calculating what benefits can be acquired for some through one loss, in this case her own.

Dounia's attempt to follow Christ in a shameful self-sacrificial marriage is linked to Sonia's self-sacrifice through prostitution in Raskolnikov's imagination. "Sonia, Sonia Marmeladova, the eternal victim so long as the world lasts," Raskolnikov exclaims. "Have you taken the measure of your sacrifice, both of you?" he addresses Sonia and Dounia. "Is it right? Can you bear it? Is it any use? Is there any sense in it? And let me tell you, Dounia, Sonia's life is no worse than life with Mr. Luzhin" (*CP*, 42–43). Raskolnikov perceives demeaning, even ugly qualities in great acts of self-sacrifice. Sonia "sold herself for us," Katerina Ivanovna says (*Pss*, 6:304). "*She* sacrificed herself for her family," he reflects about Sonia. "My God! Even in the greatest sacrifice there is ugliness and vileness [*bezobrazie i pakost'*]. Fate so demeans the humiliated that even in their most noble sacrifice there is shame and ugliness!" Raskolnikov exclaims in Dostoevsky's notes (*Pss*, 7:91). Raskolnikov's obsession with the degradation he perceives to be an inextricable part of self-sacrifice seems to echo the concerns of his author, who was famously fixated by the degradation of Christ in the tomb portrayed by Holbein.

The straightforward kind of cost-benefit logic motivating Dounia's imitation of Christ is espoused by Luzhin, whom Razumikhin calls "a Yid" (*Pss*, 6:156). It also informs the sociopolitical order of Russia. Russian society, as Raskolnikov perceives it, is built on the principle that some can be sacrificed for the benefit of others; the authorities who maintain that order claim the right to decide who should be sacrificed for whom. Russian society, the novel suggests, rests partly on the sacrifice of sexually exploited children. The tumult his mother's letter awakens in him drives Raskolnikov out into the streets; while wandering, he encounters "a quite young, fair-haired girl—sixteen, perhaps not more than fifteen years old," still "quite a child!" drunk and apparently sexually abused (*CP*, 45). The sight of this sexually abused child prompts Raskolnikov to question his relationship to sacrificial exchange logic. First he tries to intervene on her behalf; but after trying to help her and enlisting a kind policeman to get her home, Raskolnikov questions his desire to intervene. "And why did I want to interfere?" he asks himself. "Have I any right to help?" (*CP*, 48).

His brief swing toward callousness—"Let them devour each other alive—what is it to me?"—is immediately silenced by grief-stricken reflections about how society functions on the basis of sacrificial victims (*CP,* 48). Sociopolitical authorities tell us to accept the sacrifice of a few as the price of the well-being of the whole, Raskolnikov realizes. "That's as it should be, they tell us. A certain percentage, they tell us, must every year go . . . that way . . . to the devil, I suppose, so that the rest may remain chaste, and not be interfered with" (*CP,* 49). Utilitarian logic, the novel suggests, has simply replaced a religious concept of sacrificial victims with the pseudoscientific notion of percentages. "A percentage! What splendid words they have; they are so scientific, so consolatory. . . . Once you've said 'percentage' there's nothing more to worry about. If we had any other word . . . maybe we might feel more uneasy" (*CP,* 49).

These thoughts of unredeemed Raskolnikov—the Raskolnikov contemplating the murder—echo in the January 1876 issue of the *Diary.* The "kingdom of thought and light" will begin, Dostoevsky proclaims, when society rejects the principle that some people are mere "material and means" for the happiness of others. Renunciation of this moral error will happen first in Russia, he believes, for Russia distinguishes itself from Europe by rejecting the worship of sacrificial percentages Raskolnikov addresses. "I could never understand the notion that only one-tenth of people should get higher education while the other nine-tenths of people should serve only as their material and means while themselves remaining in darkness," Dostoevsky writes in the *Diary* (*WD,* January 1876, 332).

> I do not wish to think and live in any other way than with the belief that all our ninety million Russians (or however many will subsequently be born) will all someday be educated, humanized, and happy. . . . I even believe that the kingdom of thought and light is possible to achieve here, in our Russia, even sooner, perhaps, than anywhere else, for even now no one here will stand up for the idea that we must bestialize one group of people for the welfare of another group that represents civilization, such as is the case all over Europe. (*WD,* January 1876, 332)

Dounia's ascent to the cross, Russian society, and the older generation exemplify the principle of sacrificial exchange. The morality of the fathers— Raskolnikov's deceased biological father and the authorities who sanction building society on the basis of sacrificial percentages—is the command to look away from injustice in exchange for one's own well-being. *Crime and Punishment* contrasts a paternal morality that renounces intervention against injustice as the price to pay for one's own well-being to a child morality of total identification with suffering. In his dream about the horse,

Raskolnikov's father tells him to abandon the horse to a violent death in exchange for their own safety from the crowd. Mikolka is angry at the little old horse because she consumes resources but doesn't contribute anything. She is "twenty if she is a day" and "has not had a gallop in her for the last ten years," so Mikolka resents the bread she eats—"I feel as if I could kill her. She's just eating her head off" (*CP,* 54).

As the child in his dream, Raskolnikov tries to elicit some kind of reaction from his father regarding the horse beating. "'Father, father,' he cried, 'father, what are they doing? Father, they are beating the poor horse!'" The response he gets is the command to look away. "'Come along, come along!' said his father. 'They are drunken and foolish, they are in fun; come away, don't look!' and he tried to draw him away, but he tore himself away from his hand, and, beside himself with horror, ran to the horse" (*CP,* 55). Raskolnikov physically joins himself to the horse and suffers some of the abuse she receives. He escapes from his father, runs to the horse, clings to her neck, and is struck by the whip; various adults from the crowd try to pull him away. Figures from the crowd join in and use anything they can get their hands on to beat her—"whips, sticks, poles"—and the horse finally dies (*CP,* 56). Raskolnikov tries to attack Mikolka, but his father prevents him.

> At that instant his father, who had been running after him, snatched him up and carried him out of the crowd.
>
> "Come along, come! Let us go home," he said to him.
>
> "Father! Why did they . . . kill . . . the poor horse!" he sobbed, but his voice broke and the words came in shrieks from his panting chest.
>
> "They are drunk . . . they are brutal . . . it's not our business! *[ne nashe delo!]*," said his father. He put his arm around his father but he felt choked, choked. He tried to draw a breath, to cry out—and woke up. (*CP,* 57)

Raskolnikov refuses to accept that the suffering of others is "not our business," refuses to acquiesce to the paternal injunction to look away from injustice.

The forces driving Raskolnikov to the murder are complex. His family's suffering, the suffering of society's sacrificial victims such as the girl on the street, and his own position as the recipient of a sacrifice, the target of his family's benefactions—all these compel him to find a solution. His dissatisfaction with the morality of the fathers—the belief that the suffering of others is "not our business"—also contributes.

Raskolnikov comes to the conclusion that another sacrifice is necessary in order to put an end to the sacrifices and "percentages" he sees around him. For all his unpleasant qualities, Raskolnikov is someone acutely aware of the suffering of others, someone who finds being a passive witness to their fate unbearable. Several times in the notes for *Crime and Punishment,* Dostoevsky returns to the idea that Raskolnikov saves children in a fire; in the final version this is alluded to as a reason why his sentence is softened (*Pss,* 7:321). "Something must be done now, do you understand that?" he asks himself regarding his mother and sister (*Pss,* 6:36).

He perceives two options that recall Devushkin: he can either lose his own life from grief or insanity caused by the state of affairs, or he can do something, specifically, he can perform an extremely complex gift-event that contains elements of self-sacrificial generosity and aggressive self-assertion. The first option is to "accept one's lot humbly as it is, once and for all stifle everything in oneself, giving up all claims to activity, life and love!" (*CP,* 44). Raskolnikov concludes that "he must not now suffer passively, worrying himself over unsolved questions, but that he must do something, do it at once, and do it quickly" (*CP,* 44). Failing to intervene, failing to bring what he thinks of as his new word or gift, would mean giving up his own life, revealing the coexistence of helping oneself and others in the act of giving. Instead of letting Dounia play Christ, he decides to take on that role himself. "If there's sin there, I decided to take it on myself, but only so that you would be happy," he concludes while thinking of his "poor mother, poor sister" (*Pss,* 7:38).

The solution he comes up with shows that he is confused about his relationship to self-sacrifice, as exemplified in Christ, and to sacrificial exchange logic, which will be shown to be the exclusive prerogative of higher authorities. The murder is complicated because it is an attempt to resist and overcome sacrificial exchange logic, *and* represents an exercise in this logic. Raskolnikov is caught in a contradiction; he rejects the idea that some can be sacrificed for the good of others, even while intending to commit the murder, which he justifies as the sacrifice of one for the benefit of others.

For Raskolnikov, the murder is a confusing knot of victimization and perpetration he can't untangle. In his dream, Raskolnikov's desire to prevent suffering links him to the victim, the horse; on waking, however, he understands that his desire to prevent suffering through the murder puts him in the position of the horse's killers—he equates the old woman with the horse and himself with the crowd. "'Good God!' he cried, 'can it be, can it be, that I shall really take an axe, that I shall strike her on the head, split her skull open . . .'" he moans (*CP,* 57). Yesterday, making my experiment, "I realized completely that I could never bear to do it. . . . I said to myself that it was base, loathsome, vile, vile . . . the very thought of it made me feel sick and filled me with horror," he admits (*CP,* 57–58).

He continues to identify with the horse/victim, however, even after committing the murders. After burying the stolen items under a rock and then visiting Razumikhin, he wanders the streets. A coachman suddenly "gave him a violent lash on the back with his whip," because "for some unknown reason he had been walking in the very middle of the bridge, where the carriages drive, and not where people walk" (*Pss*, 6:89). The narrative then intensifies his status as a victim by portraying him receiving alms from figures associated with Lizaveta and Sonia. An old woman in "goatskin shoes," associated with Lizaveta, and her daughter who is "wearing a hat, and carrying a green parasol," like Sonia, give him alms (*CP*, 108). Raskolnikov tosses their coin into the river and goes home; there he undresses and, shaking like an overdriven horse, lies down. The narrator seems to share Raskolnikov's confusion about roles by associating him with horses and portraying him as the (unwilling) recipient of charity from true victims.

Raskolnikov reverses the relationship between himself and the pawnbroker; he inserts himself into the position of victim she rightfully occupies. He suggests that she has tried to take his life: "My life has not yet died with that old woman!" he exclaims; "The Kingdom of Heaven to her—and now enough, madame, leave me in peace!" (*CP*, 177). She has been the victim of his murderous impulse, but he denies her this status, claiming that he has attacked himself, not her. "Did I murder the old woman? I murdered myself, not her! I crushed myself once and for all, forever . . ." he tells Sonia (*CP*, 388).

Raskolnikov's attempt to intervene against sacrificial exchange logic simply takes the form of appropriating the right to practice it himself. In his attempt to overcome the forces he opposes, Raskolnikov merely replicates their moral error by performing the same kind of sacrificial exchange—the same high-handed dealing in percentages—that he accuses them of. It angers him that some can kill and be considered benefactors of humanity—"they destroy people by the millions, and yet are considered benefactors"—and he wants this prerogative (on a lesser scale) for himself (*Pss*, 6:323).

The murder combines elements of child morality—identifying with and trying to help victims—and adult morality: the "childish" impulse to help some inflicts suffering on others as a seemingly unavoidable consequence. The first time the idea of the murder is openly discussed, it is described as a utilitarian calculation that invites comparison to the Crucifixion. "For one life—thousands of lives; one death and a hundred lives in exchange," he overhears another student expounding the idea of killing the old woman (*Pss*, 6:54). "Listen, I want to ask you a serious question," this student continues,

> on one side we have a stupid, senseless, worthless, spiteful, ailing, horrid old woman, not simply useless but doing actual mischief, who has not an idea what she is living for herself, and who will die in a day or two in any case . . . On the other side, fresh young lives thrown away for want of help and by the thousands, on every side! A hundred thousand good deeds could be done and helped, on that old woman's money which will be buried in a monastery! Hundreds, thousands perhaps, might be set on the right path; dozens of families saved from destitution, from ruin, from vice, from the Lock hospitals—

and all with her money. Kill her, take her money and with the help of it devote oneself to the service of humanity and the good of all. What do you think, would not one tiny crime be wiped out by thousands of good deeds? For one life thousands would be saved from corruption and decay. *One death, and a hundred lives in exchange*—it's simple arithmetic! (*CP,* 57, my emphasis)

The murder is performed by a character associated with Christ.[2] Allusions to Christ are woven throughout the novel. The novel seems ambivalent about Raskolnikov's status, sometimes portraying his self-association with Christ in a way that invites criticism, yet at other times encouraging readers to associate him with Christ. Most obviously, Raskolnikov hopes that by committing the murder—by intervening to stop suffering—he will join the ranks of those like Christ and Napoleon who bring a new word, who move humanity forward (the types of progress represented by these figures are equivalent to him). After Luzhin has accused Sonia of theft, she runs home; meanwhile, Katerina Ivanovna, pushed over into insanity at last, goes onto the streets with her children. Raskolnikov follows Sonia to her rooms; when she learns from him that her stepmother and siblings are on the streets, she tries to rush off to find them. Raskolnikov paraphrases Christ's words to the disciples, telling her to stay with him because she will always have the others. "Stay a little with me," he commands. "You won't lose Katerina Ivanovna, you may be sure" (*CP,* 376).

Raskolnikov thinks of the murder as a form of taking sin and suffering on oneself in order to save others. "Is it possible to suffer for them?" he asks himself (*Pss,* 7:147). "I took sin and suffering on myself," he affirms (*Pss,* 7:166). As Christ on the cross gives his mother into John's keeping, so does Raskolnikov, on the verge of the confession that he experiences as a kind of Passion, entrust his mother and sister to Razumikhin's care (*CP,* 410). Christ on the cross refuses the water offered him; Raskolnikov refuses the water offered him at the police station before he confesses. The fact that Raskolnikov experiences his confession as a kind of reenactment of the Passion is further underscored by the way he regards his confession as a bitter cup he has to drink. Dostoevsky himself seems to conflate Raskolnikov and Christ and the confession with the Crucifixion. The thoughts of the character and creator seem to merge when Dostoevsky writes in his notes, "Sonia follows him to Golgotha at forty paces" on the way to confession (*Pss,* 7:192). Dostoevsky seems, at least at times, to share his character's confusion about his relationship to Christ.

Raskolnikov believes that a higher power calls him to perform the murder, and experiences it as a burden, a sacrifice of himself—he regards it as a "fearful burden" (*CP,* 58). In a scene that evokes, in twisted form, Christ praying in the garden of Gethsemane on the eve of the Crucifixion,

Raskolnikov asks to be relieved of the role he thinks he is called to play. "'Lord,' he prayed, 'show me my path—I renounce that accursed . . . dream of mine'" (*CP*, 58). He composes a narrative for himself similar to Christ's: after asking to be relieved of his burden, he imagines that he is compelled to go through with the deed. A chance conversation overheard between Lizaveta Ivanovna and some traders in the Haymarket plays the role in Raskolnikov's narrative that God's command plays in Christ's. Learning that the old woman will be alone the next evening causes a "thrill of horror, like a shiver running down his spine"; he believes that "he had no more freedom of thought, no will, and that everything was suddenly and irrevocably decided," and he goes home "like a man condemned to death" (*CP*, 60).

His belief that a higher power is leading him toward the murder colors the initial formulation of his idea. When he overhears the conversation between two students in the tavern about killing Alyona Ivanovna for the sake of humanity, he interprets this as a sign of "something preordained, some guiding hint" (*CP*, 64). He "doggedly, slavishly sought arguments in all directions, fumbling for them, as though some one were forcing and drawing him to it" (*CP*, 68). His path to the old woman's house, he believes, is a journey to his own execution. The random disjointed thoughts elicited by various sights along the way lead him to muse, "So probably men led to execution clutch mentally at every object that meets them on the way" (*CP*, 70).

The principle of sacrificial exchange on which the murder is based isn't repudiated; what's repudiated is Raskolnikov's right to practice it. This is the fundamental paradox, I believe, that produces dissatisfaction with the novel. The Christian faith through which Raskolnikov is regenerated does not represent a moral alternative to the sacrificial exchange logic of the murder; it simply represents a renunciation of the individual's right to practice such logic, while conceding this right to higher authorities.

Sonia accords Providence the right to decide who should live and who will die. The novel does not flinch from enumerating the horrific potential consequences of her submission to God. She is willing to sacrifice herself to save her family but would not arrogate the right to take life as part of a calculation that would benefit her family. She would not kill Luzhin, even to save the children, for "is it for me to decide who should live or die?" she asks Raskolnikov (*CP*, 377). This right belongs to God, she shows him. "It would be interesting for me to know how you would decide a certain 'problem' as Lebeziatnikov would say," Raskolnikov says to her (*CP*, 377).

"Imagine, Sonia, that you had known all Luzhin's intentions beforehand. Known, that is, for a fact, that they would be the ruin of Katerina Ivanovna and the children and yourself thrown in—since you don't count yourself for anything—Polenka too . . . for she'll go the same way. Well, if suddenly it all depended on your decision whether he or they should go on living, that is whether Luzhin should go on living and doing wicked things, or Katerina Ivanovna should die? How would you decide which of them was to die? I ask you!"

"Why do you ask about what could not happen?"

"Then it would be better for Luzhin to go on living and doing wicked things? You haven't dared to decide even that!'"

"But how can I know the Divine Providence . . . And why do you ask what can't be answered? What's the use of such foolish questions? How could it happen that it should depend on my decision—who has made me a judge to decide who is to live and who is to die?"

"Oh, if the Divine Providence is to be mixed up in it, there is no doing anything," Raskolnikov grumbled morosely. (*CP*, 403)

Raskolnikov's redemption consists of according others the right to decide who should live or die. "To help others one must have the right to do it," he says bitterly at one point, and Sonia will finally inspire him to accept his difference from those who have that right (*CP*, 211–12). When some perish for the good of others through the actions of the state, this is in fact "not a crime," as he says about the murder at one point (*CP*, 69). Raskolnikov is so confused because the principle behind the murder is sanctioned by society and Sonia. The exchange of one for many is just, he assures himself, seeing "that there is no flaw in all that reasoning [*raschetakh*], that all I have concluded this last month is clear as day, true as arithmetic," the kind practiced by higher authorities, he thinks on waking from his dream about the horse (*CP*, 58).

What Raskolnikov senses from the beginning but attempts to disprove is the fact that such utilitarian logic is validated, although he himself is not entitled—is literally unable—to practice it. "I couldn't do it, I couldn't do it!" he exclaims in despair (*CP*, 49). The crux of *Crime and Punishment* is that this type of utilitarian arithmetic—sacrificing some, such as Sonia's little siblings, in the name of some inscrutable Providence—is not a crime when practiced by God or the tsar who abandons the self-proclaimed orphan Katerina Ivanovna, who seeks but fails to receive his support.

As portrayed in the novel, Sonia's renunciation of the right to sacrifice others actually comprises willingness to permit the sacrifice of some by others, when someone else—Providence—does the sacrificing. Raskolnikov and the novel itself openly practice the sacrificial logic Sonia condones as a prerogative of Providence. The novel accomplishes his Christian resurrection through the very logic Raskolnikov has to simultaneously renounce and accept in order to become a Christian, unabashedly using several deaths as the vehicle of his redemption. "This may be God's means for bringing you to Him," Porfiry Petrovich tells Raskolnikov, regarding the murder (*CP*, 424). In his notes for the novel, Dostoevsky makes it clear that killing the old woman is ultimately the vehicle of Raskolnikov's salvation, the catalyst through which he experiences death and resurrection. "Life ended on the one hand, but begins on the other. On the one hand burial and curses, on the other—resurrection," Dostoevsky writes of the effects of the crime (*Pss*, 7:138). It is very clear to Dostoevsky that Raskolnikov benefits from the deaths of his victims. His notes clarify that the murders provide the basis for this character's "moral development." After the crime,

> it's a fight, life didn't end completely, there will be life. His moral devel-
> opment begins with the crime itself, the possibility of such questions that
> didn't exist before. In the last chapter, in the camp, he says that without this
> crime he would not have acquired in himself *such questions,* desires, feelings,
> needs, striving and development. (*Pss*, 7:139)

The moral similarity linking Raskolnikov before and after his confession is underscored by the similarities of the murder and confession scenes. When Raskolnikov confesses to Sonia, his action affects her the way the murder affected Lizaveta; both react like frightened children at the spectacle of Raskolnikov with the axe or Raskolnikov with the cutting words. The scene suggests that Raskolnikov's confession is a form of violence against Sonia. She stares at him with the same expression he saw on Lizaveta's face, and she performs the same physical movements, backing away from him, holding her hand in front of her, "with utterly child-like fear in her face, exactly like small children" (*Pss*, 6:315). Lizaveta is associated with children—her sister keeps her "in complete bondage like a small child," and "Lizaveta was continually with child," we learn (*CP*, 62). The confused self-sacrificing figure who saves children from a fire kills them as well. The literal and symbolic murder of figures associated with children becomes the means to his salvation.[3]

The confession to Sonia in her room is described in such a way as to emphasize its similarity to the murder. "His sensations at that moment were terribly like the moment when he had stood over the old woman with the axe in his hand and felt that 'he must not lose another minute,'" Raskolnikov feels on the verge of confession to Sonia (*CP*, 378). He has the same feelings of helplessness or lack of responsibility about confessing as he did about the murder. On his way to Sonia, he thinks "he *had* to tell her who had killed Lizaveta . . . He did not yet know why it must be so, he only *felt* it, and the agonizing sense of his impotence before the inevitable almost crushed him" (*CP*, 375).

One of the most significant moral quandaries of *Crime and Punishment* resides in the absence of alternatives to sacrificial exchange logic. The reader experiences this quandary as well. The novel enacts a blood sacrifice in order to subject such sacrifices in general to critical scrutiny. The act of reading *Crime and Punishment* embroils readers in a blood sacrifice: we are the passive bystanders to a brutal murder, witnesses to the gruesome deaths of the pawnbroker and childlike Lizaveta, who may be pregnant, in the first pages; we are positioned as spectators to violence, resembling the bystanders to the beatings of Nelli and the horse.

Reading the rest of the novel is a process of deciding about the legitimacy of the sacrificial exchange the narrative performs, the exchange of two women's lives for Raskolnikov's redemption. The reader must weigh the scales and accept or reject their deaths as a reasonable price to pay for a regenerated Raskolnikov. Sacrificial exchange logic is the structural principle of *Crime and Punishment*. Any feeling of satisfaction with the epilogue rests on affirmative collusion with two murders as an acceptable price to pay for one moral resurrection, as so many critics claim that satisfaction with *The Brothers Karamazov* rests on affirming Ilyusha's death as the price to pay for the new spiritual lives for the boys who survive him.

The displeasure many readers have experienced regarding the epilogue can now be illuminated from a new angle.[4] A great deal of the debate elicited by *Crime and Punishment* arises from the fact that the success of the novel depends on our acceptance of a utilitarian exchange calculation—on our participation in the very moral activity the novel explicitly tries to repudiate. By reading the novel and embracing Raskolnikov's regeneration, we relegate Alyona Ivanovna and Lizaveta to those sacrificial "percentages" Raskolnikov so movingly rejects.

The salvation that readers *can* embrace without any ambivalence is accomplished through the suicide of a bad father and sexual exploiter of children—Svidrigailov. Contrary to Sonia's hopes, God doesn't save her siblings; Svidrigailov's money does. Katerina Ivanovna repeatedly calls on God and the tsar for justice for orphans, for herself and her children. After the wake, at which Sonia's situation comes to resemble that of the horse abandoned to the festive violence of the crowd, Katerina Ivanovna cries, "Good God!" She continues, "Is there no justice! Whom should you protect if not us orphans? We'll see!" (*Pss*, 6:311). She runs off to seek justice and truth. "The tsar will drive by," she tells everyone, "I will fall on my knees, put these children forward and point to them: 'Defend us, father.' He is the father of orphans, he is merciful, he will defend us, you'll see" (*Pss*, 6:329). God and the tsar ignore her heartbreaking pleas, but justice for orphans *is* delivered by Svidrigailov. His money fixes everything at once, the way Dostoevsky fantasized about doing for his dependents.[5] Salvation for the most sympathetic characters of *Crime and Punishment*—the children—comes from a depraved child-abusing father figure who is linked in complex ways to his spiritual son, Raskolnikov.[6]

From Prince Christ to the Russian Christ:

Problems of Resurrection in *The Idiot*

and the Development of Dostoevsky's

National Messianism

THE PROBLEM of resurrection that preoccupies Dostoevsky in his earlier works commands attention in *The Idiot* as well, but the focus shifts slightly. In this novel, the seemingly overwhelming evidence of physical obstacles to resurrection preoccupies central characters; the contest between physics and mortality, on the one hand, and spiritual life, on the other, moves to the center of attention. "If death is so horrible and if the laws of nature are so powerful," the reader must ask with Ippolit Terentiev, "then how can they be overcome?" (*I*, 419). Ippolit and the novel as a whole question the possibility of eternal life through Christ on the cross. How can the laws of physical decay be overcome, Ippolit demands, "when even He did not conquer them?" (*I*, 419).

The Idiot is, in many respects, one of Dostoevsky's most despairing works, lacking even the (to many) flawed attempt at optimism contained in the epilogue to *Crime and Punishment*; it engages in some of the most explicit questioning of the Crucifixion to be found in Dostoevsky's writings. *Crime and Punishment* performs a kind of degradation of the Crucifixion by suggesting its association with murder, crime, and Raskolnikov's psychic derangement; here, in *The Idiot,* the Passion is degraded through an obsessive focus on the element of physical death and decay to which even Christ was subjected.

Ippolit is tormented by an image of Christ that haunted Dostoevsky as well. While visiting Basel, Dostoevsky became familiar with Holbein's painting *The Body of the Dead Christ in the Tomb*; according to Anna Grigorevna, her husband would become lost in thought before this image.[1] This picture, Ippolit tells the other characters, "aroused in me a strange feeling of uneasiness" (*I*, 418). It arrests his attention, he explains, because it "seems to give expression to the idea of a dark, insolent, and senselessly eternal power, to which everything is subordinated" (*I*, 419). The contest between this "eternal power" and Christianity's promise of resurrection is graphically embodied in this painting. The Church makes great concessions to this malignant power, Ippolit points out, making its assurances of triumph over death all the more incredible.

> The Christian Church laid it down in the first few centuries of its existence that Christ really did suffer and that the Passion was not symbolical. His body on the cross was therefore fully and entirely subject to the laws of nature. In the picture the face is terribly smashed with blows, swollen, and covered with terrible, swollen, and bloodstained bruises, the eyes open and squinting; the large, open whites of the eyes have a sort of dead and glassy tint. (*I*, 419)

Overcoming the rule of the "enormous, implacable, dumb beast" of nature, to which Christ himself was at least temporarily subject, is the task Dostoevsky sets himself in works such as *The Idiot*. The difficulty of achieving unambiguous success in his novels leads to the recasting of resurrection as a communal project based in antisemitic nationalism in the *Diary*.

The redemptive efficacy of Christ and a figure associated with him are subjected to intense critical scrutiny in this novel. Despair about the difficulty of resurrection through Christ pervades *The Idiot* and is worth reexamining in light of how it contributes to Dostoevsky's eventual articulation of a distinction between Russians and Jews as an alternative guarantee of salvation in the *Diary*. The skepticism about Christ's resurrection that haunts this novel through the background presence of Holbein's *The Body of the Dead Christ in the Tomb* is closely linked to the articulation of the Russian people's alternative self-sacrificial triumph over the Jews that followed in the 1870s.

Composed on the threshold of the 1870s, the decade that witnessed the emergence of Dostoevsky's Russian religious chauvinism and antisemitism, *The Idiot* is in many ways a transitional and seminal work, documenting sources of significant future developments. The positive intentions for the character Dostoevsky calls "PRINCE CHRIST" in his notes, which are only ambiguously realized through the character of Myshkin in the novel, go into the portrait of the Russian people in the *Diary*.[2] "Just one more such minute, and I will be resurrected [*voskresnu*]," Ippolit says in Dostoevsky's notes, but this moment never comes for any characters in the novel (*Pss*, 9:275). The incredible pathos of the dying boy's unsatisfied longing for life is one source of the pent-up desire for transfiguration that is finally satisfied in the *Diary*, when the Russian people and the community of *Diary* readers experience moments of resurrection during a few heady months of the Balkan War.

Dostoevsky's notes for *The Idiot* show that he was working with conflicting intentions.[3] Even after the fundamental reconception of the novel that produced meek Prince Myshkin in place of the proud, domineering Idiot of his original plans, Dostoevsky continued to have contradictory goals for this character. On the one hand, he intended his Christlike figure to be an instrument of moral resurrection for others. "He restores [*vosstanovlaet*] Natasha Filippovna and has influence on Rogozhin. He leads Aglaia to humanness [*dovodit Aglaiu do chelovechnosti*]," Dostoevsky writes of Myshkin (*Pss*, 9:252). The novel will provide "the full story of Natasha Filippovna's rehabilitation" through her interactions with the Prince, Dostoevsky notes: "When he marries Natasha Filippovna, the Prince declares that it's better to resurrect one [*luchshe odnu voskresit'*], than all the victories of Alexander of Macedon" (*Pss*, 9:268).

Such clear indications of Dostoevsky's desire to portray Myshkin as a successful agent of moral resurrection coexist with notes indicating the futility of his ministry, however. "But *that* which he was able to do and undertake, *it all* died with him," Dostoevsky likewise writes of Myshkin (*Pss*, 9:242). Dostoevsky seems to have been unaware of the contradiction, for at times opposing intentions coexist within a single passage. Several lines after indicating that all of Myshkin's effects died with him, Dostoevsky writes, "But wherever he touched—everywhere he left ineradicable traces."[4]

Whatever Dostoevsky's intentions for Myshkin may have been, the version that was ultimately published portrays this Christlike figure failing to redeem those around him. Aglaia, who was supposed to have a remarkable future, converts to Catholicism, a fate worse than death in Dostoevsky's universe; Rogozhin becomes a murderer; and Natasha Filippovna, far from rising up, allows herself to be killed. Myshkin not only fails to save those around him but also himself succumbs to "the laws of nature" Ippolit cites as the rival power contending with Christ over humanity. His period of activity in Russia turns out to be merely a brief interlude of lucidity sandwiched between the long periods of darkness that are his life at Schneider's clinic in Switzerland. "Everything that developed in the Prince was extinguished in the tomb," Dostoevsky writes at one point in his notes (*Pss*, 9:242).

Dostoevsky's profound doubts about the possibility of redemption through a "Prince Christ" express themselves through the contradictory intentions he has for Myshkin; these doubts are also evident in the contrast between Myshkin and Ippolit. The notebooks for *The Idiot* indicate that Dostoevsky wavered as to who should be the novel's primary character. "The main task: the character of the Idiot. Develop him. That's the idea of the novel," Dostoevsky writes at one point about the character who would eventually become Myshkin (*Pss*, 9:252). Somewhat later, however, he tells himself, "IPPOLIT—the main axis of the whole novel" (*Pss*, 9:277).

The fact that Myshkin and Ippolit contend for primacy in Dostoevsky's conception of the novel is significant. Despite the ambiguity of his ultimate legacy, the character of Myshkin contains impulses toward the possibility of redemption; Ippolit, however, embodies utter despair over its absence. He serves as a spokesman for one of Dostoevsky's most cherished beliefs—the conviction that life is senseless if there is no personal immortality—and he tends toward the view that there is no life after death. For Ippolit, life is the contrast between "Meyer's wall and everything that is so frankly and openly written on it"—the end point of death without resurrection—and an "illusion of life and love" that sometimes screens that wall from his vision (*I*, 423).

Illness links Myshkin and Ippolit as privileged figures who experience the tension between life and death daily; epilepsy and consumption position them on the boundary between light and darkness. Myshkin's first conversation with the Epanchins revolves around the topic of the boundary between life and death. He explains that his life was broken in two by illness and describes how he slowly emerged from darkness into light and consciousness in Switzerland. He talks about how people who are insane sometimes suddenly recover their sanity; he describes the experiences of a man on the way to the scaffold.

Their special status as figures living in proximity to darkness bestows certain privileges on Myshkin and Ippolit; a combination of pity and respect for their closeness to another world compels other characters to tolerate their eccentricities. Mortal illness, Ippolit says, releases him from the usual standards of behavior. "Here's a beautiful girl—but you're dead—dead—introduce yourself as a dead man, tell her, 'A dead man may say anything,'" he says of his situation (*I*, 311). Myshkin commits numerous transgressions of the social code with relative immunity.

Through his illness, Myshkin experiences the contrast between "dazzling light . . . joy and hope," and heightened awareness, on the one hand, and "stupor, spiritual darkness, idiocy," on the other (*I*, 244). Ippolit likewise experiences life as a series of transitions between light and darkness; he frequently "emerged from his state of almost real delirium suddenly, for a moment, and then, regaining full consciousness, suddenly remembered and talked, mostly in disconnected phrases, which he had perhaps thought out in the long, weary hours of his illness, in bed, during his sleepless nights" (*I*, 310).

As "a man under sentence of death" at eighteen years old, Ippolit is understandably preoccupied with the question of eternal life (*I*, 405). At times he believes that life on earth is valuable in and of itself. "It is life, life that matters, life alone—the continuous and everlasting process of discovering it—and not the discovery itself!" he exclaims at one point (*I*, 406). But he much more frequently questions the value of a life that is not followed by immortality. A brief life followed by oblivion, he declares, is not worth living; why should I exist for a few more weeks, he demands, when I am excluded from eternity, "when all that festival, which has no end, has begun by refusing admission to me and me alone?" (*I*, 423).

Impulses toward embracing his brief life or accepting as his "last conviction" the idea that life is senseless without immortality coexist and torment Ippolit (*I*, 403, 406). "The first moment the idea took full and absolute possession of me was on the Prince's veranda, at the very instant when I had taken it into my head to make a last trial of life, when I wanted to see people and trees," he tells the guests gathered in Pavlovsk (*I*, 403). He circles around the belief that "it is not worth while living for a fortnight"—without immortality—and seems unable to overcome the feeling that death is an end point (*I*, 399).

Like Myshkin, Ippolit assumes a ministry of sorts. Where Myshkin attempts to bring new life to others, however, Ippolit tries to share his experience of the reality of Meyer's wall. He tells the guests, "When you were saying good-bye just now, I suddenly thought: here these people are, and they will never be there again—never! And the trees too—there will be just the brick wall—the red brick wall of Meyer's house—opposite my window—well, tell them all about it—just try and tell them." He concludes that he accomplishes "nothing!" (*I*, 311, 312).

The novel shares Ippolit's obsession with the experience of being condemned to death and implies that the horror of living under a death sentence may not be limited to condemned criminals or the mortally ill. To live or die, Ippolit reads from his manuscript, "is pretty much the same thing for a man in my condition," which the novel shows is actually the universal condition of mortal beings (*I*, 398). In Ippolit's case, this condition has been created by God, but the novel shows that political authorities can create this condition as well; the criminal condemned to death endures agonies similar to those experienced by the mortally ill. Raskolnikov perceived that society and God or Providence practiced sacrificial or utilitarian exchange logic; *The Idiot* invites us to associate the political state that condemns men to death with a God who possibly authors their hopeless condition as well.

Myshkin seems preoccupied by the spiritual suffering inflicted by capital punishment. "The chief and worst pain," he tells the Epanchins' servant with whom he chats during his first visit to their home, "is perhaps not inflicted by wounds, but by your certain knowledge that in an hour, in ten minutes, in half a minute, now, this moment your soul will fly out of your body, and that you will be a human being no longer, and that that's certain—the main thing is that it is *certain*." Myshkin maintains that execution, "murder by legal process," is a greater evil than the original crime. A man who is murdered by thieves, he explains, always has hope that he may be saved. "But here all this last hope, which makes it ten times easier to die, is taken away *for certain*; here you have been sentenced to death, and the whole terrible agony lies in the fact that you will most certainly not escape, and there is no agony greater than that," he concludes (*I*, 46).

The spiritual torture of facing certain death, borne by Ippolit and criminals awaiting execution, is a central theme of *The Idiot,* refracted on many levels of the novel. Lebedev may be a lying swindler, but he prays for the Countess du Barry, who he recalls cried out before the guillotine, "'*Encore un moment, monsieur le bourreau, encore un moment!*' which means, 'Wait one more moment, Mr. *bourreau,* just one little moment!' And for that little moment the Lord will perhaps pardon her, for a greater *misere* than that it is impossible to imagine" (*I,* 215). Lebedev, too, understands what Myshkin, Ippolit, and the novel show—that the certainty of death may be the worst agony a human being can suffer.

This dilemma is shown to have Russian national dimensions. *Crime and Punishment* creates associations between the political power that builds society on sacrificial percentages and the divine power that accomplishes salvation for some through the sacrifice of others. *The Idiot* likewise associates God, who subjects humanity to an existence overshadowed by the possibility of death without hope of resurrection, and the political authorities who inflict capital punishment. Everyone knew that Dostoevsky had faced the firing squad for a political crime. In *The Idiot,* he aligns himself with Christ and criminals as someone who has special knowledge of the agony of facing certain death. Myshkin says:

> Possibly there are men who have sentences of death read out to them and have been given time to go through this torture, and have then been told, "You can go now, you've been reprieved." Such men could perhaps tell us. It was of agony like this and of such horror that Christ spoke. No, you can't treat a man like that! (*I,* 46)

Through Myshkin, Dostoevsky protests against the outrageous abuse he had personally endured and implies that it derives from God and the tsar.

The novel initially holds out some hope that Russia may be a special space within which new life is possible. During his first visit to the Epanchins, Myshkin suggests that Russia may be superior to the West—that Russia may be a privileged space where death is not so certain—because of the absence of capital punishment (*I,* 44). This hope is rescinded, however, and Russia emerges as a space of spiritual degeneration, a place to which redemption hasn't come. Myshkin's fate and the experiences of the other characters belie any hope in Russia.

The relationship between Russia and the West portrayed in *The Idiot* fails to bear out Myshkin's claims about Russian spiritual superiority or the claims Dostoevsky makes in some of his other writings, for the lucidity Myshkin acquires in Switzerland is extinguished in Russia. Myshkin initially believes that a "new life has begun for me" on his return to Russia (*I,* 97).

He came to Russia with hopes, he tells Mrs. Epanchin, "hopes of the future" (*I*, 332). "In that murky darkness I dreamed—I seemed to catch a glimpse of a new dawn," he tells Aglaia (*I*, 446). Myshkin believes he overcomes death in a sense when he survives Rogozhin's attack and a terrible epileptic fit; my birthday "seems to have come at the right moment," he tells Rogozhin, "for my new life has started today, hasn't it?" (*I*, 379). In his notes, Dostoevsky writes that Russia exercises positive influence on Myshkin—"*Russia influenced him gradually*," in positive ways, Dostoevsky writes there—but it turns out differently in the novel (*Pss*, 9:242).

The novel teases other characters with hopes for regeneration as well. Hope invested in the national-spiritual community of Orthodox Russia fails Myshkin, as hope in God for a reprieve from mortal illness fails Ippolit. Ippolit initially seems to have gotten a reprieve in Pavlovsk, for he tells the Prince "that he could not help being surprised himself how three days ago he was expecting to die, for he had never felt better in his life than that evening" (*I*, 381). Ippolit dies after temporarily feeling better; Russia pushes Myshkin back into spiritual darkness and Schneider's clinic.

Totsky tries to convince Natasha Filippovna to embark on a new life, telling her that "what she was suffering from was a general depression of spirits and an utter disbelief in the chance of a new life, which might dawn for her so beautifully in love and a family of her own" (*I*, 70). At times she agrees, saying "she wished she could start her life all over again, for she realized that she had to find a new aim in life, if not in love, then in a family of her own" (*I*, 71). She, too, believes that her birthday marks a new beginning. "Tomorrow I'm starting a new life," she tells the guests at her party, "and today is my birthday and I'm my own mistress for the first time in my life!" (*I*, 176). She never experiences any moral regeneration, however. "Sometimes I was successful in making her see the light around her again," Myshkin explains to Aglaia, "but all at once she felt so resentful that she accused me bitterly of putting myself far above her" (*I*, 444).

The Idiot begins with a tease, with things that are supposed to bring new light and life but don't. The opening paragraphs encapsulate the discrepancy between appearances of life and light and the reality of darkness— the novel starts with a false thaw and a morning that brings no light. When the novel opens, Myshkin and Rogozhin are approaching Petersburg. It is a brief thaw at the end of November; even after it grows light at nine in the morning, the narrator says, the persistent fog makes it difficult to see anything. Their fates are already reflected in their faces: Rogozhin displays "deathly pallor" and a "look of utter exhaustion," and Myshkin's face is "colorless" and "blue with cold" (*I*, 27, 28).

The novel implies that there is no reprieve from the laws of decay and degeneration and that when such reprieve seems to become possible, either its potential goes unrealized or the thought of it drives people mad. While on his way to the scaffold, the condemned criminal Myshkin thinks that if he were given life again, he'd treasure every minute; he is in fact reprieved, but he doesn't experience his new life the way he thought he would. When the Prince offers Natasha Filippovna a new life—moral rehabilitation; no recriminations, no consequences from the past, for "you are not to blame for anything," he tells her; "It's impossible that your life should be utterly ruined"—she goes crazy (*I*, 189). "They all maintained afterwards that Natasha Filippovna went mad from that precise moment" (*I*, 187).

Behind these various absent or failed resurrections is the Crucifixion. *The Idiot* is structured by irresolvable choices, by different ways of viewing the same picture. Myshkin tells the Epanchins that he has a subject for a painting. He would portray a man at the moment of execution, he explains: "his head, his face is as white as paper, the priest is holding up the cross, the man greedily puts out his blue lips and looks and—*knows everything*. The cross and the head—that is the picture" (*I*, 88). But a picture of what? Of hope or despair? What does this face kissing the cross know and communicate?

The message of Holbein's painting remains indeterminate as well.[5] By portraying Christ's utter physical degradation, does Holbein convey the impossibility of overcoming death or intensify the triumph of Christ's feat? Ippolit wonders how anyone who witnessed this death could believe in its reversal. "How could they possibly have believed," he asks of the witnesses, "as they looked at the corpse, that that martyr would rise again?" (*I*, 418). He also speculates as to whether Christ would have assented to such a death if he had seen this image: "if, on the eve of the crucifixion, the Master could have seen what He would look like when taken from the cross, would he have mounted the cross and died as he did?" (*I*, 420). Ippolit's questions about this image of Christ in the tomb remain unanswered in *The Idiot*.

Christ failed when personified—the results of trying to embody moral perfection in Myshkin were ambiguous at best—but a nation messiah might succeed where a Prince Christ failed. Dostoevsky's letters and notebooks from the late 1860s, the period of work on *The Idiot*, show that he increasingly endowed the problem of redemption with explicitly national-historical dimensions. While he was articulating some of his most profound doubts about the possibility of resurrection through the Crucifixion in his novel, Dostoevsky was identifying a specifically Russian Christ and Russia itself as alternative means to salvation. In 1868, he writes Maikov that "the definitive essence of the Russian mission . . . consists of revealing the Russian Christ to the world . . . that is the whole essence of our future civilizing and resurrecting of all Europe" (*Pss*, 29.1:30). "The essence of the Russian calling," he writes Strakhov in March 1869, "consists of the revelation of the Russian Christ before the world"; and "the resurrection of all Europe" might come through us, he tries to persuade Strakhov (*Pss*, 29.1:30).

The increasingly explicit faith Dostoevsky places in Russia as a vehicle of resurrection is spurred partly by his experiences in Europe. Encountering other Russians professing faith in the West galvanizes Dostoevsky to become an ever-more-strident believer in Russia. Russian émigrés with their "belief in Europe and civilization" annoy him, he writes Maikov in August 1867. When I had to leave Russia, he tells Maikov, "I left then with death in my soul: I didn't believe in Europe, that is, I believed that its moral influence would be very bad" (*Pss*, 28.2:204).

A desire arises in the wake of *The Idiot* that dominates Dostoevsky for the rest of his creative life. From the late 1860s forward, he aspires to give artistic form to the loss and reattainment of Christian faith, embedding this narrative of moral resurrection within a specifically Russian national context. Belief in the entwinement of spirituality and nationality was, of course, not new for Dostoevsky. His notes for *The Idiot* reveal that he conceived of the personal and national merging in his "Prince Christ." He reminds himself, "In his most extremely tragic and personal minutes the Prince is occupied with solving general questions" (*Pss*, 9:366). These intentions for Myshkin are only faintly present in the novel, however. Myshkin believes that "the essence of religious feeling" exists "most clearly in a Russian heart" and tells the Epanchins' guests, "It is necessary that our Christ should shine forth in opposition to the ideas of the West," but these sentiments—Dostoevsky's own, expressed as his most cherished convictions in his contemporaneous letters—are problematized by the character who serves as their vehicle (*I*, 238, 549).

The autumn of 1867 was a trying time for Dostoevsky; he was dissatisfied with his original conception of the Idiot as a proud, arrogant figure. While he was struggling with his novel, Dostoevsky was also working on a project his notes refer to as "One thought (a *poema*): a theme under the name 'Emperor.'" Dostoevsky's projected *poema* "Emperor" was inspired by an essay by M. I. Semevsky that appeared in *Notes of the Fatherland* in 1866. Semevsky presented two alternative views of Ivan Antonovich, a shadowy figure who was kept in isolation before being declared emperor on the death of Anna Ivanovna, hidden when Elizabeth Petrovna took the throne in 1741, and killed by Catherine's guards during an attempt to free him and set him on the throne.

Dostoevsky's engagement with the story of Ivan Antonovich during October and November 1867, the period of his greatest difficulties with *The Idiot*, influenced this novel and Dostoevsky's future work in significant ways. He never wrote any "Emperor," but he endows the character who becomes Myshkin with aspects of a popular folk image of Ivan Antonovich, the shadow tsar. According to popular legend, Ivan Antonovich spends his early years "in darkness" and "unable to speak" but is brought into society as its hope. Catherine's dependents, on the other hand, propagated an image of Ivan Antonovich as "dull-witted, tongue-tied, an idiot," Semevsky writes; but "the voice of the people proclaimed that his mind and noble feelings made Ivan entirely worthy of that crown worn by others" (*Pss*, 9:487).

The image of Ivan Antonovich contributed to the characterization of Myshkin specifically and to the Russianization of Christ in Dostoevsky's writings more generally. Like Ivan Antonovich, the Russian Christ is underestimated by the elite but appreciated by the people. Although he is simple, this underestimated Russian turns out to be morally superior to those who persecute him; he draws on native sources of enlightenment—"constant conversation with his own heart" developed him "more than any European teachers could have" (*Pss*, 9:487).

Dostoevsky's goal of nationalizing Christ and framing the problem of resurrection in national-historical terms continues to evolve in the years during and immediately following composition of *The Idiot*. It seems spurred by the gap between his intentions for his characters and what he is capable of portraying within the genre of the novel. His greatest ambition is to create a character who articulates his own ideas about the relationship between Russia and Christian redemption, but he seems incapable of realizing this goal. As Dostoevsky's editors observe, "Realizing the idea of 'overcoming sinfulness' stubbornly eluded the writer" (*Pss*, 9:518). In Dostoevsky's notebooks from the period after composition of *The Idiot*, A. L. Bem observes, "The criminal countenance of the hero is drawn in great detail, clearly and psychologically convincingly, whereas the spiritually illuminated countenance is sketched vaguely" (*Pss*, 9:518). Perhaps Dostoevsky can portray rebels more successfully because these characters articulate his own anxieties about the faith he so desperately wanted to affirm.

The contrast between his positive intentions for his major characters and how his novels undermine those intentions becomes increasingly sharp. The distance between Dostoevsky's original ambition to create a spokesman-hero for Russian Christianity and the complexity of what he actually writes is perhaps greatest in the case of Stavrogin. The unfulfilled desire to champion a Russian Christ and the Russian people at the basis of some of Dostoevsky's greatest novels is the inspiration behind the *Diary* as well.

In December 1869, not done yet with *The Idiot*, Dostoevsky writes Maikov that he is planning a work that will link spiritual resurrection to national identity. He has an idea for a "huge novel, called 'Atheism,'" he tells Maikov (*Pss*, 28.2:329). Work on *Atheism* occupies Dostoevsky for much of 1868–69. The main character is "a Russian of our background," he explains to Maikov, "who suddenly loses faith after an unremarkable life" (*Pss,* 28.2:329). "The loss of faith in God has a colossal effect on him," sending him on a spiritual quest (*Pss,* 28.2:329). After searching everywhere—among the young generation, atheists, Europeans, even Poles and Jesuits, "at the end he acquires Christ and the Russian earth, the Russian Christ and Russian God" (*Pss,* 28.2:329). Statements about the connection between Russian soil and his own creativity begin to appear in Dostoevsky's letters during this period as well. "If I don't write it, it will torment me," he tells Sofia Ivanova regarding *Atheism.* "But it's impossible to write it here" in Europe, he insists (*Pss,* 9:500).

The title *Atheism* disappears from his notes in the summer of 1869, replaced by a plan for a series of novels that acquires the name *Life of a Great Sinner* in December 1869. The name is significant, for it signals Dostoevsky's attempt to tighten the connection between faith and nationality. The genre of the "Life" played an important role in Russian culture during the first centuries after conversion to Christianity, and it was rediscovered by intellectuals in the nineteenth century as an alternative to Western spiritual influence. By calling his projected series of novels a "Life," Dostoevsky draws attention to the specifically Russian nature of the faith he is trying to portray. Dostoevsky claims an especially personal relationship to this project. Writing to Maikov in the spring of 1870 about the *Life,* he says, "The main question which will run through all its parts is the very one I have suffered from consciously or unconsciously all my life—the existence of God. The hero, over the course of his life, is an atheist, then faithful, then a fanatic and sectarian, then again an atheist" (March 25, 1870, *Pss,* 29.1:117). "This novel is all my hopes [*upovanie*] and the hope of my whole life—not only in the financial sense," he explains to Sofia Ivanova in December 1869. "It is my main idea, which only expressed itself in me in the last two years" (*Pss,* 29.1:93). "This idea is everything for which I've lived," he declares, but "in order to write this novel I would have to be in Russia" (*Pss,* 29.1:503–4).

Neither *Atheism* nor *Life of a Great Sinner* was ever written, but these projects form the basis out of which Dostoevsky's future writings grow. His future characters, from Alyosha Karamazov and Father Zosima to Stavrogin, Ivan, and Russia in the *Diary,* all evolve out of Dostoevsky's desire to portray connections between nationality and redemption.

"This Is What I Cannot Bear":

The Obliteration of Moral Distinctions

Through the Crucifixion in *Demons*

LIKE RASKOLNIKOV, Nikolai Stavrogin is trying to understand the nature of Christian redemption and is particularly concerned with his relationship to Christ and the Crucifixion. Raskolnikov is troubled by the suspicion that the Crucifixion is based on the kind of utilitarian logic he both abhors and attempts to practice. It is a different aspect of the Crucifixion that troubles Stavrogin, however; he suspects that it plays a role in human affairs similar to that played by money. The nineteenth-century German philosopher and sociologist Georg Simmel provides an analysis of money's effect on human relations that is useful for approaching Stavrogin's anxieties about the Crucifixion. Money, Simmel argues, is a terrifying leveler of differences.

> By being the equivalent to all the manifold things in one and the same way, money becomes the most frightful leveler. For money expresses all qualitative differences of things in terms of "how much?" Money, with all its colorlessness and indifference, becomes the common denominator of all values; irreparably it hollows out the core of things, their individuality, their specific value, and their incomparability.[1]

Stavrogin suspects that the Crucifixion functions as a similar leveler of differences in moral life. The universal forgiveness offered to humankind through Christ's death on the cross, he fears, obliterates distinctions among human actions; the general equivalence established by money has a parallel for him in a perceived moral equivalence of actions established by the Crucifixion.

The moral vacuum Stavrogin finds himself in results not just from deracination or the pernicious influence of Western ideas but from the Crucifixion itself. If all sins are washed clean by Christ's blood, Stavrogin wonders, then aren't all actions robbed of their significance? If the child rapist and the violated child are equally embraced by the Lamb, as Tikhon says they are, if such basic distinctions are suspended, then what remains except to hang oneself in the attic?

Crime and Punishment implicates readers in a kind of salvational exchange transaction. Like Raskolnikov in the epilogue, readers must accept the suffering of many individuals—Lizaveta, Alyona Ivanovna, and Raskolnikov's mother, whose fatal illness is precipitated by his crime—as the price to be paid for his Christian redemption if they are going to find satisfaction in the novel. The cost of Christian faith preoccupies Stavrogin as well. Reading *Crime and Punishment* implicates readers in the reduction of human life to utilitarian calculation; reading *Demons* implicates readers in making a decision about the significance of child abuse. Tikhon, "the bearer of Christian morality" in the novel, tells Stavrogin that God is willing to make the violation and suicide of a child an element in his, Stavrogin's, salvation narrative.[2] Tikhon is capable of accepting the violation of a child as something to be used in an adult's redemption narrative: he encourages Stavrogin to make his crime and repentance the basis of his eventual reconciliation with God. Stavrogin, on the other hand, wants to believe that some crimes can't be forgiven, and it is just this idea that Tikhon's version of Christianity denies.

Stavrogin is struggling to decide what attitude he should adopt to his crime against Matrena. He has seduced her and then tormented her with his indifference, leaving her to figure out what has happened. "She still understood nothing," he tells Tikhon; "there was despair in her face, such as was impossible to see in the face of a child."[3] Matresha spends several days in feverish delirium before hanging herself while Stavrogin lurks in the background, knowing what she is doing but making no attempt to help her.

The crux of his dilemma, as he presents it to Tikhon, is what to do with such an enormous debt. Tikhon urges him to turn it over to Christ, who will redeem it for him. Stavrogin rejects the Christian redemption Tikhon offers because he perceives that the forgiveness extended to him is based on the logical and philosophical bases of money—the erasure of differences. He rejects, in other words, the intrusion of the spirit of money—the principles of mediation and abstract exchange equivalence—into spiritual affairs. He believes that his debt to Matrena is nontransferable—Christ cannot mediate or pay for him. He also believes that the magnitude of his sin and the amount of Matrena's suffering resist translation into any sort of comparable units or a scale that would enable comparison and calculation. Tikhon agrees with Stavrogin that the crime is a heinous one: "There is not and cannot be any greater and more terrible crime," he acknowledges (*D*, 707). Stavrogin perceives that Tikhon is trying to compare crimes, and he objects, "Let's quit putting a yardstick to it [*Ostavim meru na arshiny*]" (*Pss*, 11:25). Only he, Stavrogin, can redeem the debt, and payment must be made in kind, not the cash of the Crucifixion: his life for hers.

Stavrogin's infamous debauchery was one response to the moral vacuum caused by his anxious fear of a general equivalence established by the

Crucifixion. He is capable of a quite different response, however. He desperately wants to believe in the moral significance and differences of actions.[4] The scene at Tikhon's is painful to read partly because Stavrogin has come in search of consequences—he wants Tikhon to censure him—but instead of the condemnation he so passionately desires, which would establish meaning and order in human affairs, this representative of Christianity tells him that all things are the same. All human actions, Tikhon tells him, float with equal weight in God's infinite forgiveness.

Perhaps Stavrogin claims the status of sinner with such bravado because he wants to bear the consequences of his crimes. He anticipates and prevents recourse to fashionable theories to exonerate him. "I am always master of myself when I want to be," he asserts before embarking on his confession. "And so, let it be known that I do not want to seek irresponsibility for my crimes either in the environment or in illness" (*D*, 693). Why Stavrogin wants to hold on to his guilt and why Tikhon, on the other hand, urges him to relinquish it are questions of central importance for understanding Dostoevsky's anxieties about Christianity.

Stavrogin knows that his crime against a child is blocking his redemption. One day, long after he thought he had forgotten all about Matresha, he had a remarkable dream. Dostoevsky endows Stavrogin with his own fascination with Claude Lorrain's painting *Acis and Galatea,* or "The Golden Age," as Stavrogin calls it. This painting inspired a vivid dream, Stavrogin tells Tikhon, in which he saw "the most incredible vision," one to which

> mankind throughout its life has given all its forces, for which it has sacrificed everything, for which prophets have died on crosses and been killed, without which people do not want to live and cannot even die. . . . It was as if I still saw it when I woke up and opened my eyes, for the first time in my life literally wet with tears. A feeling of happiness, as yet unknown to me, went through my heart until it hurt. (*D*, 703)

This baptism of tears is interrupted by a vision of Matresha, however. "It was as though something pierced me," Stavrogin remembers; "I saw Matresha, wasted and with feverish eyes. . . . And nothing had ever seemed so tormenting to me!" (*D*, 703).

I have many memories of vile behavior, Stavrogin admits, but "none of these memories evokes anything of the kind in me" (*D*, 704). There is something irreducibly unique, concrete, and intolerable about the memory of Matresha. "What is unbearable to me is only this image alone, and precisely on the threshold, with its raised and threatening little fist, only that look alone, only that minute alone, only that shaking head. This is what I cannot bear," he confides (*D*, 704). Why, he wants to know, does "the pitiful despair of a helpless ten-year-old being" stand out as something apart among his memories (*D*, 703)? He senses the answer: this crime against a child is unique because it offers the last chance to establish meaning, to generate consequences amid the moral absurdity inaugurated by the universal forgiveness held out by Tikhon.

Stavrogin contradicts himself when he tries to explain what he wants to do about the memory of Matresha. At one point he says he wants to free himself from the memory by forgiving himself. "'Listen, Father Tikhon: I want to forgive myself, and that is my chief goal, my whole goal!' Stavrogin said suddenly, with grim rapture in his eyes. 'I know that only then will the apparition vanish'" (*D*, 710). But he also wants to hold on to the image of Matresha and his guilt, even though holding on to them makes life impossible. "It does not appear on its own," he concedes, regarding Matresha's image, "but I myself evoke it, and cannot help evoking it, even though I cannot live with it" (*D*, 704). "I know I can remove the girl even now, whenever I wish," he explains. "But the whole point is that I have never wanted to do it, I myself do not want to and will not want to; that I do know" (*D*, 704). Allowing her image to live despite the anguish this causes him has become a type of penance.

Belief in universal forgiveness is a cornerstone of Christian faith in Dostoevsky's novels; yet there is evidence that he feared that the concept of universal forgiveness, especially forgiveness of crimes against children, might harbor sinister dimensions. Some of the clearest indications of Dostoevsky's uneasiness with the notion of universal forgiveness occur in the *Diary* and "At Tikhon's," regarded by his biographer Konstantin Mochulsky as "Dostoevskii's loftiest artistic creation."[5] "At Tikhon's" and the figure of Stavrogin have commanded enormous respect, and what they reveal about Dostoevsky's faith is of critical importance. Linnér shares Mochulsky's enthusiasm for "At Tikhon's." This chapter enjoys exceptional, independent significance, Linnér believes: "It can be read as a short story, and as such it is one of the most fascinating Dostoevsky ever wrote."[6] Dostoevsky "attached exceptional significance" to Stavrogin's confession, Dolinin writes.[7]

Stavrogin himself, "this prestigious being [*cet être prestigieux*]," does more than impress readers with his significance; it would not be exaggerating to say that "this fallen Lucifer" has in fact seduced many readers.[8] He is "a character whose complexity is rare even for Dostoevskii," Richard Pope and Judy Turner enthuse; a "marvelous aura of mystery" surrounds him.[9] Even those who share Leonid Grossman's view that this character is "a ruined and wingless soul," a figure who bears a "deformed word," are likely to concede with Mochulsky that Stavrogin is "Dostoevsky's greatest artistic creation."[10] Recognizing with Dolinin "the fact that for Dostoevsky a crime such as the rape of a child probably constituted an irremediable act, that there could be no forgiveness for such a crime even in terms of God's highest order," we must come to terms with why Dostoevsky would endow one of his most compelling figures—and one with whom he enjoyed such an intimate relationship—with this most heinous crime.[11]

Tikhon assures Stavrogin that all crimes, even the greatest, are forgiven, for there is no debt so great that Christ can't redeem it. Father Zosima in *The Brothers Karamazov*, like Tikhon, propagates the view that God has an infinite amount of love, enough to cover all human debts. "There is no sin, and there can be no sin on all the earth, which the Lord will not forgive to the truly repentant," Zosima says. "Man cannot commit a sin so great as to exhaust the infinite love of God," he insists (*BK*, 43). The real Saint Tikhon, who inspired the portraits of Tikhon and Zosima, said, "There is no kind of sin, and there cannot be any such on earth, that God would not pardon to someone who sincerely repents."[12]

Stavrogin responds to Tikhon's promise of forgiveness for even the most grievous sin by distinguishing between God and Christ. He concedes that God, himself a practitioner of child sacrifice, may indeed forgive a child abuser, but Christ will not. He has come to Tikhon as his last recourse, hoping that Tikhon will assert the Gospel of the Son on the cross as a source of moral absolutes.

> "Christ, incidentally, will not forgive," Stavrogin asked, and a light shade of irony could be heard in the tone of the question, "for it is said in the book; 'Whoso shall offend one of these little ones'—remember? According to the Gospel, there is not and cannot be any greater crime. In this book!"
> He pointed to the Gospel. (*D*, 711)

Tikhon disappoints him, however. "'I have glad tidings for you about that,' Tikhon spoke with tender feeling. 'Christ, too, will forgive'" (*D*, 711). Stavrogin does not *want* Christ, himself the victim of child sacrifice, to betray children and forgive their trespassers; he does not want Christ to condone the use of a dead child as a token for purchasing someone else's redemption.

The contest between Tikhon's belief in universal forgiveness, on the one hand, and Stavrogin's insistence that crimes against children are irredeemable, on the other, represents a significant chapter in the aesthetic embodiment of Dostoevsky's Christian anxieties. This chapter, Dolinin and Tikhomirov persuasively argue, reveals the increasing distance between Dostoevsky's understanding of Christianity and official doctrine—a gap that would soon give rise to antisemitic passions. Dostoevsky, Tikhomirov writes, sees "the attitude toward children as the most important criterion to be taken into consideration on the Day of Judgment."[13] By comparing the original gospel passages that are quoted by Stavrogin (and by Versilov in notes for *The Adolescent* as well), Tikhomirov reveals that Dostoevsky does something remarkable: Dostoevsky actually equates children with the Holy Spirit.

When Stavrogin insists that whoever offends a child will not be forgiven, Tikhomirov points out, he is creating a new mixture out of two gospel sources. Matthew 12:32 declares, "And whosoever speaketh a word against the Son of Man, it shall be forgiven him: but whosoever speaketh against the Holy Ghost, it shall not be forgiven him, neither in this world, neither in the world to come." Matthew 18:6 warns, "But whoso shall offend one of these little ones which believe in me, it were better for him that a millstone were hanged about his neck, and that he were drowned in the depth of the sea." Stavrogin's insistence that offenders of children will not be forgiven is "an instance of a most interesting *contamination*," Tikhomirov observes. "This is yet another example of an 'act of exegesis' by Dostoevsky: . . . as a result of the contamination created by the author, offending a child is *equated* with the unforgivable 'sin of sins'—abuse of the Holy Ghost."[14]

The chapter "At Tikhon's" is structured by tension between the belief that anything can be forgiven and the view that some transgressors are beyond hope, Dolinin argues. As for Stavrogin's crime against Matresha, "The person who committed it would bear within him such irradicable sources of primordial evil that he would be incapable, no matter how he tried, of true repentance"; yet "according to Dostoevsky's religious views there is no sin that cannot be forgiven, just as there is no absolutely hopeless sinner."[15] At one point, Dolinin observes, Stavrogin seems to "suddenly come to life with an act of living religious will," his desire for repentance; but then he perishes nevertheless. "If Dostoevsky did provide him with the capacity for repentance, thus bringing him very close to the Church and to Christ," Dolinin wonders, "then how can this be reconciled with his shameful death: 'The citizen of the Canton of Uri was hanging there behind the little door.'" Dolinin continues, "But why death and not resurrection, if what we have here is an act of living religious will?" *Demons* "ends with this act of harsh retribution" and is "unusually harsh even for Dostoevsky's tragic outlook."[16]

To Tikhon and the Christianity he represents, there is a more heinous sin than violating and being complicit in the suicide of a child. Stavrogin would commit a worse sin, Tikhon explains, if he refused to accept that Christ is capable of forgiving him. Christ can forgive such a crime, but only if Stavrogin forgives himself first. "Christ, too, will forgive, if only you attain to forgiving yourself," Tikhon tells him (*D,* 711). "'If you believe that you can forgive yourself and can attain to this forgiveness in the world, then you believe everything!' Tikhon exclaimed rapturously. 'How is it that you say you do not believe in God?'" (*D,* 710). Forgiving himself, Stavrogin fears, means accepting that the Crucifixion made all actions equal as already forgiven and canceled all debts human beings are capable of incurring against each other. Self-forgiveness attains such importance in this conversation about Christian faith and redemption because it is equivalent to acknowledging Christ as sole possessor of the right to redeem debts.[17]

Raskolnikov has to abdicate the right to perform sacrificial exchanges; Stavrogin has to relinquish the right to collect debts. His desire to collect his own debt against Matresha by taking his life is a kind of contest with Christ. For Tikhon, collecting his debt, not driving Matresha to suicide, is "the most terrible crime" Stavrogin could commit (*D,* 713). Other characters comment on Stavrogin's spiritual pretensions. Shatov observes that he has "a passion for martyrdom" (*Pss,* 10:201–2). Tikhon tells him, "You are wrestling with a desire for martyrdom and self-sacrifice; subdue this desire also . . . and then you will conquer everything" (*Pss,* 11:29). The idea that the stain of all crimes has been washed clean by Christ's blood is what Stavrogin cannot accept. Accepting this idea, Tikhon perceives, would represent the greatest humiliation for him: "Your deed, if done in humility, would be the greatest Christian deed, if you could endure it," he tells Stavrogin (*D,* 712).

Tikhon believes that Stavrogin has a choice. Stavrogin could perform an "astonishing deed" in the name of Christian faith—he could let Christ pay his debts (*D,* 706). He describes salvation through Christ in commercial language, painting for Stavrogin the benefits he will receive if he agrees to participate in the merchant God's economy. "Make a vow to yourself, and with this great sacrifice you will buy everything that you long for, and even what you do not expect, for you cannot understand now what you will receive! [*seiu velikoiu zhertvoi kupite vse, chego zhazhdete*]" (*D,* 713). God is like an accountant, Tikhon explains, one who will carefully record Stavrogin's payments toward salvation. Turning your debt over to Christ would be difficult, he concedes, but the benefits will outweigh the expenses. "Even if you were unable to endure it all, all the same the Lord would count your initial sacrifice. Everything will be counted: not a word, not a movement of the soul, not a half thought will be in vain [*Dazhe esli b i ne vyderzhali, vse ravno vam pervonachal'nuiu zhertvu sochtet gospod'. Vse sochtetsia: ni odno slovo, ni odno dvizhenie dushenvnoe, ni odna polumysl' ne propadut darom*]" (*D,* 712; *Pss,* 11:29).

Stavrogin rejects the exchange Tikhon offers him—he refuses to let Matresha's death buy his reconciliation with God. He chooses instead to remain unredeemed, excluded from the harmony he glimpses in his dream, rather than be the beneficiary of a child's death. Once his crime has been committed, he seems to believe, refusing to accept Christ's forgiveness may be the only way to show respect for Matresha's loss. Against Tikhon's urging, Stavrogin does not allow her death to become part of a transaction between himself and God but asserts that her experience is irredeemable.

Stavrogin hopes that Christ's gospel is the last bulwark of moral absolutes in a world of general relativity, but he is disappointed. His aching suspicion that the Crucifixion itself is actually a source of moral equivalency is confirmed by Tikhon. Tikhon robs Stavrogin of his last hope that some actions have meaning. There is nothing at all that can't be equalized in universal forgiveness, Tikhon insists; there is in fact almost no way to *elude* forgiveness. It initially seems that refusing to forgive oneself might be a way to avoid complicity in the salvational economy based on child suffering, but Tikhon takes this possibility away as well. Christ will forgive you if you forgive yourself, he says, but then he robs even this action—refusing self-forgiveness—of potential significance.

> Even if you do not attain to reconciliation with yourself and forgiveness of yourself, even then He will forgive you for your intention and for your great suffering . . . for there are no words or thoughts in human language to express *all* the ways and reasons of the Lamb, "until his ways are openly revealed to us." Who can embrace him who is unembraceable, who can grasp the *whole* of him who is infinite! (*D*, 711)

Far from consoling Stavrogin, these words confirm his worst fears and leave him "agitated and half crazy" (*D*, 711).

The fact that Dostoevsky articulates these fears about Christianity through Stavrogin is significant. The character who eventually bears the name Nikolai Stavrogin begins in Dostoevsky's notes as a spokesman for some of his most cherished beliefs about personal resurrection, Russian Orthodoxy, and its role in the world. The Prince, as Stavrogin is initially called, expresses views that Dostoevsky had been advancing in his correspondence and notebooks and later puts forth as his own in the *Diary*. Stavrogin begins as Dostoevsky's mouthpiece, a spokesman for Russia and Christian faith. What the private Dostoevsky calls "Russian" and "Christian" seems to acquire surprising dimensions when launched into the world of a novel, however.

This character's spiritual troubles arise from his depth, Russianness, and intimate relationship to Dostoevsky. "This is a Russian and tragic character," Dostoevsky writes Katkov in October 1870; "I took him from my heart" (*Pss*, 29.1:142). Stavrogin is *"our* type, Russian," trying to "renew himself and begin to believe" (*Pss*, 29.1:232). Dostoevsky conceived of this character as a Russian hero, an answer to the pervasive Westernization he perceived shaping the types being portrayed in Russian literature.

The initial period of work on what became *Demons* shows Dostoevsky planning a novel and main character that conform to his stated intentions. Many of the ideas Dostoevsky was developing as his own during this period receive their earliest literary embodiment in the Prince.[18] He voices Dostoevsky's cherished belief that Orthodoxy alone represents Christianity. "We consider Orthodoxy to be the sole preservation of Christ's image, and nowhere else, and Russia is the bearer of Orthodoxy," Stavrogin says (*Pss*, 11:187). He likewise expresses Dostoevsky's conviction that building a Christian society was the primary task facing Russia. "What's to be done?" Shatov asks, regarding the disorder of the present moment in national and individual life, to which the Prince answers, "Build the Kingdom of Christ" (*Pss*, 11:178).

It was during this period of the late 1860s and early 1870s that Dostoevsky began to believe that Russia was called to build the Kingdom of Christ not just in Russia but over the whole world. Stavrogin articulates Dostoevsky's developing confidence in Russia's messianic destiny. The Prince tells the ward, the character evolving into Dasha, "that from now on he is a Russian man and that it's necessary to believe . . . that Russia and the Russian idea will save humanity" (*Pss*, 11:133). Europe "has blinded us," the Prince says, but we will disperse their ideas "like a spiderweb, and we will finally realize everything consciously, that never has the world, the earth, the land—never has it seen such a grand idea as what now goes from us in the East to replace the European masses, to renew the world" (*Pss*, 11:167). Christ is "sine qua non, and the basis of the future existence of the whole world, and consists of three words: the *word became flesh* [*slovo plot' byst'*]. . . . Sooner or later everyone will agree with this" (*Pss*, 11:179).

It was during this period as well that Dostoevsky was beginning to believe in a looming apocalyptic clash between Orthodox Russia and Europe. His apocalyptic visions take shape through the Prince. "Christ has been distorted in the West," the Prince says; the West is "the Kingdom of the Antichrist. We have Orthodoxy" (*Pss*, 11:177). "From us go Enoch and Ilya to fight with the Antichrist," the Prince says, "that is with the spirit of the West" (*Pss*, 11:168). During this period, Dostoevsky increasingly identified the Russian people with Christ, and one of the cornerstones of the Prince's character is likewise belief in renewal through the Russian people. Dostoevsky sought "to present a man who has realized that he lacks native soil"; in the notes, Stavrogin desires moral resurrection through hard work and contact with the people and soil (*Pss*, 11:135).

The Prince offers one of Dostoevsky's earliest articulations of the concept of Russians as the god-bearing people. It is important to note that here, in one of its initial formulations through Stavrogin, belief in the god-bearing people as a vehicle of resurrection is independent of belief in God; indeed, it seems to serve as a substitute for belief in God. Dostoevsky never satisfactorily addresses the conflict between faith in the Russian people and faith in God that begins with Stavrogin. When he advances the Russian people as a vehicle of resurrection in the *Diary,* his own position remains riddled with the same moral ambiguity that characterizes this belief when it comes from the mouth of Stavrogin.

Arguments between the Prince and Shatov revolve around the question as to whether any personal or communal resurrection is possible outside faith in Russia and Christ. The Prince comes to Dostoevsky's conclusion, the conviction that there is no salvation outside Christ and the Russian people. The Prince "searches for truth; found truth in the ideal of Russia and Christianity" (*Pss,* 11:116). He advances Dostoevsky's conviction that the world will be renewed through Orthodoxy alone. "We are bringing the world . . . the only thing needed: Orthodoxy . . . the teaching of Christ and full moral renewal [*polnoe obnovlenie nravstvennoe*] through his name" (*Pss,* 11:167).

Dostoevsky's awareness of the Prince's importance increases alongside his realization that this character has a strange relationship to faith. "It turns out that the main hero of the novel is the Prince. He comes together with Shatov, enflames him to enthusiasm, but doesn't himself believe," he plans in his notes (*Pss,* 11:135). Even while he serves as Dostoevsky's mouthpiece, the Prince is a highly problematic figure. "The Prince was the most depraved man and haughty aristocrat," Dostoevsky writes (*Pss,* 11:130). Stavrogin comes to embody a strange kind of absence; he acquires the traits of a skeptic, a Don Juan, who is occupied "only with playing with life," although he is "deeper than anyone else" (*Pss,* 11:119). "He is a noble nature, and to be nothing dissatisfies and tortures him. He finds no foundations within himself, and he is bored" (*Pss,* 11:134).

In the early stages of Dostoevsky's work on the novel, the figures of the Nihilist revolutionary Sergei Nechaev and a self-educated mystic theologian, a peasant Old Believer named Konstantin Efimovich Golubov, figured prominently. They recede in importance before the Prince, however. The more complex the Prince becomes, the more he dominates the novel. "*Golubov is unnecessary,*" Dostoevsky emphatically writes several times in his notes in spring 1870 (*Pss,* 11:135). "AND SO ALL THE PATHOS IN THE NOVEL IS IN THE PRINCE, he is the hero. Everything else revolves around him, like a kaleidoscope. He replaces Golubov. Limitlessly arrogant [*vysoty*]" (*Pss,* 11:136).[19]

Even as he becomes more problematic, however, the Prince remains a spokesman for Dostoevsky's views. Well after Dostoevsky's revaluation of this character was under way, the Prince continues to voice some of Dostoevsky's most cherished religious and political convictions. The more ambiguous the Prince's stance toward Dostoevsky's religious and national convictions became—the more this character evolved into the moral enigma of Stavrogin—the more importance Dostoevsky ascribed to him. Surely this fact—that this character gained in importance in Dostoevsky's estimation, even as he adopted a skeptical attitude toward his creator's religious and national commitments—attests to Dostoevsky's own extremely complex, perhaps even ambivalent feelings regarding the articles of his faith.

The relationship between the Prince and Dostoevsky is perhaps more intimate than the writer's relationship to any other character. Stavrogin (as he begins to be called) expresses Dostoevsky's contempt for some of the foundational principles of liberal democracy, such as legal rights. "The Prince's ideas. A new idea. This is not Anglo-Saxon rights, not democracy and the formal equality of the French (the Roman world). This is true brotherhood. The tsar at the head, slave and free (apostle Paul)" Dostoevsky writes in his notes (*Pss,* 11:167). Russia, the Prince says, embodies the idea of Orthodoxy, according to which slaves and masters are spiritual equals: "Russia is simply the embodiment of the spirit of Orthodoxy (slave and free). Christianity. The peasants live in it" (*Pss,* 11:167).

Stavrogin asserts that Christianity is incompatible with science and refutes the view, popular among some of Dostoevsky's radical contemporaries, that the practice of Christian morality can be independent of belief in the miraculous dimensions of Christianity. "You and I know, Shatov," he says, "that Christ is not a man but the Savior and source of life, and science alone will never fulfill the human ideal." The core of Christian faith, he asserts with his creator, is belief in Christ's divinity. The Prince derides "the conviction of many that Christianity is compatible with science and civilization." Many mistakenly think that "if you don't believe in the resurrection of Lazarus or the Immaculate Conception, even so you can still be a Christian. But you and I know, Shatov, that this is all nonsense and that one flows from the other—and it's impossible to remain a Christian not believing in the Immaculate Conception" (*Pss,* 11:180). "Many think that it is enough to believe in the moral of Christ to be a Christian," the Prince objects. "Not the moral of Christ, not Christ's teaching will save the world, but belief that the word became flesh," he asserts. "It is necessary to believe that this is the final ideal of man, the embodied word, God embodied [*bog voplotivshiisia*]" (*Pss,* 11:187–88). He expresses Dostoevsky's cherished belief in personal immortality. "There is no death. There is life, but there is no nonexistence at all [*Bytie est', a nebytiia vovse net*]" (*Pss,* 11:184).

Dostoevsky initially plans a novel that will illustrate how faith in these ideas—in Russia's messianic destiny, personal immortality, and resurrection through the people—brings redemption. The Prince, Dostoevsky initially asserts, represents the redeemed man of Russia's future. "He's a *new* man," Dostoevsky believes (*Pss,* 11:133). The Prince and the ward are "*new people,* enduring temptation and deciding to begin a *new,* renewed life" (*Pss,* 11:98). The possibility of resurrection for the Prince stands at the center of interest in Dostoevsky's notes from the beginning. "New people, renewed life!" Dostoevsky writes rapturously (*Pss*, 11:125).

The Prince is trying to figure out the bases of renewal. "The prince gets together with Nechaev and talks with him about resurrection" (*Pss*, 11:123). He tells the ward "that he observed her, that he became convinced that he loved her and that he will be resurrected with her, if she shares his convictions" (*Pss*, 11:133). Stavrogin fails to be resurrected, however. He tells the ward they'll be resurrected through contact with the soil, "and then he suddenly shoots himself" (*Pss*, 11:133). Dostoevsky presents a specific explanation in his notes for the Prince's failure to be resurrected, but this explanation differs greatly from some of the reasons evident in the novel. Why there should be such a disjunction between how Dostoevsky explains a failed salvation narrative to himself in his notebooks and the obstacles to resurrection suggested by the novel is a question of critical significance for understanding the ambivalence about Christianity that leads to Dostoevsky's antisemitism.

Stavrogin is fallen and needs resurrection, Dostoevsky writes in a March 1872 letter to Liubimov, because he is deracinated: he has lost touch with the Russian soil and faith, is "a person who has lost touch with everything native, and, most important, faith, he is depraved out of *toska*" (March 1872, *Pss*, 29.1:232). "Renewal and resurrection are closed to him," Dostoevsky writes in his November 1870 notes, "only because he is divorced from the soil, consequently, he does not believe and does not acknowledge the people's morality" (*Pss*, 11:239). In the notebooks, Stavrogin shoots himself and writes in his suicide letter, "I opened my eyes and saw too much and—could not bear it that we are without soil" (*Pss*, 11:132). He understands that "we, the *bare* [gentlemen] are worse than anyone, torn from the soil, and therefore we, we before everyone else must be reborn [*pererodit'sia*]; we are the main rot [*gnil'*], the main curse is on us and everything happened because of us" (*Pss*, 11:126).[20]

"Everything is contained in the character of Stavrogin. Stavrogin is *everything*," Dostoevsky writes in his notes (*Pss*, 11:207). The character of Stavrogin does indeed contain a great deal of information about Dostoevsky's experience of Christianity. In *Demons* as Dostoevsky originally wrote it, with the chapter "At Tikhon's" at the fulcrum point of the novel, Stavrogin fails to be resurrected at least partly because he refuses to be saved by the Crucifixion. Dostoevsky appears to have sensed the complexity of this character's relationship to his own cherished convictions. He acknowledges that the character he endows with his own beliefs, who has an incomparably profound understanding of Russia, is precisely the character who fails to believe. "It's curious [*liubopytno*], that he was able to understand the essence of Rus' so deeply, when he explained it to Shatov and enflamed him with it, but it's even more curious and incomprehensible that he, it seems, didn't believe any of this," Dostoevsky writes of his hero (*Pss*, 11:149).

Stavrogin's ability to entertain simultaneous belief and disbelief becomes more comprehensible, and sheds light on Dostoevsky's own lifelong vacillation between belief and doubt, when we appreciate the anxieties about the Crucifixion at the basis of their shared dilemma. This "prestigious being" seems to have a superior understanding of his creator's ambivalence about redemption through the child on the cross. When Katkov remained deaf to Dostoevsky's entreaties and refused to allow the novel to be published with "At Tikhon's," Dostoevsky acquiesced.[21] He never tried to restore the censored chapter to the novel, a fact that has puzzled scholars and for which there may be several plausible explanations. There is general consensus that the chapter is an integral part of the novel. "We consider the chapter 'At Tikhon's' an integral and indispensable part of the novel," Pope and Turner write.[22] Grossman and Richard Peace each likewise assert the importance of "At Tikhon's" for the novel. Omitting the chapter, Peace writes, "disturbs the balance of the novel."[23]

Why Dostoevsky would have left such a crucial episode out of future editions, when he presumably had the freedom to restore it, is a question that has elicited a great deal of speculation. V. L. Komarovich believes Dostoevsky's decision to omit the chapter was based on the author's realization that the episode was an ideological failure: far from extolling Tikhon of Zadonsk, the prototype for Tikhon, the chapter casts him in an ambiguous light.[24] W. J. Leatherbarrow suggests that the aura of mystery around Stavrogin was enhanced by the absence of this chapter. "The dramatic requirement that Stavrogin remain an enigma must have informed Dostoevskii's decision not to reinstate the confessional chapter 'At Tikhon's' when he had the chance," Leatherbarrow writes.[25]

Demons is certainly a gripping novel without "At Tikhon's," and Dostoevsky may have understood this. Komarovich's suggestion that Dostoevsky was aware of this chapter's sharp criticism of precisely the Christian faith he hoped to promote may be close to the mark. Perhaps Dostoevsky refrained from reinserting this chapter because he sensed, on some level, what it suggests about redemption through a child on a cross.

"You Can Buy the Whole World": Zosima's Christian Faith and the Jewish Idea in the *Diary of a Writer*

BY THE TIME DOSTOEVSKY composes *The Brothers Karamazov,* the conception of God as a merchant and of redemption as something purchased with innocent suffering has become so well established in his fictional universe that it is simply assumed by figures as different as Ivan Karamazov and Father Zosima. Ivan and Zosima both believe that redemption is an economic transaction between the merchant God and his adult customers. The choice between these two characters is not between different conceptions of God and redemption but between acceptance or rejection of God as a merchant and redemption as an item for sale for the right price in innocent suffering in general and dead children specifically. Zosima accepts a relationship between humanity and the divine founded on the exchange of children; Ivan rejects it.

The stances adopted by Zosima and Ivan become more complex when we read the novel the way Dostoevsky's original Russian readers did, in light of the ideas put forth in the *Diary of a Writer.* The sixteen installments of the novel that appeared in the *Russian Messenger* from January 1879 through November 1880 were sandwiched between issues of the *Diary,* which Dostoevsky suspended in December 1877 and resumed in January 1881 (with one special issue appearing in August 1880). Failing to take the *Diary* into account when assessing the central concerns of both works—suffering children and theodicy—denies the significant organic connections that link them.

The essence of Ivan's rebellion, as he expounds it to Alyosha in the tavern, is a rejection of the use of child sacrifice as currency for the purchase of redemption.[1] He perceives the Crucifixion as a kind of foundational transaction at the basis of Christianity, an exchange of innocent suffering for the benefit of others. He barrages Alyosha with excruciating examples of child abuse and implies that the suffering experienced by children pays for redemption—"eternal harmony"—for others. After reciting this litany of traffic in the suffering of contemporary children, he slips into language that suggests a parallel between their many torments and the paradigmatic, singular torment of the Passion. "Is there in the whole world a being who would have the right to forgive and could forgive?" Ivan asks (*BK*, 226), and stridently asserts: "A blameless one must not suffer for another, and such a blameless one! [*Nel'zia stradat' nepovinnomu za drugogo, da eshche takomu nepovinnomu!*]" he protests to Alyosha (*Pss*, 14:217).

Ivan doesn't bother explaining his perception that a salvational economy is at work but simply assumes its existence and states his response to it. The role children play in the salvation economy is a stumbling block for him. "But then there are the children, and what am I to do about them? That's a question I can't answer," he tells Alyosha (*BK*, 225). "Listen!" Ivan commands Alyosha. "If all must suffer to pay for the eternal harmony, what have children to do with it, tell me, please? It's beyond all comprehension why they should suffer, and why they should pay for the harmony" (*BK*, 225). "Too high a price is asked for harmony; it's beyond our means to pay so much to enter on it" [*Da i slishkom dorogo otsenili garmoniiu, ne po karmanu nashemu vovse stol'ko platit' za vkhod*] (*BK*, 226; *Pss*, 15:223).

Much of the conversation between the two brothers in the tavern consists of Ivan expressing horror at the use of children's suffering to buy salvation for others.[2] "And if the sufferings of children go to swell the sum of sufferings which was necessary to pay for truth, then I protest that the truth is not worth such a price," he asserts (*BK*, 226). "I renounce the higher harmony altogether. It's not worth the tears of that one tortured child who beat itself on the breast with its little fist and prayed in its stinking outhouse, with its unexpiated tears to 'dear, kind god'!" (*BK*, 225).

The crimes against innocents graphically described by Ivan and Dostoevsky in the *Diary* contribute to a sum of suffering with which redemption is purchased from God; they concretize the Crucifixion as an exchange transaction in real time and history. By assaulting Alyosha with real examples of cruelty against children drawn from the press and familiar to Dostoevsky's readers, Ivan insinuates that the sacrificial exchange of the Crucifixion inaugurated a system of relations between God and humanity based on the circulation of children. God sacrificed his son, and now humanity submits its children to suffering, in an unjust system that remains in place between the merchant God and adult humanity seeking to buy salvation with the redemptive coin of child sacrifice.

Readers have noted the important role economic metaphor plays in Ivan's theological discourse. Ivan, Jackson points out, believes that salvation is for sale, purchased with the strange coin of children's suffering. "In the clever design of Ivan," Jackson writes, "an evil God, one who tolerates the intolerable, one who trades salvation in the coin of the tears and suffering of children, is no God at all . . . indeed, scorching is the metaphor of commerce that Ivan awakens in his discussion of religious redemption."[3] While noting that economic language permeates Ivan's indictment of God, however, readers have overlooked the fact that Zosima relies on a similar vocabulary to encourage faith; he joyfully embraces what Ivan rejects. According to Zosima, God is like an accountant. "Do what you can," Zosima tells distraught Madame Khokhlakova, who confesses her inability to love her fellow human beings, "and it will be reckoned unto you" (*BK*, 49).

Like Ivan, Zosima believes that redemption is an item for sale, the object of an exchange transacted between God and his customers. "With love everything is bought, everything is saved [*liubov'iu vse pokupaetsia, vse spasaetsia*]," he tells a pilgrim at the monastery (*Pss*, 14:48). This pilgrim, a young woman who has killed her husband, fears that her soul is irredeemable, but Zosima assures her that an infinite amount of love, functioning as a kind of redemptive currency, circulates between God and humanity. There is enough to pay for even her sin, he insists. "Love is such a priceless treasure that you can buy the whole world with it, and redeem not only your own but other people's sins [*liubov' takoe bestsennoe sokrovishche, chto na nee ves' mir kupit' mozhesh', a ne tol'ko svoi, no i chuzhie grekhi eshche vykupish'*]." He sends her on her way with words of encouragement: "Go, and be not afraid" (*Pss*, 14:48).

How significant is Zosima's recourse to mercantile language in talking about salvation? Are the linguistic vehicles merely incidental, or do they indicate something substantial about his faith?[4] Close examination of Zosima's relationship to God, as set forth in his exegesis of Job, reveals that his faith is in fact profoundly shaped by a kind of spiritual exchange logic. "Dostoevsky shows more than he argues," Father George Florovsky maintains.[5] By juxtaposing Ivan's perception of a salvation economy based on the circulation of suffering children with Zosima's faith, Dostoevsky accomplishes something remarkable. He shows that children do in fact function in Zosima's relationship with God the way Ivan alleges they do, as a kind of coin that buys harmony or reconciliation for others. Despite Zosima's assertion that the basis of our relationship with God is love, this relationship turns out to be based on dead children. In his vision, humanity accepts the suffering and death of its children as the price that has to be paid for its relationship with God. Through his juxtaposition of Ivan's conversation with Alyosha and Zosima's exposition of Job, Dostoevsky illuminates this familiar biblical story from a new angle.

Like Father Tikhon in *Demons*, Zosima assures those who seek his counsel that all actions, even murder, have been equalized as forgiven and that it is actually impossible to escape forgiveness. "Man cannot commit a sin so great as to exhaust the infinite love of God," he assures the murderer. "Believe that God loves you as you cannot conceive; that He loves you with your sin, in your sin" (*BK*, 43). The implications of Zosima's universal forgiveness are explored in depth in the *Diary* as well as in the novel.

> *Kto zhaleet obidchika,*
> *tot ne zhaleet obizhennogo.*
> Whoever pities the offender
> doesn't pity the offended.
> —Dostoevsky (*Pss*, 24:209)

During the years when he worked on *The Brothers Karamazov* and the *Diary of a Writer,* Dostoevsky seems to have been progressing toward the conclusion that the interests of victims and their transgressors may be irreconcilable.[6] Forgiving perpetrators, he seems to have suspected, may entail an ability to forget about their victims that is neglectful at the very least and may even be a form of moral depravity. He was turning the idea of this irreconcilability around and around in his notes, writing it many times in slightly different forms.

A good deal of his contemplation about the possibly irreconcilable perspectives of offenders and the offended was elicited by the contemporary court cases Dostoevsky found so fascinating. One case that gripped his imagination was the attempted murder of a woman by her husband's mistress. Dostoevsky devoted extensive *Diary* coverage to analysis of the Kairova case, as it was known. He suggests a connection between Kairova's victim (who survived the attempt on her life) and others, including himself, who have experienced near-death experiences, by ascribing thoughts to her similar to those Myshkin speculates may run through the head of a condemned man on the scaffold. Preparing the *Diary* entries in his 1876–77 notebooks, he writes, "Whoever pities the killer doesn't pity the victim [*Kto zhaleet gubitelia, tot ne zaleet zhertvu*]" (*Pss*, 24:207).

Zosima, like the West as Dostoevsky portrays it in the *Diary*, focuses on those who benefit from or themselves cause the suffering of others, whereas Ivan is concerned with victims. The choice between Zosima and Ivan is between the perspective of the (adult) survivor who profits from the death of others, which provides the basis of a relationship with God, or the perspective of the suffering or dead (often child) victim. Donald Palumbo's perception that "suffering is not meaningless but leads to salvation" in Dostoevsky's works is accurate but incomplete: suffering is frequently shown leading to salvation *for others*, not the sufferer him- or herself.[7] There is often a direct payoff from a child's death for a survivor, as Palumbo notes regarding how Zosima benefits from his brother's death: "Markel's death not only saves Zosima from committing a grave sin, it also results in all the good Zosima does in his career as a holy man."[8] Zosima focuses on humanity's sins against God and says that humanity can pay for, make up for its transgressions with its children; Ivan focuses on adult and divine crimes against children and doubts that these transgressions can be remedied *for the victims.*

A fundamental difference between Zosima and Ivan is dramatized through their engagement with the story of Job. The limits to Zosima's response to the problem of suffering and the unbridgeable difference between his position and the views adopted by Dostoevsky in the *Diary* and Ivan in the novel are illustrated by Zosima's exegesis of Job. Job's first children are the victims of Zosima's perspective, which Dostoevsky implies is also the "correct" perspective of the biblical original. Zosima remains within the parameters of the original Job story, and Dostoevsky suggests that those parameters are dissatisfying. Neither the book of Job nor Zosima's explication of it offers a response to the problem of child suffering that satisfies Dostoevsky. The *Diary* offers a response, and it is one that adopts Ivan's perspective. Ivan and Dostoevsky in the *Diary* move beyond the original parameters by trying to write the story of Job's first children. Through Ivan, Dostoevsky is doing nothing less than challenging the finality of the biblical word.

Dostoevsky experienced the dilemmas portrayed in the Job story in his own life, and he reached no easy conclusions. He claims that an early childhood experience with the Job story was a significant milestone in his spiritual development. Writing from Ems, of which he says, "It is literally torture, it's worse than imprisonment in jail," he tells Anna, "I'm reading the book of Job, and it brings me to ecstasy: I stop reading and pace the room for hours, almost crying. . . . This book, Ania, it's strange—it was one of the first that impressed me in life, I was at that time still almost an infant! [*ia byl eshche togda pochti mladentsem!*]" (*Pss*, 29.2:43).

Dostoevsky, like Job, witnesses his children die due to what he believes are elements of his own personal narrative with God. He writes Pasha from Vevey in June 1868, "I am very unhappy now, Pasha! God has struck me. My Sonia died, and we already buried her" (*Pss*, 28.2:301). "It's all because of my sins," he believes (*Pss*, 28.2:301). At times he muses that his own death would be the appropriate response to Sonia's loss. "Ach, Pasha, things are so difficult and bitter for me, it would be better to die!" (*Pss*, 28.2:301).

Dostoevsky believed that each of his dead children had an exceptional link to him. Alyosha inherited Dostoevsky's epilepsy; Sonia, he believed, inherited his looks, especially the novelist's look of creative concentration. In March 1868, while Sonia was still alive, he writes Maikov that she is "very pretty, even though she looks like me to an impossible, even ridiculous extent. Even to strangeness. I wouldn't believe it if I didn't see it. The baby is only a month old, but completely has my look on its face, my whole physiognomy, down to the wrinkles on the forehead—she lies there—like she's writing a novel!" (*Pss*, 28.2:277).

He experienced the pain of being told that one child could be substituted with another, and he insists that no other child could ever take her place and console him. "This small, three-month-old creature, so poor, so tiny—was for me already a personality and character [*litso i kharakter*]," he writes Maikov of Sonia. "She started to know me, love me, and smile when I approached" (May 1868, *Pss,* 28.2:297). "And now they tell me as consolation that I will have more children. But where is Sonia?" he asks. He continues, "Even if there will be another child, I don't understand how I will love it; where I will find the love; I need Sonia. I can't understand that she doesn't exist and that I will never see her" (*Pss,* 28.2:297). He can't reconcile himself to her death, he tells Pasha: "To this time I can't adjust to this unhappiness one bit or become unaccustomed to Sonia [*otvyknut' ot Soni*]" (*Pss,* 28.2:301). He would go to the cross himself, he declares, if that would bring her back to life: "Where is that little person for whom, I dare to say, I would take on the suffering of the cross, if only she were alive? [*Gde eta malen'kaia lichnost', za kotoruiu ia, smelo govoriu, krestnuiu muku primu, tol'ko chtob ona byla zhiva?*]" (*Pss,* 28.2:302).

The principle of reconciliation through substitution—the essence of the Job story, as Zosima interprets it—stands at the center of the novel. When the celebrated Moscow doctor concludes that Ilyusha doesn't have long to live, Snegiryov mutters wildly, "I don't want a good boy! I don't want another boy! . . . If I forget you, Jerusalem, let my tongue . . ." Attention to the biblical reference is further strengthened by Kolya Krasotkin's interest. "What was that he said about Jerusalem? . . .What did he mean by that?" Kolya asks. "It's from the Bible," Alyosha explains. "'If I forget you Jerusalem,' that is, if I forget all that is most precious to me, if I let anything take its place, then may . . ." (*BK,* 531).

The problem of reconciliation through substitution—one child or person for others, as Zosima's Job accepts—was one Dostoevsky had encountered even before the death of his daughter. Before Sonia's death, Dostoevsky had already experienced losses that he felt could not be made up with anything. He expresses the desire not to live on if his beloved brother Mikhail should die. He writes Mikhail in June 1858 from Semipalatinsk, "Ten times a day I pray to God that he protect you. If you die—I will die, I don't want to live after you" (*Pss,* 28.1:328). In spring 1865, he writes a long letter to his old friend A. E. Vrangel' about the deaths of Mikhail and his first wife, Maria Dmitrievna. As she suffered her extended death agonies, he writes, he was tormented by the thought of what he would lose with her; after her death he found that the pain of his loss was even greater than he could have imagined:

I could not have imagined how empty and painful it would become in my life when they covered her with earth. And now it has been a year, and I feel exactly the same thing, it doesn't lessen. . . . Having buried her, I threw my-self at my brother, to Petersburg—he alone was left to me, but within three months he died too. (*Pss*, 28.2:116)

And so I am left alone, he tells Vrangel', and life has broken in two parts. Dostoevsky emphatically rejects the principle of substitution and de-clares his adherence to the dead.

In one half, the one I passed through, was everything that I lived for; in the other, still unknown half, everything is alien [*vse chuzhoe*], everything is new and there is not one heart that could replace those two for me. Literally—there is nothing left for me to live for. Make new ties, think up a new life! The very thought of it is disgusting to me. I felt for the *first time* that *they* can't be replaced by anyone, that I loved only them in the world and that you don't make a new love, even shouldn't make a new love. (*Pss*, 28.2:116)

But he also confesses a conflicting will to survival and new beginnings. Later in the same letter, he writes, "I, a forty-year-old, don't have any of my former ones or former things. And meanwhile it seems to me that I am just getting ready to live. Funny, isn't it? The longevity of a cat" (*Pss*, 28.2:120).

As he reflects on his life, Father Zosima identifies two formative experiences pointing him toward God: the death of his brother Markel and exposure to the Job story. It was in church during Holy Week, Zosima recalls, when he was eight years old, that he heard the priest read the book of Job, and "for the first time in my life I consciously received the seed of God's word into my heart." He recalls, "For the first time I understood something" (*BK*, 270). God hands Job over to Satan, "and the devil smote his children and his cattle and scattered his wealth," but Job cried out to God, "Blessed be Thy name, although Thou dost punish me!" Zosima tells the monks, "I've never been able to read that sacred tale without tears" (*BK*, 270).

The lesson he derives from each experience is that accepting the prin-ciple of exchange, especially the exchange of children, is the key to faith. Markel himself bequeathed the principle of child substitution to him, Zosima explains. As his brother was dying, Zosima tells the monks, he "called me to him, took me by the shoulders, looked at me lovingly, and finally said: 'go now, play, and live for me'" (*Pss*, 14:263). Without the boy "who died before my eyes at seventeen," Zosima explains, "I might never have taken religious vows" (*BK*, 264). My brother was "a guidance and a sign from on high for me," Zosima believes; without him, I might not have "entered on this pre-cious path" (*BK*, 264).

The story of Markel conveys a further lesson as well: the survivor who accepts the principle of exchange will be rewarded with a satisfying substitute for the lost child. My dead brother, Zosima explains, who long ago commanded me to live for him, "seems to have come to me over again," in the person of Alyosha (*BK,* 264). Alyosha "seems to me so like him spiritually, that many times I have actually taken him for that young man, my brother, mysteriously come back to me at the end of my pilgrimage, as a reminder and inspiration" (*BK,* 264).

Zosima distills the book of Job down to a tale similar to his own. The essence of the Job story, as Zosima interprets it, is reconciliation with exchange logic—Job gets new children in exchange for the original family God took away. By focusing on Job's ability to reconcile himself to the loss of some children and acceptance of others, Zosima places the biblical story within a psychological rather than religious paradigm. Zosima, Nathan Rosen points out, "shifts to a psychological question: how can Job recover from the loss of his first children and love the new children which God has provided for him?"[9] If we assess Zosima's exegesis of Job in religious terms, Harold Bloom contends, it fails to impress.

> His interpretation of the Book of Job is the weakest failure in the history of theodicy. What is least acceptable about the Book of Job, its tacked-on conclusion in which God gives Job a perfect set of new sons and daughters, every bit as good as the old, is saluted by Zosima as the height of holy wisdom. It is difficult to answer the Grand Inquisitor with such sublime idiocy.[10]

What strikes one critic as sublime idiocy is frequently identified by others as the laudable core of Zosima's teaching, however. Zosima's understanding of Job's acceptance of his new children and hence reconciliation with God, many critics assert, is based in profound mystery.[11] But close analysis of this passage reveals that there is nothing mysterious about Job's reconciliation *as Zosima describes it;* instead of mystery, there is exchange logic. "God raises Job again, gives him wealth again. Many years pass by, and he has other children and loves them," Zosima explains (*BK,* 271). The pious servant Grigory exemplifies this acceptance as well. He takes the orphaned infant Smerdiakov in exchange for his own dead child, telling his grieving wife, "Our little lost one has sent us this, who has come from the devil's son and a holy innocent. Nurse him and weep no more" (*BK,* 89).

The impressions stirred by Ivan's obsessive focus on victimized children are still fresh when the reader encounters Zosima's exegesis of Job, and they put it in a curious light. Zosima's attention is focused entirely on how Job reacts to the death of his children—how their suffering affects *him*—rather than on the victims themselves, the children whose lives are taken away. "How could he love those new ones . . . ? . . . how could he be fully happy with those new ones . . . ?" Zosima asks with concern about Job (*BK,* 271).

In his exegesis of Job and his homily in general, Zosima evades the challenge set by Ivan and Dostoevsky, the challenge to explain innocent suffering. Zosima does not address innocent suffering; instead, he addresses the issue of the survivors' response to it. Job's original children lose their lives as the price of their father's narrative with God, but Zosima pays no attention to their loss at all; his interest is focused exclusively on how their death affects the survivor, their father Job, and his relationship to God.[12] Job's children exist for Zosima only as a function in their father's redemption narrative. For Zosima, Job's first children are expendable goods in their father's redemption story. Zosima does not consider the children's death; they are objects in the inventory of Job's possessions, one of the goods that can be seized, traded, or lost in the relations between adult humanity and God. Zosima's only concern is whether Job can still be happy after their death. What concerns him is whether Job can reconcile himself to their death, as to the loss of his cattle and wealth; they have no story of their own, their death is merely one element of the survivor's narrative.

The novel prods readers to notice that Zosima pays *no* attention to the fate of Job's first children, who lose their lives as part of their father's salvation narrative. Without the new context provided by Ivan's concern with dead children circulating between God and humanity, we might be inclined to read this biblical book as Zosima does, glossing over the sacrificial children. The novel's concern with the linked problems of utilitarian logic, children, and salvation, however, prompts us to notice that Job's first children are reduced to a marker or coin exchanged between Job and God in Zosima's telling, and that they suffer what the novel calls the worst fate—being forgotten.

The true mystery of the Job story, as *The Brothers Karamazov* illuminates it, is not, as Zosima claims, Job's acceptance of his new children. The survivor's response to loss remains within reason in Zosima's telling—the rationality of exchange logic.

> God raises Job again, gives him wealth again. Many years pass by, and he has other children and loves them. But how could he love those new ones when those first children are no more, when he has lost them? Remembering them, how could he be fully happy with those new ones . . .? (*BK*, 271)

"But he could, he could"—it is possible for Job, the survivor, to accept their death, Zosima ecstatically proclaims. He joyfully describes the beatitude that awaits the survivor who makes it to the sunset of life.

> "It's the great mystery of human life that old grief passes gradually into quiet tender joy. The mild serenity of age takes the place of the riotous blood of youth. I bless the rising sun each day, and, as before, my heart sings to meet it, but now I love even more its setting, its long slanting rays and the soft tender

gentle memories that come with them, the dear images from the whole of my long happy life—and over all the Divine Truth, softening, reconciling, forgiving!" (*BK*, 271)

The real mystery, which Ivan alone probes, is why Job's children lose their lives for the sake of their father's story with God and why no one pays attention to them. The children's loss, not the adult survivor's reaction to it, is the locus of mystery. Ivan's discourse on suffering children represents an attempt to recover submerged narratives of forgotten victims; through this character, Dostoevsky may actually be challenging the authority of the biblical word by writing the story of Job's forgotten first children.[13]

Zosima asserts that God has something for the dead children to make up for their loss, and he shifts attention from the suffering of the victims to the emotional anguish of the survivor. To the pilgrim woman blackened with grief over her little dead son, he says her son is with God—"remember that your little son is one of the angels of God"—and tells her that her grief will heal with time and eventually save her from sin. "That great mother's grief . . . will turn in the end into quiet joy, and your bitter tears will be only tears of tender sorrow that purifies the heart and delivers it from sin" (*BK*, 42).

The fact that Zosima's faith is based on the rational principle of exchange, the logic of substitution, has enormous consequences. The common perception that Zosima's faith is based in mysticism requires amendment, as does the widespread belief that Ivan's rebellion against God is based in reason. "Ivan," Frank writes, "represents . . . the supreme and most poignant dramatization of the conflict between reason and faith at the heart of the book."[14] "The validity of Ivan's challenge rests on a rational foundation," Silbajoris writes, but Zosima's answer "is not given in rational terms."[15] Ivan's "indictment is not answered, and could not be answered, on the rational plane," E. H. Carr asserts; it "can only be answered by transferring the issue to another and super-rational plane."[16] "In Ivan we find completed the age-old development of the philosophy of reason from Plato to Kant," Mochulsky writes; "Ivan is proud of his reason and for him it is easier to renounce God's world than reason. If the world is not justified by reason, it is impossible to accept it."[17]

Ivan himself has confused the issue by suggesting that God's harmony rests on nonrational principles, which he cannot accept. Critics have remained within Ivan's self-understanding, accepting his perception that he rejects a nonrational, non-Euclidean harmony. "The framework of Ivan's rebellion is horror at the unjustified suffering of children and his refusal to participate in a non-Euclidean geometry of forgiveness," Miller writes; "Zosima does not counter Ivan's arguments through reason or logic, but through the heart."[18] Yet Ivan's self-understanding is unreliable here.

Ivan rejects both reconciliation and revenge as responses to injustice because he rejects the utilitarian calculations, based in exchange logic, which this novel shows to be at their basis. "I must have retribution," he is frequently quoted as saying (*BK*, 225), but he immediately retracts this statement; the continuation of his thought is less frequently discussed.[19] "But how, how will you redeem them? Is it really possible? By their being avenged?" he asks regarding the little girl's tears (*Pss*, 14:223). "But what do I care if they are avenged, what do I care about hell for the torturers, what can hell make right, if these little ones have already been tortured?" (*Pss*, 14:223). Retribution belongs to a rational system that contains God and adults; hell may gratify adult witnesses and their sense of reciprocity, but Ivan is uninterested in them.

Ivan rejects reconciliation as well as revenge. Unlike Zosima, he cannot love sinners or reconcile himself to suffering and injustice; he cannot accomplish these spiritual feats because he refuses to engage in the mental operation that makes them possible for characters in this novel, the practice of exchange logic. The child whose young life was taken away, Zosima tells a grieving mother, receives the privilege of being an angel in heaven; the adult who bears his losses through life finds the "quiet tender joy" and "mild serenity of age" waiting for him (*BK*, 271). Ivan acknowledges the possibility that Zosima is correct—that there is something that balances all accounts in the end—but rejects the rationality of the final payout, the "compensation of eternal harmony [*ne poniatnoe nam vozmeshchenie vechnoi garmonii*]" (*Pss*, 15:229).

Adult experience, Ivan concedes, may make sense. In addition to the rewards Zosima enumerates for them—new family, wealth, and serene old age—"they have retribution" for the sin of eating the apple (*BK*, 218). Children's suffering, on the other hand, can't be explained through reason, though the attempt to do so is often made. Zosima rationalizes innocent suffering by balancing it out with the promise of adequate compensation (being angels in heaven). Some readers suggest that the novel explains children's suffering by doing what Ivan claims is impossible: situating their torment within the logic of reciprocity.

The novel makes a halfhearted effort to show that children do in fact sin, which presumably would rationalize their suffering as a logical consequence within a system based on exchange logic. Terras, for example, believes that Dostoevsky has a "strategy to diffuse the power of Ivan Karamazov's charge that God allows innocent children to suffer"; this strategy, Terras argues, consists of showing that "the Devil is not absent from the world of children."[20] According to readings like that of Terras, the novel makes no attempt to deny the reality of children's suffering; instead it raises questions about the victims' character, specifically their innocence. It is true that the novel portrays an incipient capacity for evil in some children. Kolya Krasotkin orchestrates the death of a goose, and little Ilyusha himself feeds a dog a needle. Ilyusha's "edifying death," Terras writes, "may be read as an answer to Ivan's arguments regarding the sufferings of innocent children. Note that the little boy in Ivan's 'rebellion' dies for having hurt a dog. Iliusha says: 'It's because I killed Zhuchka, dad, that I am ill now. God is punishing me for it.' . . . The point is, of course, not that Iliusha deserves to die, but that the actual facts are more complex and deeper than Ivan had thought."[21]

The overwhelming evidence of the novel as a whole, however, speaks of a grotesque imbalance between whatever capacity for evil children might harbor and the cruelty inflicted on them. The attempt to contain children's suffering within a rational exchange economy remains only halfhearted; the "crimes" committed by children in this novel pale before the savagery of their abuse. The fact that Ilyusha fed a needle to a dog and might have grown up to do something worse seems feeble grounds for a death sentence. The potential for evil harbored within Kolya Krasotkin or Liza Khokhlakova seems irrelevant to the anguish of Balkan infants impaled on daggers by Turkish forces, whose suffering forms one of the topics of Ivan's conversation with Alyosha in the tavern and occupies Dostoevsky's attention in the *Diary*.

Ivan describes the discrepancy between a childish crime and the adult punishment it provokes in order to illustrate the obscenity of explaining children's suffering by pointing to some alleged evil in their nature. By contrasting the triviality of a child's crime to the atrocity of the punishment meted out by an adult in response, this episode effectively repudiates the objection that children actually have done something to deserve their suffering. The contention that children are capable of such crimes as would justify their role as sacrificial victims in the salvation economy is shown to be a comforting delusion. Such childish crimes as do exist are not matched by the ferocity of the divine-adult system.

Ivan recounts an incident of child torture that was well known to the pubic from the press.[22] Shortly before the emancipation, an eight-year-old serf boy accidentally injured his master's favorite hound while playing. "He was taken," Ivan recounts for Alyosha,

> "taken from his mother and kept shut up all night. Early that morning the general comes out in full pomp, mounts his horse with the hounds, his dependants, dog-boys, and the huntsmen, all mounted around him. The servants are summoned for their edification, and in front of them all stands the mother of the child. The child is brought from the lockup. It's a gloomy cold, foggy autumn day, a capital day for hunting. The general orders the child to

be undressed; the child is stripped naked. He shivers, numb with terror, not daring to cry . . . 'Make him run,' commands the general. 'Run! Run!' shout the dog-boys. The boy runs . . . 'At him!' yells the general, and he sets the whole pack of hounds on the child. The hounds catch him, and tear him to pieces before his mother's eyes!" (*BK*, 223–24, ellipses in original)

What, Ivan asks Alyosha, should be done with a man who does this to a child? "What did he deserve? To be shot?" Ivan demands. "To be shot," Alyosha replies (*BK*, 224). It is Ivan who points out that the desire to shoot a wrongdoer comes from the devil—"So there is a little devil sitting in your heart," he tells Alyosha (*BK*, 224).

Justifying the suffering of children, Ivan perceives, entails performing a kind of *reasoning* abstraction and mediation among unlike things. "If they also suffer terribly on earth, it's of course for their fathers, they are punished for their fathers, who ate the apple—but that is reasoning from another world, for the human heart here on earth it's incomprehensible" (*Pss*, 14:216–17). Behind Ivan's rejection of exchange and the principle of transference or mediation that makes exchanges of the sort Zosima recommends possible lurks a challenge to the Crucifixion. "A blameless one must not suffer for another, and such a blameless one!" Ivan objects (*Pss*, 14:217). One child cannot live and play for another; the slaughter of babies in one part of the world can't be explained through reference to the crimes of children somewhere else; and one precious being cannot die for or save anyone else.

Zosima forgives and accepts because he embraces the rational principle of exchange or substitution, whereas Ivan rejects both forgiveness and vengeance because he adheres to something irrational. Faith and forgiveness as portrayed in the novel are based on a distinctive type of logic with extraordinary significance in Dostoevsky's universe, a utilitarian calculus dealing in substitutions and exchange. Ivan rejects the logical reasoning of exchange and the reconciliation and revenge that it makes possible. He perceives that the salvation economy leaves a remainder of unrequited suffering, that there is something left over after all the substitutions and calculations, and that the system requires the existence of this remainder.

Ivan's challenge doesn't rest on reason; it's Ivan who transfers the discussion to a superrational plane. "When the mother embraces the fiend who threw her child to the dogs, and all three cry aloud with tears, 'Thou art just, O Lord,' then, of course, the crown of knowledge will be reached and all will be made clear," Ivan concedes. But there is a catch, he continues: "I can't accept that harmony" (*BK*, 225). Hell and retribution do nothing for the victims and so are of no interest to Ivan; heaven and harmony are likewise simply beside the point. It is entirely possible, Ivan admits to Alyosha, that it all makes sense in the end.

"I believe like a child that suffering will be healed and made up for, that all the humiliating absurdity of human contradictions will vanish like a pitiful mirage, like the despicable fabrication of the impotent and infinitely small Euclidean mind of man, that in the world's finale, at the moment of eternal harmony, something so precious will come to pass that it will suffice for all hearts, for the comforting of all resentments, for the atonement of all the crimes of humanity, of all the blood they've shed; that it will make it not only possible to forgive but to justify all that has happened with men—but though all that may come to pass, I don't accept it. I won't accept it." (*BK*, 216–17)

This eternal harmony—rejected by Ivan, embraced by Zosima—is entirely rational: there is something we don't know about yet that pays off all debts, balances all accounts. Ivan rejects this rational system in the name of unreason.

Ivan tells Alyosha he will not address the topic of adult suffering because "besides being disgusting and unworthy of love, they have retribution—they've eaten the apple and know good and evil, they have become 'like God'" (*BK*, 218–19). What happens to adults, in other words, makes sense. What happens to them is a logical consequence of their actions. The adult suffering that concerns Zosima is likewise part of a rational system, an economy that makes sense, one of reciprocity and exchange: those who reconcile themselves to the suffering of innocents and make it to the end find a joyful reward awaiting them. According to both Ivan and Zosima, in other words, the experience of adults takes place within a rational exchange economy.

Children's suffering, on the other hand, represents something mysterious. Their suffering remains unrecompensed for them; it is used to buy something for someone else. "But the children haven't eaten anything, and are so far innocent," Ivan points out (*BK*, 219). Innocent children absorb, carry the burden of an abysmal leftover, the remainder of cruelty and suffering generated by the rational adult-divine economy. For Ivan, the suffering of children is impermissible because it exists outside of, yet makes possible, the system in place between God and adults.

Ivan, like Stavrogin, believes that suffering and forgiveness are nontransferable, and it is this belief that stands between them and acceptance of the Crucifixion. Assuming the opposite perspective from Zosima, whose concern is focused on (adult) survivors, Ivan asks how the child's suffering will be made up to *him*, not to the mother for whom the spectacle of death by dog pack was orchestrated. "Let her forgive him for herself, if she will, let her forgive the torturer for the immeasurable suffering of her mother's heart. But the sufferings of her tortured child she has no right to forgive" (*BK*, 226). It is not just appallingly presumptuous for anyone other than the actual victim to offer forgiveness, Ivan implies. Allowing the adult survivors/beneficiaries to forgive in the child's name implies acceptance of and participation in certain logical operations. For one person to forgive the suffering experienced by another assumes that human experience can be subjected to abstraction, translation, and mediation, whereas Ivan and Stavrogin uphold the principles of irreducibility and nontransferability. These principles, Dostoevsky's novels imply, may be incompatible with Christian faith as Dostoevsky understands it.

Dostoevsky grapples with similar quandaries in the *Diary*. Once atrocities have been committed, he asks with Ivan, what can be done to set things right? Appointing Russia to be an avenger of outraged innocence poses familiar moral dilemmas for Dostoevsky in the *Diary*. How he approaches the apparent conflict between the interests of victims and transgressors is significant for assessing Ivan and Zosima in the novel.

Dostoevsky tries to distinguish between retribution or vengeance, which he rejects, and activist identification with victims, which he upholds. He argues that Russia is motivated exclusively by compassion for the victims of injustice and that compassion dictates action. Through the Balkan War, he explains to *Diary* readers, the Russian people have been confronted with atrocities and accomplished facts that demand a response. Dostoevsky adopts a role with his readers similar to that taken by Ivan with Alyosha: he graphically describes atrocities in order to compel his listeners to formulate a response. "We found our wounded soldiers and officers robbed and naked, with noses, ears, and lips cut off, stomachs cut out, their bodies charred after having been burned on stacks of straw and hay to which the Turks had dragged them, still alive, and then set afire," Dostoevsky reminds his readers (*WD*, November 1877, 1196–97). In response, Russia will go "to save the oppressed, the humiliated, the downtrodden, and the suffering," not to punish wrongdoers, although championing the victims of injustice may entail righteous violence (*WD*, November 1877, 1194).

Dostoevsky is furious with Tolstoy for suggesting, through the character Levin in *Anna Karenina*, that the Balkan War is merely a crude desire for revenge and violence. "This is unjust," Dostoevsky retorts: "there is no *vengeance* involved here at all" (*WD*, July/August 1877, 1097). This war was "initiated against monsters for the liberation of unhappy nationalities," he asserts (*WD*, November 1877, 1201). Violence against women and children commands intervention, Dostoevsky insists.

Was it to seek vengeance, was it only to commit murders that the Russian People rose up? And when was it that helping whole provinces of those being massacred and exterminated, helping women and children who are being violated and who have no one else on earth to stand up for them—when was

171

it that this was considered a crude, ridiculous, almost immoral action, a thirst for vengeance and blood? And what a lack of feeling, side by side with sentimentalism! Why, Levin himself has a child . . . So why doesn't his heart bleed when he hears and reads about mass killings, about children with crushed heads crawling after their raped mothers . . . (*WD*, July/August 1877, 1099)

How could Tolstoy have us abandon the Bulgarians, "those oppressed and harassed people for whose sake we journeyed from the shores of the gulf of Finland and all the rivers of Russia to shed our blood," Dostoevsky wonders (*WD*, November 1877, 1194). He mocks Levin: "as a sensitive man, he's afraid to kill . . . a Turk," Dostoevsky writes contemptuously. Levin's sympathy is misplaced, Dostoevsky writes: "He's awfully sorry for the Turks," despite the atrocities they commit (*WD*, July/August 1877, 1096).

Zosima loves those who are most sinful, even those who have blood on their hands. "The monks used to say that he was more drawn to those who were more sinful, and the greater the sinner the more he loved him" (*BK*, 23). This tender love of sinners acquires different ramifications in light of the *Diary*. Concern for the perpetrators of injustice, Dostoevsky tells *Diary* readers, is a degenerate Western idea. He decries what he calls a false liberal sentimentality that masquerades as mercy but is actually complicity with injustice. It comes from Europe, he believes, and has infected Russia's elite. "Good manners toward Europe prevail everywhere among us. The Turkish prisoners demanded white bread, and white bread was given to them" (*WD*, November 1877, 1189). The Turks unleashed brutal savagery on Russian prisoners of war, whereas Turkish prisoners received humane treatment from their Russian captors. This latter fact elicits Dostoevsky's disapproval, not his support. Russian "ladies threw flowers and candies at the train full of Turks," he observes with disgust (*WD*, November 1877, 1189). "The kindness of ladies toward the Turks was merely hysterical sentimentalizing and pseudo-liberal Europeanism," he objects (*WD*, July/August 1877, 1098).

Certain kinds of forgiveness are simply Western degeneracy, Dostoevsky insists; overcoming the tendency to forgive wrongdoers would represent Russia's emancipation from Western tutelage. The problem is "good manners toward Europe, 'good manners' toward the debt of European enlightenment in which we were raised, in which we've become mired to the point of losing our independent personality and from which we'll be a long time breaking free," he complains (*WD*, November 1877, 1193). Russian truth, Dostoevsky insists, is adherence to victims against their trespassers, even to the point of performing an action that Ivan rejects: shooting the wrongdoer.

Diary readers witnessed Dostoevsky orchestrate a dialogue about the nature of justice that has intriguing parallels to the dialogue Ivan spins out.

Dostoevsky initially rejects reprisals on the grounds that they cannot change what has already happened, cannot reverse the suffering that has already been endured. Of course, he concedes, "It would be best not to resort to reprisals against Turks found guilty of murdering prisoners and wounded," for "this would hardly diminish their savagery" (*WD*, July/August 1877, 1097). He finds himself in a quandary, however; like Ivan, he struggles to understand what *should* be done with transgressors. Unlike Zosima, who offers universal blanket forgiveness, Dostoevsky insists that the suffering of victims demands something. "It would be better not to have the Russians' noble and humane conduct of this war besmirched by reprisals," he concedes. "But piercing the eyes of infants must not be allowed; and for this infamy to be stopped forever the oppressed people must be promptly liberated and the tyrants disarmed once and for all" (*WD*, July/August 1877, 1097). "But taking away their weapons means engaging them in battle. But battle is not vengeance; Levin need not worry about the Turk" (*WD*, July/August 1877, 1098). Dostoevsky works himself into a position more extreme than that adopted by Ivan.

> Reprisals are a cruel thing, of course, the more so that in essence they lead nowhere, as I have already said in one of the preceding issues of the *Diary*; but severe measures against the commanders of these beasts would not be out of place. We could state bluntly, aloud and to the whole of Europe . . . that if atrocities are committed, the immediate superiors of the Turks responsible will, if taken captive, be tried on the spot and placed before a firing squad. (*WD*, November 1877, 1197)

Ivan associated the urge to shoot with the devil, but in the *Diary*, Dostoevsky affirms the desire to shoot as the authentically Russian, Christian response to injustice. "A surprise like that, rather than a carriage with springs, might inspire some wisdom in many of them," he writes of the Turks (*WD*, November 1877, 1197).

Ivan and Dostoevsky in the *Diary* are engaged in similar projects. Raskolnikov perceived the Crucifixion being reenacted around him and tried to create a Passion narrative for himself. Ivan and Dostoevsky perceive that the Job story is continually being reenacted on multiple levels, from the family to Russian society to geopolitics, and they try to rewrite it. Trying to ascertain which perspective on Job wins—Ivan's or Zosima's—is a project that should take the *Diary* into account. It's often been said that the novel repudiates Ivan's views by showing their consequences (parricide); but the consequences of Zosima's views are portrayed in the *Diary*, where they are held by Jews and Judaized Russian liberals and justify the massacre of innocents.[23]

Ivan's views, on the other hand, are remarkably similar to the Russian idea Dostoevsky advocates in the *Diary*.[24]

One of Dostoevsky's foremost roles in the *Diary*, bequeathed to Ivan, is that of self-appointed child advocate with the Russian reading public. Children function in the *Diary* the way they do in Ivan's narrative: they are innocent sacrificial victims of the sins of others. Dostoevsky assumes a role with Russian readers similar to the role Ivan plays in *The Brothers Karamazov*: he indicts delinquent biological and political "fathers" and defends their children's/victims' right to justice. He suggests that the existing system is inadequate and implies that people should appropriate the right to judge paternal and political crimes in a moral court.

Ivan and Dostoevsky in the *Diary* try to speak for those who lack a voice because they are children, dead, Christian Slavs in Muslim Turkey, and so on. Dostoevsky's notes from these years reveal that he experienced this phenomenon—the suffering of the voiceless—as an irresistible call to action. The suffering of a child who could not defend herself torments him. In his notes for the Kroneberg case, in which a father was tried for beating his six-year-old daughter with excessive brutality, Dostoevsky compulsively returns again and again to the child's need for an adult champion. "Before you is a child, who is going to defend it?" [*pered vami rebenok, kto za nego zastupitsia?*] he addresses the adult community (*Pss*, 24:140). "Well, who is going to defend the little child? It's terrible, terrible!" [*kto zhe zastupitsia za ditia? Ved' zhalko, zhalko!*] (*Pss*, 24:140). The phenomenon of the well-off father-transgressor being represented by a skillful lawyer who denies his client's guilt enrages Dostoevsky, who demands to know who will defend the child. "Who is going to defend those of little strength?" he asks (*Pss*, 24:144). "We are sorry that you torture the child in your speech, because it has no one to defend it" (*Pss*, 24:139). Let us keep our sympathy for the child, he demands: "Leave us our pity" (*Pss*, 24:151).

The Brothers Karamazov encourages readers to associate Ivan with Dostoevsky. They have similar backgrounds and are advocates for children. Dostoevsky's biography was common knowledge, and he could ascribe his own experiences to his characters, confident that readers would make the connection. Like Ivan, Dostoevsky had been an impoverished young man who arrived in St. Petersburg with little more than his literary talent and ambition; both quickly became successful authors of topical feuilletons. Ivan refers to an experience in prison that recalls a similar observation made by the narrator of *Notes from the House of the Dead*, whom the Russian public identified with Dostoevsky. "I knew a robber in prison: he happened, in the course of his career, while slaughtering whole families in the houses he broke into and robbed, to have put the knife to several children as well [*Ia znal odnogo razboinika v ostroge: emu sluchalos' v svoiu kar'eru, izbivaia tselye semeistva v domakh, v kotorye zabiralsia po nocham dlia grabezha, zarezat' zaodno neskol'ko i detei],"* Ivan tells Alyosha.[25]

The grammar of the original Russian passage allows two interpretations: Ivan was either in prison or visiting one when he made this observation of a child murderer. Whether Ivan himself was incarcerated (of which there is no other indication) or simply visited a prison, this passage associates him with Dostoevsky, a former inmate who maintained a well-known interest in crime and the penal system his entire life. Dostoevsky often endowed elements of his fiction with ambiguous status, hovering inconclusively between autobiography and invention. The narrator of *Notes from the House of the Dead,* for example, is in prison for murdering his wife, whereas Dostoevsky was convicted of a political crime, but the narrator otherwise resembles Dostoevsky enough to defy any simple conclusions as to their true relationship.[26] Almost two decades before the conversation between Ivan and Alyosha Karamazov, that narrator had written of Gazin, one of the most terrifying inmates of the dead house:

> It was also said that he had the habit of slitting the throats of little children solely for pleasure; he would take the child to some convenient place and frighten and torment him; then, when he had sufficiently enjoyed the terror and anguish of his wretched little victim, he would slowly, quietly, voluptuously cut his throat. (*MHD*, 55–56)

The connections between Ivan and Dostoevsky, like the connections between Stavrogin and Dostoevsky, run deep. Dostoevsky endows Ivan with his own well-known belief that the basis of all moral conduct is faith in immortality, the belief that "there is no virtue if there is no immortality" (*BK*, 60). In the December 1876 *Diary,* Dostoevsky had declared "that love for humanity is even entirely unthinkable, incomprehensible, and *utterly impossible without faith in the immortality of the human soul to go along with it.*"

> I even affirm and venture to declare that love for humanity *in general* is, *as an idea,* one of the most difficult ideas for the human mind to comprehend. . . . Feeling alone can justify it. But such a feeling is possible only with the conviction of the immortality of the human soul to accompany it. (*WD,* December 1876, 736, italics in original)

Ivan, Miusov explains, has "solemnly declared"

> that there was nothing in the whole world to make men love their neighbors. That there was no law of nature that man should love mankind, and that, if

there had been any love on earth hitherto, it was not owing to a natural law, but simply because men have believed in immortality. (*BK*, 60)

Ivan went on to say, Miusov recounts,

if you were to destroy in mankind the belief in immortality, not only love but every living force maintaining the life of the world would at once be dried up. Moreover, nothing then would be immoral, everything would be lawful, even cannibalism. (*BK*, 60)

For the person "who does not believe in God or immortality," Miusov recalls Ivan stating,

The moral law of nature must immediately be changed into the exact contrary of the former religious law, and that egoism, even unto crime, must become, not only lawful but even recognized as inevitable. (*BK*, 60)

"Yes, I asserted that," Ivan affirms. "There is no virtue without immortality" (*Pss*, 14:65). Ivan likewise voices Dostoevsky's public disdain for the "wild conclusion" that Christ's teachings and socialism coincide. "European liberals in general," Ivan says, "and even our liberal dilettantes, often mix up the final results of socialism with those of Christianity" (*BK*, 60).

It is as impassioned champions of children that Ivan and Dostoevsky most resemble each other. I am preoccupied with the fate of children, Dostoevsky tells his *Diary* readers, "I dream of them and see them in my fancies" (*WD*, 1873, 309). "Are you fond of children, Alyosha?" Ivan asks, and assures him, "I am awfully fond of children too" (*BK*, 219). "I, over these two years, have spoken up about children in my *Diary*," Dostoevsky points out to his readers (*WD*, December 1877, 1241). "I have collected a great, great deal about Russian children, Alyosha," Ivan claims (*BK*, 222).[27]

Because of their vulnerability—because their well-being depends on the right conduct of adults—children function for Dostoevsky and Ivan as a gauge by which the moral health or sickness of individuals and whole societies can be measured. Graphically describing a real case of child abuse, recognizably the same Kroneberg case to which Dostoevsky devoted so much attention in the *Diary*, Ivan ascribes a propensity to abuse children to Western influence, much as Dostoevsky ascribed the depraved desire to forgive killers to Western influence.

It is a peculiar characteristic of many people, this love of torturing children, and children only. To all other types of humanity these torturers behave mildly and benevolently, like cultivated and humane Europeans; but they are very fond of tormenting children, even fond of children themselves in that sense. It's just their defenselessness that tempts the tormentor, just the angelic confidence of the child who has no refuge and no appeal, that sets his vile blood on fire. (*BK*, 222)

Before Ivan constructs his case against God with evidence of crimes against children, Dostoevsky cultivates a deep sense of horror and outrage at the suffering of children in his *Diary*. The groundwork for Ivan's rage against those who offend children and his refusal to be reconciled to it is laid in the *Diary*. The contemporary reader's experience of *The Brothers Karamazov* was intensified by the fact that Ivan's examples of child abuse are drawn from the contemporary press, many from Dostoevsky's *Diary* itself. When Ivan takes the witness stand for the victims of a world guilty of incurring irredeemable debts against its most vulnerable members, the pathetic power of his testimony is greatly enhanced by the readers' recognition of his examples as real events and by their knowledge of Dostoevsky's own views on them.[28]

The case of the boy torn apart by his master's dogs, for example, had appeared in an 1877 issue of *Russian Messenger*, the same journal in which *The Brothers Karamazov* was published beginning in January 1879. Responding to his editor Liubimov's objection that he had imbued Ivan with excessive persuasive force and that Ivan's examples of child abuse strained credulity and the boundaries of decency, Dostoevsky retorts, "The character of my hero is real in the highest degree. . . . All my hero says in the text I sent you is based in reality. All the stories about children occurred, were printed in the newspapers, and I can show you where; nothing was invented by me" (*Pss*, 30.1:64).

Dostoevsky and Ivan adopt the same chatty, anecdotal tone when speaking of the most brutal crimes; the effect created by the contrast between their light tone and the horrific content of their words is chilling. "We've come to anecdotes, so here's one more. I noticed it in the *Petersburg Gazette*," Dostoevsky writes (*WD*, November 1877, 1191). "I am fond of collecting certain little facts," Ivan tells Alyosha; "I even copy anecdotes of a certain sort from newspapers and stories" (*BK*, 220).

They both draw attention to the atrocities against Slavic children being committed in the Balkans with Disraeli's approval. "Children are tossed in the air and caught on the point of a bayonet," Dostoevsky reports to his readers, "one two-year-old boy had his eyes pierced while his sister watched and then was impaled on a stake so that he did not die quickly but screamed for a long time" (*WD*, July/August 1877, 1095). "These Turks," Ivan informs Alyosha, "took a pleasure in torturing children, too; cutting the unborn child from the mother's womb, and tossing babies up in the air and catching them on the points of their bayonets before their mothers' eyes" (*BK*, 219).

I have information from a "friend who has come back from Moscow,"

Dostoevsky tells his *Diary* readers in February 1877. Among the Balkan refugee children brought to Russia is an eight-year-old girl suffering from fainting spells; "she faints because of her recollections: last summer, with her own eyes, she watched a group of Circassians flay the skin from her father, and do it completely" (*WD,* February 1877, 859). "By the way," Ivan tells Alyosha, "a Bulgarian I met lately in Moscow . . . told me about the crimes committed by Turks and Circassians in all parts of Bulgaria . . . they burn villages, murder, rape women and children" (*BK,* 219).

Lest his readers draw the mistaken conclusion that child abuse exists only in far-off war zones, Dostoevsky draws their attention to the many ways Russia is failing its children. Writing in the summer of 1873 of his Sunday evening strolls about St. Petersburg, Dostoevsky turns his attention to the shabby working-class families out walking with their pathetic little children. "How haggard, pale, sickly, and anemic they are, and what gloomy little faces they have, especially those who are still being carried; those who are already walking all have crooked legs and flounder along rocking from side to side," Dostoevsky comments (*WD,* 1873, 261). There are many sickly children in Petersburg, he observes, "and people say that terrible numbers of them die off here. As I could see, they are mostly very young and have barely learned to walk or cannot yet walk at all. Could it be that there are so few older children because they do not survive infancy?" (*WD,* 1873, 259). "A child is like a little flower or a leaf on a tree in spring," he objects; "it needs light, air, freedom, room to grow, fresh food; but instead of all these things there is the stuffy basement with some odor of kvass or cabbage, a dreadful stench at night, food that does not nourish, cockroaches and fleas, raw dampness that seeps from the walls, and outside only dust, bricks, and lime" (*WD,* 1873, 261).

The first issue of the *Diary* as an independent monthly opens with Dostoevsky's profession of interest in children and his intention to write a novel about the relations between Russian fathers and children. "There was a Christmas tree and a children's party at the Artists' Club, and I went to have a look at the children," he begins the January 1876 issue.

> Even formerly I always watched children, but now I pay particular attention to them. For a long time now I have had the goal of writing a novel about children·in Russia today, and about their fathers too, of course, in their mutual relationship of today. . . . I will take fathers and children from every level of Russian society I can and follow the children from their earliest childhood. (*WD,* January 1876, 301–2)

Over the next two years of the *Diary*'s publication, Dostoevsky would use all his rhetorical power to condemn the abusive authorities who supposedly enjoyed sacred authority over children and other helpless groups.

The *Diary* draws attention to the children who are "the miscarriages of society," the sacrificial victims of a social order built on the debts it incurs against its weakest members (*WD*, January 1876, 302). There are the two orphaned brothers, little boys age twelve and nine, who witness how their mother's boyfriend "stabbed her barbarically at night, deliberately and with premeditation; then he cut his own throat" (*WD*, January 1876, 302). "We absolutely must help them . . . these innocent children," Dostoevsky implores, and he believes the debt is one that can't be paid off in money: "surely we won't just collect some seventy or a hundred rubles and then forget about them?" (*WD*, January 1876, 303).

There are the "hordes" of little street urchins exploited and abused by the drunken adults who send them out begging for vodka money "even in the most terrible cold, and if they collect nothing, they can probably expect a beating" (*WD*, January 1876, 309).

> In the days before Christmas and on Christmas Eve itself I kept meeting on a certain street corner a little urchin who could have been no more than seven. In the terrible cold he was wearing clothes more fit for summer. . . . There are many like him; they hang about you, whining some well-rehearsed phrases. But this boy didn't whine; his speech was innocent and unpracticed and he looked trustingly into my eyes. (*WD*, January 1876, 309)

Once such a child has collected a few kopecks, Dostoevsky explains, he returns "with red, numbed hands to a cellar where some 'dodgers' are drinking."

> In the cellars their hungry and beaten wives drink with them; their hungry babies cry here too. Vodka, filth, and depravity, but vodka above all. With the kopecks he has collected in hand, the urchin is at once sent to a tavern and he brings back more vodka. Sometimes, for the fun of it, they pour half a bottle into his mouth and roar with laughter when, his breath catching, he falls to the floor scarcely conscious. (*WD*, January 1876, 309)

The future holds only exploitation and total oblivion for such a child. Dostoevsky observes, "When he gets older he's quickly packed off to a factory somewhere, but he's forced once again to bring all that he earns back to the dodgers, and they drink it up." The only alternative to such a life of slavery is the danger of the streets. These children "roam about the city and know places in various cellars into which they can crawl to spend the night unnoticed." Cast off by society, the children endure "hunger, cold, beatings" and are forgotten: "one boy slept several nights in succession in a basket in the quarters of a janitor who never even noticed him." Dostoevsky concludes, "A wild creature such as this sometimes knows nothing at all—neither where he lives, nor what nation he comes from; whether God exists, or the tsar" (*WD*, January 1876, 310).

This passage recalls one of the most powerful pieces of writing from Dostoevsky's preexile days, *Poor Folk,* a text associated with Dostoevsky the radical critic of injustice, the Belinsky protégé. Here, in the *Diary,* Dostoevsky speaks words almost identical to those of Devushkin, the original character-nexus in whom the morally ambiguous father figure, sacrificial victim, and critic of injustice are combined. Devushkin writes in his September 5 letter of his impressions while watching an organ grinder on the street:

> I noticed a little boy, a tiny thing of about ten, he would have been a nice looking child but he looked so sick, so puny, wearing nothing but a shirt and something else, with virtually nothing on his feet, and he was standing there open-mouthed listening to the music . . . his arms and legs were numb with cold and he was shivering and chewing the end of his sleeve. (*PF,* 113)

The boy gives Devushkin a note that reads:

> "Take pity on the poor, dying mother of three children, her children are starving . . ." Well, it was clear what I had to do, but what could I give him? Well, I gave him nothing. But how sorry I was! Such a poor little boy he was . . . The only thing that was wrong with it was the way these vile mothers send their children out half-naked in the cold with notes instead of looking after them. (*PF,* 113)

Perhaps the mother is stupid and weak, perhaps she is really ill, Devushkin muses. "Still, she should seek help from the right people" (*PF,* 114). And maybe she's out to trick people and is abusing her child, "sending a starving, sickly child out on purpose to deceive the public, and making him ill" (*PF,* 114).

What does such begging teach the boy?

> All that's happening to him is that his heart is hardening, he just goes around, rushing from place to place, begging for help. People go by and have no time for him . . . the heart of a child grows hard, and the poor, frightened little boy shivers in vain in the cold like a fledgling which has fallen out of its broken nest. His arms and legs are chilled to the bone, he is breathless. Whenever you look at him he's coughing. He won't have long to wait before sickness like some foul vermin creeps into his chest and before you know it death will be standing over him as he lies in some stinking corner somewhere, helpless and with no escape—and that's all there is to his life. (*PF,* 113–14)

Dostoevsky presents as his own in the *Diary* sentiments that clearly link him to the incipient freethinker, rebel Devushkin of the September 5 letter.

In the spring of 1876, Dostoevsky visited a foundling home, a place "I had long wanted to see," and wrote about his impressions in the May issue of the *Diary* (*WD,* May 1876, 491). Reflecting on how such neglected children call upon society's sense of moral duty to its weakest members, Dostoevsky muses that the demand for charity such helpless children unwittingly place on adults probably irritates some people, sometimes even their own parents. Look at that orphaned infant "crying, squalling," carrying on "as if he had the right to disturb you . . . and a right to be cared for," Dostoevsky directs his reader's gaze. "You look around and right away, like it or not, the thought comes that what if he really does offend someone?" He continues, "And what if someone should suddenly decide to take him in hand and say, 'Look here, you little tyke, do you think you're the son of a prince or something?'" (*WD,* May 1876, 492).

> This isn't some idle fancy of mine. Children are even thrown out of windows, and once some ten years ago another stepmother, I think (I've forgotten, but it would be better if she were a stepmother), got tired of dragging around a child, born of the former wife, that was continually crying from some sort of pain; she went up to the boiling, bubbling samovar, held the child's little hand right under the tap . . . and opened it. (*WD,* May 1876, 492)

Most of the *Diary*'s examples focus on the sins of the fathers, but this trip to the foundling home elicits Dostoevsky's reflections about mothers.

> An interesting, attractive young girl will creep into some dark corner; and suddenly she has a fainting spell and can remember nothing more; sud- denly—just how, no one can tell—her little child, an arrogant, squalling little fellow, just accidentally gets into the water and chokes. Choking, still, is more pleasant than the samovar tap, isn't that so? (*WD,* May 1876, 492–93)

The *Diary* does not confine itself to graphic examples of physical vio- lence against children; Dostoevsky is equally concerned with their spiritual abuse. "I have a secret conviction," he writes, "that our young people are suffering and longing because of the absence of higher aims in the life of our society. The higher aims of life are scarcely mentioned at all within our families" (*WD,* December 1876, 738). The contemporary disintegration of the family harms children more than anyone else, he writes. "Never has the Russian family been more unsettled, more disintegrated, more disarranged and unformed than it is now" (*WD,* July/August 1877, 1034).

> This isolation of our younger generation, this abandonment of them to their own devices is something dreadful . . . Our young people have been so placed that they have absolutely nowhere to get advice about the higher meaning of life . . . and these things are so necessary, so essential to young people;

young people everywhere and in every age have craved and sought after these things! (*WD*, December 1876, 738–39)

"Truly, we run across some amazing fathers in our day!" he exclaims. A gentleman and his son, "no more than eight, perhaps even younger" enter Dostoevsky's railway car. The boy is well dressed, and "it was obvious that the father took good care of him." But "as soon as they had taken their seats the boy suddenly said to his father, 'Papa, can I have a cigarette?' The father at once reached into his pocket, took out a mother of pearl cigarette case, took out two cigarettes, one for himself, the other for the boy, and both began to smoke with the most normal air." Fifteen minutes later the scene is repeated, and Dostoevsky reports that he witnessed the child smoke "at least four cigarettes." I was astonished, he admits: "the weak, tender, still quite undeveloped chest of such a small child had already been accustomed to such a horror. And where could such an unnaturally precocious habit come from? From watching his father, naturally . . . but how could the father have allowed his youngster to use such poison?" The father's misconduct will result in "consumption, catarrh of the respiratory tract and pulmonary cavity—that's what certainly awaits the unfortunate boy" (*WD*, July/August 1877, 1040).

Such abusive irresponsibility attests to the spiritual bankruptcy of the fathers, Dostoevsky writes, and he suggests that abuse of authority nullifies the bond between parents and children. "The accidental nature of today's Russian family consists in the loss among contemporary fathers of any common idea about their families—an idea common to all fathers that binds them together" (*WD*, July/August 1877, 1041). The absence of such an idea results in "listless, lazy fathers; egoists"; a father whose only goal is to show "his scorn for prejudices" and let his child smoke (*WD*, July/August 1877, 1041, 1040). He reports on his visit to "a colony of young offenders," whom he refers to as "fallen angels" and "children who have been 'wronged,'" and asks, "Who is to blame, and how, and for what?" and "Will they forgive us?" (*WD*, January 1876, 314).

The sins of the fathers provoke Dostoevsky to declare that it is possible for the traditional bonds of family to be suspended. Neglectful fathers, Dostoevsky proclaims, are no father at all, and their children have no family. The children of "these lazy fathers" indeed "never had a father, they never had a family; the young fellow enters life utterly alone; he has never lived with his heart; his heart is not bound in any way to his past, to his family, to his childhood" (*WD*, July/August 1877, 1043).

There are striking similarities between the *Diary*'s story of rebellion—Russia's rebellion against Disraeli's Europe—and Ivan's rebellion against

God.[29] Ivan's rejection of what he calls God's "eternal harmony" resembles the *Diary*'s rejection of what it identifies as a Judaized Western civilization. Zosima urges people to reconcile themselves to the fact of others' suffering as the basis of a higher good, their relationship with God. His attitude toward the suffering of others and what can be gained from it reappears in the *Diary*. Zosima's reconciliation with harmony resembles the reconciliation with civilization advocated by the Jews and liberals whom Dostoevsky excoriates in the *Diary*.

Ivan's rebellion against God and the *Diary*'s rebellion against Europe share a similar structure. The *Diary* conceives of Western civilization as a higher order constructed through calculations of what can be purchased with innocent suffering; Ivan conceives of God's eternal harmony as a higher order constructed through calculations of what can be purchased with innocent suffering. Ivan ascribes the Christian God, as the architect of harmony, with qualities similar to those Dostoevsky in the *Diary* ascribes to Disraeli, the Jewish architect of the European order.

Russia's Christian protest against an unjust historical order in the *Diary* resembles Ivan's protest against an unjust divine order in the novel. The grounds Dostoevsky cites for Russia's rebellion against Disraeli's civilization are the same reasons Ivan cites as grounds for rebellion against God: Western civilization and God's harmony are built on utilitarian calculations of what can be gained for the majority at the expense of a sacrificial minority; they are built on transgressions against individual morality, especially against the taboo of child sacrifice; civilization and harmony are both presided over by a bad Jewish authority figure who condones child sacrifice and claims to be unaccountable to individual morality.

The passages in which Dostoevsky contemplates the cost of civilization are an important parallel to the passages in which Ivan contemplates the cost of divine harmony. Civilization, Dostoevsky concludes, requires a bad peace or reconciliation with injustice, much as Ivan decides that God's harmony requires reconciliation with injustice. In the *Diary*, Dostoevsky points to atrocities committed against Balkan Slavs, especially their children, as examples of the suffering Europe is willing to allow in the interest of gaining a higher end, the balance of power that allegedly promotes peace and prosperity for some; and he identifies a certain type of calculating reason, which he associates with Jews, as the source of this European mentality that condones the suffering of others in the pursuit of one's own advantage.

Dostoevsky assumes the role of spokesman for the victims of Western civilization; he excoriates Disraeli, the architect of a European order built on the abuse of innocents; and he urges Russians to refuse their right of entry into Europe. Ivan's refusal to be reconciled to the merchant God and his economy of salvation parallels Russia's refusal to be reconciled to the merchant-diplomat Disraeli and the sacrificial exclusions on which Western civilization is based. Neither refusal is definitively repudiated anywhere in Dostoevsky's writings.

Ivan and Dostoevsky in the *Diary* insist that higher entities are not exempt from the strictures of individual morality. Higher entities—whether states or the architect of divine harmony—may not practice utilitarian or sacrificial exchange logic, they may not justify bad means with good ends. The refusal to allow higher entities to transgress individual morality is an essential component of the Russian idea in the *Diary*. "This is what I think," Dostoevsky writes in the *Diary*: the fact that Russians "in essence reject Europe" reveals "the protesting Russian soul which always, from the very time of Peter the Great, found many, all too many, aspects of European culture hateful and always alien" (*WD*, June 1876, 517). One of the most important aspects of European culture that Russians find hateful, he asserts, is the belief that the ends justify the means, especially when allegedly transcendent ends are pursued by higher entities.

The *Diary* valorizes the "Russian instinct" that "has protested precisely in the name of its downtrodden and Russian principle" (*WD*, June 1876, 517). The Russian principle is also Ivan's principle. The ends do not justify the means, Dostoevsky and Ivan insist; you cannot sacrifice some for the good of the whole, the present for the future, children for adults, Slavs for the rest of Europe. "Surely I haven't suffered, simply that I, my crimes and my sufferings, may manure the soil of the future harmony for somebody else?" Ivan asks (*BK*, 225). It cannot be, Ivan insists, that this principle of sacrificial exclusions is correct. There can be no future good for the sake of which the present individual should be sacrificed; there can be no harmony for the sake of which children are sacrificed. "Why should they, too, furnish material to enrich the soil for the harmony of the future?" Ivan asks, regarding children (*BK*, 225).

European civilization is guilty of justifying atrocities against children and innocents through the principle of sacrificial exclusions. Ivan will mercilessly subject Alyosha, and the reader, to a litany of God's crimes against innocents for the construction of some higher harmony; before Ivan does so, Dostoevsky subjects *Diary* readers to a litany of civilization's crimes against its sacrificial victims. "What we have learned over the past year and a half about the tortures suffered by the Slavs goes beyond the fantasies of even the sickest and most frenzied imagination," he tells *Diary* readers (*WD*, July/August 1877, 1094–95). "The Turks have shown their fury and are devastating Bulgaria entirely," but Europe accepts this devastation as the price to be paid for peace (*WD*, November 1877, 1198). "They murder prisoners and wounded after subjecting them to ghastly tortures such as cutting off noses and other organs. Specialists in the extermination of nursing infants have appeared among them, experts who seize the child by both legs at once and tear it in half, to the amusement and laughter of their comrades, the *bashibazouks*" (*WD*, July/August 1877, 1097).

> People are being exterminated by the thousands and tens of thousands. Tortures have been refined to such a degree as we have not read or heard before. The skin is stripped from living people while their children watch; children are tossed in the air and caught on the point of a bayonet while their mothers watch; women are raped, and during the act the woman is stabbed with a dagger; worst of all, infants are tortured and abused. (*WD*, July/August 1877, 1095)

> It was not by the tens nor by the hundreds, but by thousands and tens of thousands that the Bulgarians were exterminated with fire and sword; their children were torn to bits and died in torment; their wives and daughters were violated and were either beaten after the act or taken away as captives to be sold. (*WD*, November 1877, 1196)

These atrocities do not disturb the Judaized Europeans, however, because Europe "has indisputably reached the point where she places supreme value on her current advantage . . . no matter what the price" (*WD*, February 1877, 867). That price is paid by others.

> The question is plainly put: which is better—for many tens of millions of workers to be thrown onto the street or for a few million Christians to suffer at the hands of their Turkish rulers? The numbers are set forth; the figures are used to frighten people.
> Let them skin people. What do these skins matter in any case? Is the tranquility of Europe worth the hides of some two or three people—or of some twenty or thirty thousand—what's the difference? (*WD*, February 1877, 865)

International harmony—"the interests of civilization"—requires these atrocities.

Dostoevsky challenges the idea that a state has higher pursuits that place it above moral account. Allowing states to claim such exemption, he understands, enables them to commit what to our limited individual view appear to be injustices. The *Diary* upholds the limited, individual perspective and claims that it is Russia's mission to put an end to the transgressions committed by higher entities. Consider the case of Austria, Dostoevsky suggests. The liberal Westernized intellectual Timothy Granovsky defends the Austrian Empire's pursuit of realpolitik. Dostoevsky writes of Granovsky's enthusiasm for Austria:

To justify Austria's action with such fervor, and not only to justify it, but to prove plainly that she *should* have acted in no other way—well, say what you like, but this is like cutting your mind in two. There is something here that one simply cannot agree with, something that prohibits agreement. (*WD*, July/August 1876, 552, italics in original)

Granovsky accuses Russians of inappropriately trying to hold Austria to the strictures of individual morality. Granovsky holds the view that "the state is not a private individual," as Dostoevsky puts it. "A private person, apparently, is one thing, and a state something else" (*WD*, July/August 1876, 552). Dostoevsky contemptuously paraphrases Granovsky's position:

There exists, they say, a rule, a doctrine, an axiom that says that the moral principles of one person—a citizen, an individual—are one thing, and the moral principles of a state are another. Accordingly, what can be considered wickedness on the part of a single individual may, when related to the state, take on the appearance of the greatest wisdom! (*WD*, February 1877, 865)

Westernized, liberal rationalizations of the state's unaccountability form an intriguing parallel to the justifications of God offered by positive characters such as Sonia and Zosima, to their acquiescence to "mystery."

Dostoevsky imagines how the torture of innocent Balkan civilians might affect Disraeli, the consummate Jewish practitioner of realpolitik. "Not long ago I read that the bashibazouks crucified two priests; the victims died after twenty-four hours of torment that exceeds all imagination," he recounts for *Diary* readers (*WD*, September 1876, 609). Dostoevsky ponders what thoughts might enter Disraeli's mind as he prepares for sleep, and he imagines this scene:

"Well," Beaconsfield will think, "the blackened corpses on those crosses . . . hmm . . . well, of course. . . . However, 'the state is not a private individual; it cannot sacrifice its interests out of sensitivity, the more so that in political affairs magnanimity itself is never disinterested'". . . And Beaconsfield falls asleep, sweetly, tenderly. (*WD*, September 1876, 609–10)

Opposed to such calculation and justification is the spectacle of Russian intervention on behalf of Disraeli's victims. Next to the image of Disraeli "preparing for slumber in his richly appointed bedroom," Dostoevsky juxtaposes "old veterans of Sevastopol and the Caucasus, in their rumpled, worn, old frock coats with white crosses in their buttonholes" and urges the reader to "look at how he dies in battle; what a hero he is at the head of the battalion, bringing glory to the Russian name and through his example transforming cowardly recruits into heroes!" (*WD*, September 1876, 609, 610). The portraits of Russian outrage and quixotic resistance against Western reason Dostoevsky paints in the *Diary* may be one source of Ivan's character.

Dostoevsky perceives sacrificial or utilitarian exchange logic, justified because it is practiced by a higher authority and serves a higher end, contaminating the positions of un-Russian, un-Christian parties. He accuses the socialists, for example, of striving to create an order built on sacrificial exclusions. They "entirely exclude the bourgeoisie from their brotherhood: 'Brotherhood will develop later, among the proletarians, but you—you are the 100 million heads condemned to extermination, and nothing more. You must pass from the scene, for the good of humanity'" (*WD*, February 1877, 880).

The ultimate source and practitioner of this logic is Disraeli. It is he, a fellow novelist, who is Dostoevsky's most serious competition for the right to compose humanity's narrative. "Viscount Tarantula," as Dostoevsky refers to him in the *Diary*, offends children and innocents in the name of a higher good, the balance of power in Europe (*WD*, September 1876, 638). "This massacre of the Bulgarians was something he permitted, after all," Dostoevsky writes of Disraeli's role in the atrocities, "—he plotted it himself; he is a novelist, and this is his chef-d'oeuvre" (*WD*, July/August 1876, 609).

Dostoevsky does not blame the Europeans for their role in the Balkan tragedy, for they too are Disraeli's victims. "Were the Jewish idea not so powerful in the world, that same 'Slavic' question (last year's question) might have been resolved in favor of the Slavs, not the Turks," he explains (*WD*, March 1877, 904–5). Disraeli is "a spider, to be sure, a *piccola bestia*," that has infected Europe with its poison (*WD*, July/August 1876, 609). In *Time*, Dostoevsky expressed the belief that European culture was disintegrating as the various national cultures diverged from one another, and he complained about an apparent European unwillingness to understand Russia. The reasons for this cultural disintegration and hostility toward Russia were left vague in *Time*; here in the *Diary*, he discusses these exact problems but has now found an explanation for them: Jewish influence in Europe.

> It seems that everyone has been bitten already. The bite of this piccola bestia quickly brings on the most extraordinary fits: people in Europe, it seems, now no longer understand one another. . . . There is only one thing that unites them all: they all immediately point to Russia. (*WD*, July/August 1876, 606)

"This Israelite, this new adjudicator of honor in England," the *Diary* charges, opposes "human progress and the humanization of all humanity, as understood by the Russian People" (*WD*, July/August 1876, 609, 598).

Led by Disraeli, Western civilization has become a society built on what can be gained through trading in the misfortune of others, specifically the massacre of Balkan Slavs, Orthodox Christians, in exchange for peace or harmony in Europe. The *Diary* identifies "Viscount Beaconsfield, an Israeli by birth (ne d'Israeli)" as the preeminent representative of the calculating approach to what can bought with innocent suffering and argues that the Jewish idea of sacrificial exclusions is the source of Europe's current depravity (*WD*, July/August 1876, 608).

Under the influence of the Jews, the Europeans have accepted the principle of sacrificial exclusions. In Europe, "One cannot fail to note the effective triumph of Jewry which has replaced many of the old ideas with its own," specifically "the idea of the Yids, which is creeping over the whole world in place of 'unsuccessful' Christianity" (*WD*, March 1877, 915). The people of Europe cannot grasp Russia's selflessness because they are under Disraeli's sway. "Europe believes neither in Russia's nobility nor in her selflessness," Dostoevsky laments, because Disraeli is telling the Europeans that the Russians fighting in the Balkans "are only a lot of socialists, communists, and communards," who threaten their peace and prosperity (*WD*, July/August 1876, 607, 608). In Disraeli's Europe, "selflessness is a blank spot, an unknown, a riddle, a mystery!" (*WD*, July/August 1876, 607).

Ivan and Dostoevsky use similar rhetorical tactics against the merchant God and earthly practitioners of sacrificial exchange logic who claim moral immunity: they initially feign reconciliation with harmony and civilization in order to then highlight their compelling grounds for rebellion. The *Diary* positions Russia in relation to Disraeli's Europe as Ivan positions himself in relation to God's harmony: they pose as those who have understood the benefits to be gained but still refuse to be reconciled. They will be voices of naive, honest outrage resisting the mental operations used to justify the innocent suffering on which civilization and divine harmony are built.

Dostoevsky urges his readers to refrain from participating in the machinations through which civilization maintains itself. The *Diary* goes further than Ivan, who remains uncomfortable with the urge to shoot even as he rejects reconciliation. The *Diary* rebels against what it perceives to be Jewish reconciliation and liberal forgiveness—Dostoevsky advocates shooting the Turks, against the advice of Jews and liberals—and confidently proclaims that military violence will usher in a new era of Christian brotherhood on earth.

Dostoevsky and Ivan begin by confessing that they experience urges to be reconciled with the order in question, despite its apparent injustice; but those urges are quickly overwhelmed by more powerful, sincere, naive impulses toward identification with the victims. The *Diary* passage about the eight-year-old Balkan refugee who saw the Turks skin her father alive is followed by Dostoevsky's musings about the price of civilization. "'Civilization!' I thought, 'who dares say a word against civilization?'" (*WD*, February 1877, 860). Ivan likewise begins with humility and acceptance. "I accept God," he starts off with Alyosha. God is greater than me, he concedes, and "I can't expect to understand about God. I acknowledge humbly that I have no faculty for settling such questions. I have a Euclidean earthly mind, and how could I solve problems that are not of this world?" (*BK*, 216).

After his brief initial moment of humility before civilization, Dostoevsky counters, "And yet, the moment I felt like exclaiming rapturously to myself 'Long live civilization!' I was suddenly overcome by doubt. . . . Isn't this, perhaps, entirely a mirage, and aren't we deceiving ourselves?" (*WD*, February 1877, 861). "I have believed," Ivan says; "I want to see with my own eyes the hind lie down with the lion and the victim rise up and embrace his murderer" (*BK*, 225). "Yet," Ivan likewise switches direction, "in the final result I don't accept this world of God's," he challenges (*BK*, 216).

Disraeli's civilization and God's harmony do benefit some, Ivan and Dostoevsky concede. Dostoevsky paraphrases what he contemptuously calls "Yiddified" thinking, according to which it is entirely reasonable to sacrifice a few for the good of the whole. What if civilization does require the flaying of skin from some human beings, he asks *Diary* readers, as is happening in the Balkans? "From human beings? What human beings? From only a tiny number of human beings living in some obscure corner. . . . On the other hand, the rest of the organism—the huge part of it—is alive and well; it flourishes, trades, and manufactures!" (*WD*, February 1877, 860). Those of us who benefit from this system built on sacrificial exclusions, Dostoevsky concedes, can be thankful for our own safety.

> At least these children of ours who are peacefully strolling here on Nevsky Prospect will not see the skin flayed from fathers, and their mothers will not have to watch these children being tossed into the air and caught on bayonets, as happened in Bulgaria. That bit of progress, at least, can be credited to civilization! (*WD*, February 1877, 860)

But Dostoevsky, like Ivan, is concerned about the price others are paying for his well-being. "And what if it"—this civilized condition—

> does only exist in Europe, i.e., in one little corner of the globe, and in a corner which is rather small in comparison with the surface of the planet (a terrible thought!); but still, it is there, and though it may be only in some little corner, it exists; although the price we pay for it—flaying the skin from our own brothers who live somewhere off on the edge of civilization—is a high one, it exists among us, at least. (*WD*, February 1877, 860)

Dostoevsky is paving the way for Ivan, developing a logical argument against "this Israelite" Disraeli and the exclusionary civilization he represents which will reappear in the argument Ivan deploys against God and *his* harmony built on sacrificial children.

Dostoevsky emphatically rejects any complicity with sacrificial exclusions justified by utilitarian calculations. "I want only to say that despite all these rules, principles, religions, and civilizations, it is always only the most imperceptible, tiny group of people that is saved by them; true, this is the group that emerges victorious, but only in the final analysis" (*WD*, February 1877, 863). The European order Dostoevsky castigates in the journal, like the divine order castigated by Ivan in the novel, sacrifices some for the ultimate, distant salvation of others. "Better let them skin people alive way off there in the wilds" than give up our civilized harmony, Dostoevsky imagines the Europeans thinking (*WD*, February 1877, 865).

Dostoevsky declares his rejection of Western utilitarian realpolitik and encourages Russians to return their admission ticket to the European order. He even urges his compatriots to upset that order through displays of rebellion and self-sacrifice intended to usher in a new age. Self-sacrificial rebellion against injustice is celebrated in the *Diary* as the highest expression of Russian Christian faith, part of a call to transform cowards into heroes changing world history. It seems obvious to Dostoevsky that the fact of suffering demands Russian, Christian intervention, but to his amazement, many justify this suffering as part of a desirable order. He presciently understands how the mystique of expertise and the allure of higher ends can lure even decent people into barbarism.

> If some "expert" were to come up with even the most meager "proof" that there are occasions when flaying the skin from the back of some other person can even be of benefit to the common cause and, though it may be repulsive, still "the end justifies the means"; and if some expert were to say things of this sort using the appropriate style and under the appropriate circumstances, then, believe me, immediately there would be people willing to carry out the idea—very jolly people, even. (*WD*, February 1877, 861–62)

"Oh, civilization!" he exclaims. "Oh, Europe, whose interests would suffer so were she actually to forbid the Turks to flay the skin from fathers while their children watch!" (*WD*, February 1877, 859). "If its preservation demands the stripping of skin from living people," Dostoevsky concludes, "may civilization itself be damned" (*WD*, February 1877, 860).

The proximity between political and spiritual rebellion, the porousness of that boundary, would have been apparent to Dostoevsky's contemporaries. Dostoevsky's call to intransigence in the *Diary*, to a moral absolutism that has real political consequences, foreshadows Ivan's moral intransigence. "If we really don't like that sort of thing to go on here and *never do it*," Dostoevsky writes of the flayings, "then, really, we should abhor it in others as well. Abhorring it, in fact, is not enough: we should simply not allow it" (*WD*, February 1877, 864). "Russia alone cannot be seduced into an unjust alliance, not at any price," he asserts (*WD*, February 1877, 866). Given the atrocities committed for the so-called interests of civilization, he argues, "the most indignant people among us are not nearly as indignant as they ought to be" (*WD*, February 1877, 864). Like Russia, Ivan is willing to be the only one refusing reconciliation, the only one remaining outside the harmonious order.

Ivan's roots are in Dostoevsky, Russia, and Don Quixote as portrayed in the *Diary*. Europe, Dostoevsky writes, "places supreme value on her current advantage, on the advantage of the present moment, no matter what the price" (*WD*, February 1877, 867). We in Russia, however, "have always believed in an enduring moral system, not in a relative one valid only for a few days. Believe me, Don Quixote also knows where his advantages lie and is capable of a calculation: he knows that he will gain in dignity and in awareness of that dignity if he continues to remain a knight" (*WD*, February 1877, 867).

Ivan's desire to "return his ticket" to God's harmony would recall a passage from a well-known biography of the Russian literary critic Vissarion Belinsky. This biography, published in 1875 and most likely read by Dostoevsky, contained extensive passages from Belinsky's correspondence. In one letter from the early 1840s published here, Belinsky describes his relationship to the German philosopher G. W. F. Hegel and world history in terms very similar to those used by Ivan to describe his relationship to God and harmony. "Even if I attained to the actual top of the ladder of human development," Belinsky wrote, "I should at that point still have to ask [Hegel] to account for all the victims of life and history, all the victims of accident and superstition, of the Inquisition and Phillip II, and so on and so forth, otherwise I will throw myself head-downwards."[30]

Dostoevsky urges a form of national throwing oneself head-downward in the *Diary*: Russia will throw itself out of the community of so-called civilized nations to remain with the victims of the "Jewish idea." The novel plays out, within one of its personal narratives, some potential consequences of the historical narrative urged in the journal. In the *Diary*, Dostoevsky's anger is directed against a Western civilization that is Jewish; in *The Brothers Karamazov*, Ivan's anger is directed against a God whom he accuses of basing his divine order on principles associated in the *Diary* with Jews.

The *Diary* associates sacrifice for the sake of an abstraction and the claim to be unaccountable to individual morality with Jews, and it opposes this Jewish thinking to poetry and ideals. It is clear that Russia should intervene on behalf of the Balkan Slavs, but the obvious fact of their suffering and need for deliverance is obscured by Jewish influence, Dostoevsky complains. "Once there is a deed to be done, a *real* deed, a *practical* deed, everything is pushed aside and the ideals are sent to the Devil! Ideals are nonsense, poetry, pretty verses! And is it not true that the Yid has enthroned himself everywhere; indeed, that he has not only 'enthroned himself again,' but has never ceased to reign?" he asks *Diary* readers (*WD,* July/August 1876, 549). Ivan and Russia will side with ideals, with the absurdity of a single concrete fact before a grand abstraction, against what the *Diary* contemptuously calls the "so-called realistic and sober common sense" spouted by Judaized Russian liberals (*WD,* September 1877, 1125).

Ivan and the Russian people as Dostoevsky portrays them in the *Diary* will risk themselves for the sake of adhering to the suffering individual, to the fact, against the authority of any expert justifications, the allure of any harmony or civilization. The *Diary* defines the Russian mentality as one that flouts any consideration of gain, advantage, or even exchange, preferring to give to history's victims without expectation of return. We will work for "the defense of the world's weak and oppressed," the *Diary* proclaims, "even if it is sometimes at the expense of our own best and major immediate interest" (*WD,* June 1876, 598, 526).

Ivan and Russia in the *Diary* pointedly reject Zosima's injunction to humble their merely mortal sense of right and wrong and wait for the time when "you will behold all things truly then and will not dispute them" (*BK,* 299). Russia must stick to the facts, Dostoevsky declares, even if this means placing ourselves outside the higher truth of Western civilization. "Facts came to light that were striking and characteristic, that were recorded and remembered, that will not be forgotten and cannot be disputed" (*WD,* July/August 1877, 1084). In a world in which expert authority justifies flaying people alive, allegiance to concrete facts entails a rejection of reason. "'I understand nothing,' Ivan went on, as though in delirium, 'I don't want to understand anything now. I want to stick to the fact. I made up my mind long ago not to understand. If I try to understand anything, I shall be false to the fact and I have determined to stick to the fact'" (*BK,* 224). He maintains a quixotic allegiance to absurdity. "Let me tell you, novice, that the absurd is only too necessary on earth," he tells Alyosha. "The world stands on absurdities, and perhaps nothing would have come to pass in it without them" (*BK,* 224).

The Russian idea, like Ivan's, is willingness to go down for the sake of facts, for the victims of history and harmony. "We will draw our sword if need be," Dostoevsky proclaims, "in the name of the oppressed and unfortunate, even though it may be to the detriment of our own current advantage," for "Russia's real mission, strength, and truth lie" in defense of "the oppressed who have been forsaken by everyone in Europe" (*WD,* February 1877, 868).

The evils of sacrificial exchange logic have always existed, Dostoevsky concedes, but only the Jews have made them ideas worthy of emulation and veneration. "Lord Beaconsfield, and all the other Beaconsfields after him, both our own and those of Europe" ignore the massacre of the Balkan Slavs, and "they have betrayed Christ for 'the interests of civilization,'" he accuses;

"that, now, is bestiality—developed and elevated like a virtue, and people in the West and here in Russia bow down to it as if it were an idol" (*WD*, May/June 1877, 970).

"The unprecedented tortures and massacres to which the Herzegovinians were subjected became known to the whole of Europe," Dostoevsky recounts; "reports came that hundreds of thousands of people—old men, pregnant women, abandoned children—had fled their homes and were streaming out of Turkey into any neighboring country to which they could make their way," but Disraeli's Europe remains untroubled, for such tragedies are simply part of the greater design (*WD*, July/August 1877, 1082). "Eighteen centuries of Christianity, humanization, science, and progress suddenly turn out to be rubbish," Dostoevsky laments, and "their whole 'civilization' suddenly turns out to be no more than a soap bubble" (*WD*, July/August 1876, 548).

The most heinous consequence of the Jewish idea—the most heinous crime committed by the Judaized West under Disraeli's influence—is the sacrifice of history's innocents for the sake of an abstraction such as a "higher order" or "ultimate good" or interests of state.

And now the Englishman Forbes, correspondent for the *Daily News* known for his excellent and comprehensive articles from our side of the battlefield, at last has frankly expressed all his English truth. He sincerely admits that the Turks had "full right" to exterminate the entire Bulgarian population north of the Balkans once the Russian army had crossed the Danube. (*WD*, November 1877, 1198)

How can an educated and enlightened representative of Western culture express such a view, Dostoevsky wonders—"are these the last fruits and flowers of English civilization?" (*WD*, November 1877, 1198). Disraeli's Europe accepts the murder of the Balkan Slavs as a reasonable price to pay for peace.

These very same peoples and nations who cried out against slavery, who ended the trade in negro slaves; who ended their own despotic systems; who proclaimed the rights of man . . . These same peoples and nations suddenly all (almost all) at this moment turn their backs on the millions of unfortunate creatures—Christians, human beings, their own brothers who are living in dishonor and perishing. (*WD*, July/August 1876, 546)

Russia will never participate in such logic, however.

Let England's Prime Minister distort the truth before parliament for political reasons and tell it officially that the massacre of sixty thousand Bulgarians came at the hands, not of the Turks, but at the hands of Slavic emigrants. And

193

let the entire parliament, for political reasons, believe him and tacitly give approval to his lie. Nothing of the sort can or should happen in Russia. Some will say that Russia cannot, in any event, act directly against her best interest. But where is Russia's interest here? Russia's best interest is precisely to act even against her best interest if necessary; to make a sacrifice, so as not to violate justice. (*WD*, June 1876, 524)

The Russian Christian asks, "What is the point of that prosperity purchased at the price of injustice and flaying of people's skin?" and refuses to participate in such rationalizations: "let them do as they like over there in Europe, but let us do things differently" (*WD*, February 1877, 866–67, 865). "It's better to believe that happiness cannot be purchased with evil deeds than it is to feel happy knowing that you have allowed evil to happen," Dostoevsky insists (*WD*, February 1877, 865). Russian "public opinion has, it seems, declared itself and will not agree to beatings for the sake of peace of any sort," Dostoevsky notes with approval (*WD*, June 1876, 523).

Dostoevsky associates the Serbs, the sacrificial victims of Disraeli's civilization, with children. He fosters the impression that the Slavs are like children in their helplessness and vulnerability, and he draws specific attention to the abuse of Balkan children. This alleged Serbian childishness even elicits Dostoevsky's Great Russian and impatience. They dream of "a united Slavic Serbian kingdom of seven million people," he notes with condescension; "in short, they were dreamers, very like small seven-year-old children who put on toy epaulets and imagine themselves generals" (*WD*, October 1876, 662).

These Serbs, who are "very like small seven-year-old children,"

could only howl when the tormentors would take little children, and in the presence of their fathers and mothers, would cut a child's finger off every five minutes to prolong the agony; but they did not defend themselves; they could only wail in agony, as if demented, and kiss the feet of the torturers so that they would stop the torture and give them back their poor little children. (*WD*, September 1876, 632)

This image of the pathetic childlike Serbians contributes to the portrait of Ilyusha in *The Brothers Karamazov*; the sacrificial victims of Disraeli's Europe and God's harmony are linked. When Ilyusha sees Dmitry Karamazov beating his father in the street, Captain Snegiryov recounts for Alyosha, the child pleads with his father's tormentor:

He rushed up to me: "Dad," he cried, "Dad!" He caught hold of me, hugged me, tried to pull me away, crying to my assailant, "Let go, let go, it's my dad, my dad, forgive him"—yes, he actually cried: "Forgive him!" He clutched at that hand, that very hand, in his little hands and kissed it, sir . . . (*BK,* 186)

Russia must resist the allure of the Jewish idea of sacrificing others for one's own advantage. "I was musing the other day, for instance, about Russia's status as a great European power, and what didn't come into my mind on this sad topic!" Dostoevsky tells his *Diary* readers (*WD,* 1873, 234). Contemplating the cost of such status, which requires money for railroads, weapons, technology, science, and schools, Dostoevsky emphatically asserts at the outset of his discussion, "I wish only to say that this costs us too dearly" (*WD,* 1873, 234). For "the question then arises," he points out, "as to where we are to find this money," and he objects that it will be raised through the ruination of "the People" by the Jews (*WD,* 1873, 237). Russia must not agree to sacrifice future generations for the sake of great power status, he warns. "Nearly half our present budget is provided by vodka—that is, by the current drunkenness and debauch of the People—and so by the whole future of our People. We are, so to say, funding our grand budget as a great European power with our own future . . . And who is it who wanted that?" (*WD,* 1873, 237–38).

It was the Jews who wanted that, Dostoevsky avers. "We must have the budget of a great power and therefore we are greatly in need of money; who, I ask, is going to supply this money over the next fifteen years if the present state of affairs continues?" (*WD,* 1873, 238–39). The Jews will supply it through the sale of vodka, he answers. Vodka is the symbol of a calculating, acquisitive mentality willing to sacrifice others to achieve its ends, and lurking behind vodka Dostoevsky espies the Jews. The newly liberated people, he contends, were released from serfdom only to be enslaved by "cheap vodka and the Yid," growing rich as tavern keepers (*WD,* 1873, 238). "Eighty million exist solely for the support of three million Yids. Spit on them," he writes in his *Diary* notebooks (*Pss,* 24:212).

The "Jewish idea" will not triumph among the Russian people, however, for certain "inner, distinctive forces of the People" will protect them (*WD,* 1873, 235). The Russian people flout utilitarian logic, engaging in behaviors such as squandering, excess, and penitential self-abnegation. The most basic "historical trait of the people" is "their zeal for 'Godly things,' for holy places, for oppressed Christians, and, on the whole, for everything that is *penitent and Godly*" (*WD,* July/August 1877, 1091). Far from seeking their own advantage, the people seek out risky service. "I think the principal and most basic spiritual need of the Russian people is the need for suffering, incessant and unslakable suffering, everywhere and in everything" (*WD,* 1873, 161).

Their capacity for self-sacrifice links the Russian people with Christ.

The relationship between the people and Christ in the *Diary* is complex. At times Dostoevsky clearly subordinates the people to Christ, specifying that they are merely the vehicle—albeit the chosen one—of his message. "All the principles of the people have emerged entirely from Orthodoxy," he writes (*WD*, April 1876, 442). But at other times, the fact that it is a Russian word they bring to the world receives greater emphasis than the fact that it's Christ's Word, and at times, Christ is eclipsed by the people, who become themselves the object of veneration in their own right. Their self-sacrifice replaces Christ's Crucifixion as the pivotal intercession of the divine in history.

The people do not know and worship Christ; Dostoevsky concedes the possibility that they do not even know the principles of the Christian religion. They are not Christian because of their faith in Christ but because they are like him and perform his functions. Conceding that they "know the Gospels poorly and that they do not know the fundamental principles of our faith" (*WD*, 1873, 264), he protests that they know Christ "although they never attended any school. They know because for many centuries they endured much suffering" (*WD*, 1876, 440). They are a vehicle of salvation in their own right, for themselves and others. In a moment of crisis, "They would save themselves, themselves and us as well, as they have already done more than once" (*WD*, 1873, 155).

Dostoevsky equates Christianity with the Russian people. He expresses this view in his correspondence, in the *Diary,* and through Zosima in *The Brothers Karamazov.* "The huge majority of our educated classes split themselves off from the People," he writes in the 1873 *Diary;* "when they broke with the People, they naturally lost God as well" (*WD*, 1873, 126). Zosima, whom he calls "a pure and ideal Christian" in a letter to Liubimov (*Pss*, 30.1:68), reiterates the equivalence between faith in the Russian people and in God: "One who does not believe in God will not believe in God's people. He who believes in God's people will see His Holiness too, even though he had not believed in it till then. Only the people and their future spiritual power will convert our atheists, who have torn themselves away from their native soil" (*BK*, 273). "He who loses his people and nationality loses his ancestral faith and God," Dostoevsky writes in an 1870 letter to Maikov (*Pss*, 29.1:145). "All our hope is in the people [*V narode vse nashe spasenie*]," he writes in April 1878 to students of Moscow University who wrote him asking him to clarify his view of the relationship between the intelligentsia and the people (*Pss*, 30.1:22).

The Jews, who rejected the first redemptive self-sacrifice of the Crucifixion, continue to set their principle of self-interested utilitarian calculation against Christian selflessness, now embodied in the Russian people and manifesting itself as Russian self-sacrifice in the Balkans. The Jews and those who have adopted a "Jewish" outlook refuse to see that "with war and victory will come a new word, and a living life will begin"; they refuse to admit "that Russia is predestined and created, perhaps, for their salvation as well and that only she, perhaps, will at last pronounce this word of salvation" (*WD*, April 1877, 932, 936).

Neither the *Diary* nor *The Brothers Karamazov* offered a solution to the dilemma of innocent suffering that satisfied Dostoevsky, for his concern with the problem of sacrificial exclusions continued beyond publication of the novel. *The Brothers Karamazov* chapters in which Ivan challenges the authority of a God who builds his creation on the suffering of children, "The Brothers Get Acquainted" and "Rebellion," were published in the *Russian Messenger* in May 1879. On June 8, 1880, Dostoevsky spoke before the Society of Lovers of Russian Literature in Moscow, on the occasion of the unveiling of a Pushkin statue. In his address, Dostoevsky associates himself with Ivan by speaking almost exactly the same words he had placed in Ivan's mouth barely a year earlier. His "Pushkin Speech," as the address came to be known, created a sensation; Dostoevsky regarded it as the crowning achievement of his creative and public life, and he published it in a special August 1880 issue of the *Diary*.

    The speech is devoted to clarifying the national significance and legacy of Alexander Pushkin, the artist Dostoevsky revered above all others and whose art he considered to be the purest incarnation of the Russian spirit. Pushkin's *Eugene Onegin*, Dostoevsky explains, poses the question: "Can one person found his happiness on the unhappiness of another? . . . What kind of happiness can it be if it is founded on the unhappiness of another?" (*WD*, August 1880, 1287). Here, in this speech delivered barely a year after publication of Ivan's rebellion, Dostoevsky borrows Ivan's words and voices Ivan's objections to admitting innocent suffering into the pursuit of any end, no matter how worthy it may be.

    In May 1879, readers had followed Ivan's development of this argument. "Tell me yourself, I challenge you," he demands of Alyosha—

"Answer: Imagine that you yourself are building the edifice of human destiny with the goal of making people happy in the end, giving them peace and rest at last, but for this it is necessary and inevitable to torture just one tiny creature, that same little child who was beating itself on the chest with its little fist, and to build the edifice on its unavenged tears, would you agree to be the architect on the these conditions, tell me and don't lie!" (*Pss*, 14:223–24)

"No, I would not agree," Alyosha admits, and Dostoevsky strives to elicit this response from listeners and readers with his speech, adopting the same arguments and tone with his audience that Ivan used with his brother.

    In June 1880, in a speech that would reach the national reading public through publication in the *Diary,* Dostoevsky confronts Russia, claiming that Pushkin, the hallowed incarnation of the national spirit, poses the same question as the fictional deicide. Pushkin's art, Dostoevsky insists, asks us to consider a strange choice. Ivan had obliquely suggested that the Crucifixion was a reprehensible sacrificial exchange: "It is impossible that a blameless one should suffer for another." Pushkin, Dostoevsky believes, asks us to accept or reject a peace that results from the torture and death of just one human being. The position of sacrificial victim here is not occupied by a child, however. It is occupied by an older man, one who, like Devushkin, combines the status of a kind of father figure with erotic attachment to a much younger woman with that of sacrificial victim. Here the potential sacrificial victim is Tatiana's much older husband in *Eugene Onegin.* "Can you imagine that you are erecting the edifice of human destiny with the goal of making people happy in the end, of giving them peace and rest at last?" Dostoevsky believes Pushkin asks us.

> And now imagine as well that to do this it is essential and inavoidable to torture to death just one human creature . . . Will you consent on those terms to be the architect of such an edifice? That is the question. (*WD,* August 1880, 1287–88)

That is the question that evolved through Dostoevsky's fiction and journalism, reached its most eloquent articulation in the rebellions against innocent sacrifice enacted in *The Brothers Karamazov* and the *Diary,* and continued to torment Dostoevsky even after composition of the novel. *The Brothers Karamazov* was not a conclusion but rather one episode or station on a path that never reached a final destination; Dostoevsky was still seeking answers when he died. His search seems to have led him to find some certainty in the construction of a clear opposition between the "Russian" and "Jewish" ideas of his mature imagination; the ultimate direction his thinking might have taken will never be known.

Notes

INTRODUCTION

Zen'kovskii, "F. M. Dostoevsky, V. Soloviev, N. A. Berdiaev," quoted in M. A. Maslin, *Russkaia ideia i ee tvortsy* (Moscow: Respublika, 1992), 323.

1. Many excellent studies of Dostoevsky's attitudes about Jews have been made, and I draw on them throughout this work. The works on which I am building include Gary Adelman, *Retelling Dostoevsky: Literary Responses and Other Observations* (Lewisburg, Pa.: Bucknell University Press; London: Associated University Presses, 2001); Felix Dreizin, *The Russian Soul and the Jew: Essays in Ethnocriticism* (Lanham, Md.: University Press of America, 1990); Joseph Frank's foundational, five-volume biography of Dostoevsky, including *Dostoevsky: The Seeds of Revolt, 1821–1849* (Princeton, N.J.: Princeton University Press, 1979); *Dostoevsky: The Years of Ordeal, 1850–1859* (Princeton, N.J.: Princeton University Press, 1987); *Dostoevsky: The Stir of Liberation, 1860–1865* (Princeton, N.J.: Princeton University Press, 1988); *Dostoevsky: The Miraculous Years, 1865–1871* (Princeton, N.J.: Princeton University Press, 1996); and especially the final volume, *Dostoevsky: The Mantle of the Prophet 1871–1881* (Princeton, N.J.: Princeton University Press, 2002); Ronald Hingley, *Dostoevsky: His Life and Work* (New York: Charles Scribner's Sons, 1978); David I. Goldstein, *Dostoevsky and the Jews* (Austin: University of Texas Press, 1981); Felix Ingold, *Dostoevsky und das Judentum* (Frankfurt am Main: Insel, 1981); Judith Deutsch Kornblatt and Gary Rosenshield, "Vladimir Solovyov: Confronting Dostoevsky on the Jewish and Christian Question," *Journal of the American Academy of Religion* 68 (2000): 69–98; Gary Saul Morson, "Apologetics and Negative Apologetics; Or, Dialogues of a Jewish Slavist," in *People of the Book: Thirty Scholars Reflect on Their Jewish Identity*, ed. Shelley Fisher Fishkin and Jeffrey Rubin Dorsky (Madison: University of Wisconsin Press, 1996); Harriet Murav, *Identity Theft: The Jew in Imperial Russia and the Case of Avraam Uri Kovner* (Stanford, Calif.: Stanford University Press, 2003); Gary Rosenshield, "Dostoevsky's 'The Funeral of a Universal Man' and 'An Isolated Case' and Chekhov's 'Rothschild's Fiddle': The Jewish Question," *Russian Review* 56, no. 4 (1997): 487–504; Gabriella Safran, *Rewriting the Jew: Assimilation Narratives in the Russian Empire*

(Stanford, Calif.: Stanford University Press, 2000); James Scanlan, *Dostoevsky the Thinker* (Ithaca, N.Y.: Cornell University Press, 2002); and Maxim Shrayer, "Dostoevskii, the Jewish Question, and *The Brothers Karamazov*," *Slavic Review* 61, no. 2 (Summer 2002): 273–91.

2. F. M. Dostoevsky, *The Brothers Karamazov*, ed. Ralph E. Matlaw, trans. Constance Garnett (New York: W. W. Norton, 1976), 202, 217, 552 (hereafter cited in text as *BK* with page number).

3. The scholarship discussing Dostoevsky's relationship to Christian faith is vast, and I cite only a few of the works on which I have drawn here. In addition to Frank's indispensable biography, I have relied on the following works: Steven Cassedy, *Dostoevsky's Religion* (Stanford, Calif.: Stanford University Press, 2005); George Pattison and Diane Oenning Thompson, eds., *Dostoevsky and the Christian Tradition* (Cambridge: Cambridge University Press, 2001); Malcolm V. Jones, *Dostoevsky and the Dynamics of Religious Experience* (London: Anthem Press, 2005); Malcolm V. Jones, "Dostoevskii and Religion," in *The Cambridge Companion to Dostoevskii,* ed. W. J. Leatherbarrow (Cambridge: Cambridge University Press, 2002); V. N. Zakharov, ed., *Evangel'skii tekst v russkoi literature XVIII–XX vekov: tsitata, reministsentsiaa, motiv, siuzhet, zhanr; sbornik nauchykh trudov* (Petrozavodsk: Petrozavodskogo Universiteta, 2001).

4. Steven Cassedy, "The Progressive Yiddish Press in America Looks at Dostoevsky at the Turn of the Century," *Dostoevsky Studies: The Journal of the International Dostoevsky Society,* n.s., vol. 9 (2005): 53–65, quotation at 65.

5. Pattison and Thompson, *Dostoevsky and the Christian Tradition,* 7.

6. Gary Rosenshield, "Mystery and Commandment in *The Brothers Karamazov*: Leo Baeck and Fedor Dostoevsky," *Journal of the American Academy of Religion* 62, no. 2 (Summer 1994): 483–508, quotation at 484. Rosenshield provides extensive discussion of the scholarship devoted to the problem of Dostoevsky's relationship to Orthodoxy (486–87). Appreciating the radical differences that distinguish Dostoevsky's beliefs from Orthodox faith can be extremely difficult, Rosenshield explains, because Dostoevsky had such a profound impact on the subsequent development of Orthodoxy. "Russian Orthodox theologians, thinkers, and critics," Rosenshield writes, "are not in accord about Dostoevsky, yet Zenkovsky argues that however much Dostoevsky 'constituted a break with the classical formulations of the Church Fathers,' his writings were the greatest influence on the Russian Orthodox religious renaissance of the late nineteenth and early twentieth centuries" (488; for original Zenkovsky quotation, see V. V. Zenkovsky, "Dostoevsky's Religious and Philosophical Views," in *Dostoevsky: A Collection of Critical Essays,* ed. Rene Wellek [Englewood Cliffs, N.J.: Prentice-Hall, 1962], 130–45, quotation at 145).

7. Rosenshield, "Mystery and Commandment in *The Brothers Karamazov*," 487.

8. Ibid., 503.

9. Roger B. Anderson, "Mythical Implications of Father Zosima's Religious

Teachings," *Slavic Review* 38, no. 2 (1979): 272–89; Sven Linnér, *Starets Zosima in "The Brothers Karamazov": A Study in the Mimesis of Virtue* (Stockholm: Alqvist and Wiksell International, 1976). See also Sergei Hackel, "The Religious Dimension: Vision or Evasion? Zosima's Discourse in *The Brothers Karamazov*," in *New Essays on Dostoevsky*, ed. Malcolm V. Jones and Garth M. Terry (Cambridge: Cambridge University Press, 1983).

10. A. S. Dolinin, "'Stavrogin's Confession': With Reference to the Composition of *The Possessed*," *Soviet Studies in Literature* 23, nos. 3–4 (Summer–Fall 1987): 70–116, quotation at 106.

11. Ibid.

12. F. M. Dostoevsky, *Polnoe sobranie sochinenii v tridtsati tomakh*, 30 vols., ed. V. V. Vinogradov, G. M. Fridlender, and M. B. Khrapchenko (Leningrad: Nauka 1972–90), vol. 28, book 1, p. 176 (hereafter cited as *Pss*). In the text, *Pss* references include volume and page numbers, separated by a colon. Volumes 28, 29, and 30 each are split into two books. For citations from these volumes, a period and the numeral 1 or 2 follow the volume number to indicate book number, for example, *Pss*, 28.1:176. All translations from *Pss* are my own unless otherwise noted.

13. Avril Pyman, "Dostoevsky in the Prism of the Orthodox Semiosphere," in Pattison and Thompson, *Dostoevsky and the Christian Tradition*, 103–115, quotation at 103.

14. Malcolm V. Jones, "Modelling the Religious Dimension of Dostoevsky's Fictional Worlds," *New Zealand Slavonic Journal* 37 (2003): 41–53, quotation at 48.

15. Pattison and Thompson, *Dostoevsky and the Christian Tradition*, 9.

16. Valerii Alekseev, foreword to *F. M. Dostoevsky and Orthodoxy* (Moscow: Publishing House "K edinstvu!" 2003), 3, 4.

17. Maurice Baring, *Landmarks of Russian Literature* (1910), quoted in Peter Kaye, *Dostoevsky and English Modernism, 1900–1930* (Cambridge: Cambridge University Press, 1999), 17.

18. Pattison and Thompson, *Dostoevsky and the Christian Tradition*, 11.

19. See the fine discussion in Helen Muchnic, *Dostoevsky's English Reputation 1881–1936* (Northampton, Mass.: Smith College Studies in Modern Languages, 1939).

20. Pattison and Thompson, *Dostoevsky and the Christian Tradition*, 1.

21. Victor Ehrlich, "Two Concepts of the Dostoevsky Novel," *International Journal of Slavic Linguistics and Poetics* 25–26 (1982):127–36, quotation at 131–32.

22. Philip Rahv, "The Other Dostoevsky," *New York Review of Books* 18 (April 1972): 31.

23. John Middleton Murry, *Fyodor Dostoevsky: A Critical Study* (New York: Dodd, Mead, and Company, 1916), 258–59.

24. Ivan has few enthusiasts today. Victor Terras's assessment of this charac-

ter has become representative, although it is perhaps equally one-sided and so inadequate. "Behind his Grand Inquisitor's professed compassion for suffering humanity," Terras writes of Ivan, "there is hidden deep hatred of human freedom and of the image of God in man." Victor Terras, *A Karamazov Companion* (Madison: University of Wisconsin Press, 1981), 52.

25. Quoted in Pattison and Thompson, *Dostoevsky and the Christian Tradition*.

26. Irving Howe, "Dostoevsky: The Politics of Salvation," in *Politics and the Novel* (New York: Horizon, 1957), 137.

27. In "The Russian National Idea," originally published as *L'idée Russe,* 1888; Russian trans. 1909.

28. I thus concur with Maxim Shrayer's view that "the Jewish question in Dostoevsky is primarily a religious one rather than a social or ethnic one," and I share Shrayer's perception that Frank underemphasizes the religious basis of Dostoevsky's antisemitism. See Maxim Shrayer, "The Jewish Question and *The Brothers Karamazov*," in *A New Word on "The Brothers Karamazov,"* ed. Robert Louis Jackson (Evanston, Ill.: Northwestern University Press, 2004).

29. I must make this distinction absolutely clear: this study does not address problems of Orthodox or Christian theology. Under discussion are Dostoevsky's unique individual perceptions and experience of Christianity, as I believe we can reconstruct them from his texts.

30. The complexity of Dostoevsky's attitudes toward children will be addressed throughout later chapters.

31. Boris Nikolaevich Tikhomirov, "Dostoevsky on Children in the New Testament," in *Dostoevsky: On the Threshold of Other Worlds; Essays in Honour of Malcolm V. Jones,* ed. Sarah Young and Lesley Milne (Ilkeston, UK: Bramcote Press, 2006), 189–206, quotation at 195–96.

32. In my readings of Dostoevsky's novels, I will be following Robert Belknap's injunction to study the "literary density of the strong passages." Belknap believes that "it makes sense to study" not themes "but something much smaller, a passage of text that has some internal coherence and some inherent interest." Robert L. Belknap, *The Genesis of "The Brothers Karamazov": The Aesthetics, Ideology, and Psychology of Text Making* (Evanston, Ill.: Northwestern University Press Studies of the Harriman Institute, 1990), 90, 89.

33. Harriet Murav convincingly argues that "the New Testament concept of scandal," focused on the Crucifixion, is "central" to Dostoevsky's religious thought. "In Paul's view," she writes, "Christ crucified is that which both makes faith possible and destroys faith, the source of salvation and an occasion for ruin. . . . All who would believe must confront the radical demand that Christ crucified is the source of salvation." Harriet Murav, "From Skandalon to Scandal: Ivan's Rebellion Reconsidered," *Slavic Review* 63, no. 4 (Winter 2004): 756–70, quotation at 756.

34. Dostoevsky's unease with certain aspects of the Crucifixion may not be

entirely unique to him, however. Scholars who have compared Western and Orthodox iconography note that representations of the Crucifixion are much rarer in the East and emphasize different aspects of Christ's sacrifice. In Orthodox representation, G. P. Fedotov notes, "The Lord on the icon is always the Pantocrator, never a humiliated Christ" (G. P. Fedotov, *The Russian Religious Mind: Kievan Christianity: The 10th to the 13th Centuries* [New York: Harper and Row, 1960], 375). I am indebted to William Mills Todd for this observation.

35. Jones, *Dostoevsky and The Dynamics of Religious Experience,* 25.

36. Among existing explanations for Dostoevsky's antisemitism are some that likewise posit his fear of a Russian-Jewish likeness. Hingley and Dreizin postulate that Dostoevsky's antisemitism originates in the perception of similarity between his own Russian messianism and Jewish messianism. "Disliking any messianic doctrine in competition with his own, Dostoevsky denounced an alleged international Jewish conspiracy, while also condemning the Jews as exploiters—through usury, commerce and inn-keeping—of his humbler fellow-countrymen" (Hingley, *Dostoevsky,* 174–75). "Nicholas Berdyaev has pointed out that the messianic trend in Dostoevsky perceived the Russian people as 'God-bearers'—the only 'God-bearing' nation," Dreizin observes. "Such exclusively messianic consciousness cannot be called humble. This is the old-Jewish self-perception,'" Dreizin contends (Dreizin, *Russian Soul and Jew,* 64).

37. Diane Oenning Thompson, "Problems of the Biblical Word in Dostoevsky's Poetics," in Pattison and Thompson, *Dostoevsky and the Christian Tradition,* 96.

38. Fyodor Dostoevsky, *Winter Notes on Summer Impressions,* trans. David Patterson (Evanston, Ill.: Northwestern University Press, 1988), 49 (hereafter cited in text as *WN* with page number).

39. There is a good deal of scholarship dedicated to Dostoevsky's journalism and the *Diary* specifically. Frank integrates discussion of Dostoevsky's biography, novels, and journalism throughout his five volumes. Monographs dedicated to questions of journals include Deborah A. Martinsen, ed., *Literary Journals in Imperial Russia* (Cambridge: Cambridge University Press, 1997); Gary Saul Morson, *The Boundaries of Genre: Dostoevsky's Diary of a Writer and the Traditions of Literary Utopia* (Austin: University of Texas Press, 1981); and Igor Volgin, *Poslednii god Dostoevskogo* (Moscow: Sovietskii pisatel', 1986). For analysis of Dostoevsky's "self-fashioning as a persuasive public figure" in the *Diary,* see Harriet Murav, "Legal Fiction in Dostoevsky's *Diary,*" in *Dostoevsky Studies: Journal of the International Dostoevsky Society* 1, no. 2 (1993): 155–73, quotation at 164.

40. F. M. Dostoevsky, *A Writer's Diary,* trans. and annotated Kenneth Lantz, intro. Gary Saul Morson, 2 vols. (Evanston, Ill.: Northwestern University Press, 1994), 1264 (hereafter cited in text as *WD* with date and page number [page numbers run consecutively throughout the two volumes, thus volume number not included]). All *Diary* citations refer to this source unless stated otherwise.

41. Frank likewise devotes extensive discussion to the relationship between the *Diary* and *The Brothers Karamazov*. "Dostoevsky, as we know, considered his *Diary* a preparation for his next novel," Frank writes, and "the thematic outlines of *The Brothers Karamazov* begin to emerge" in its pages (*Mantle of Prophet*, 285).

42. Konstantin Mochulsky, *Dostoevsky: His Life and Work*, trans. Michael Minihan (Princeton, N.J.: Princeton University Press, 1967).

43. V. Ia. Kirpotin goes so far as to assert that the novels remain incomplete without consideration of the journals. V. Ia. Kirpotin, *Dostoevsky v shestidesiatye gody* (Moscow: Khudozhestvennaia literatura, 1966), 539.

44. The Christ-centered quality of Dostoevsky's faith has elicited a great deal of comment. "Dostoevsky early conceived a personal devotion to Jesus Christ which outlasted and outshone his doubts as to His divinity," Pyman writes ("Dostoevsky in Prism," 106). Irina Kirillova points out that "the most important spiritual experience of Dostoevsky's whole life . . . was his constant awareness of the figure of Christ, Whom he venerated throughout his life"; he doubted almost everything, Kirillova concedes, "but he never betrayed what can only be called an ecstatic faith in Christ" (Irina Kirillova, "Dostoevsky's Markings in the Gospel According to St. John," in Pattison and Thompson, *Dostoevsky and the Christian Tradition*, 43). His "redemptive vision" is "totally centered on the person of Christ, as man's only hope in life," Kirillova asserts (43).

45. Morson has provided the groundwork for my contention that mature Dostoevsky begins moving in the direction of purging Christianity not just of God the Father but even of Christ the Son. "The theology of *The Brothers Karamazov* has been little understood," Morson believes (Gary Saul Morson, "The God of Onions: *The Brothers Karamazov* and the Mythic Prosaic," in Jackson, *New Word on "Brothers Karamazov*," 107–24, quotation at 109). Ivan Karamazov, Morson argues, "refutes the very *possibility* of justifying the Creator" in the chapter "Rebellion" (118). "Alyosha at last replies that all Ivan has shown is why the question of suffering cannot be answered with only God the Father. But we are not Jews or Muslims, we have God the Son, Alyosha adds" (119). The subsequent "Grand Inquisitor" chapter then proceeds to repudiate God the Son, Morson argues, after "Rebellion" has discredited God the Father. The "diatribe against two persons of the Trinity" articulated in the novel, Morson believes, is effective: Ivan successfully "attacks God the Father," and the Grand Inquisitor "shows what is wrong with God the Son" (122).

46. V. E. Vetlovskaia, "Rhetoric and Poetics: The Affirmation and Refutation of Opinions in Dostoevsky's *The Brothers Karamazov*," trans. Diana Burgin, in *Critical Essays on Dostoevsky*, ed. Robin Feuer Miller (Boston: G. K. Hall, 1986), 233. Reprinted from *Issledovanie po poetike i stilistike*, ed. V. V. Vinogradov et al. (Leningrad: Nauka, 1972), 163–85.

47. Ibid.

48. The intimate connections linking Dostoevsky with his spiritual skeptics have commanded attention. Of Stavrogin, Dolinin writes, "Yet he, who rises above both of them [Kirillov and Shatov], longs, like 'parched grass,' for their limitations, their ability to give themselves wholly to a single idea—and cannot, as Dostoevsky, too, could not" ("Stavrogin's Confession," 108). Caryl Emerson underscores Dostoevsky's "authorial love" for his skeptics like Ivan Karamazov. Dostoevsky, she argues, "never assumes this belief zone," the place of faith from which Zosima speaks, "as a given. His most fervent authorial love is devoted to struggles for faith on, as it were, the second day, after the Crucifixion and before the Resurrection, when Jesus was reduced to the bruised and dead body trapped in Hans Holbein's painting" (Caryl Emerson, "Zosima's 'Mysterious Visitor': Again Bakhtin on Dostoevsky, and Dostoevsky on Heaven and Hell," in Jackson, *New Word on "Brothers Karamazov,"* 155–79, quotation at 166).

49. Pattison and Thompson, *Dostoevsky and the Christian Tradition,* 18.

50. Fyodor Dostoevsky, *The Idiot,* trans. and intro. David Magarshack (London: Penguin, 1955), 551 (hereafter cited in text as *I* with page number).

51. These are among "the most revealing of all Dostoevsky's words," Dolinin maintains, and he gives them to Stavrogin. "Only to Stavrogin did he give this thought of his and the ability to draw all subsequent conclusions about the Russian people as a 'God-bearing' people 'who will come to renew and save the world in the name of a new God.' . . . Dostoevsky surrounds these thoughts, which he places in Stavrogin's mouth, with his own halo of suffering, with that same 'crucible of doubt' through which his own hosanna has passed" ("Stavrogin's Confession," 107).

52. Murray Krieger, "Dostoevsky's *Idiot*: The Curse of Saintliness," in Wellek, *Dostoevsky: Critical Essays,* 39–52, quotation at 43.

53. Cassedy, *Dostoevsky's Religion,* 73.

54. Ibid., 66.

55. Ibid., 68.

56. See, for example, the letter to one N. E. Grishchenko from February 28, 1878, in which Dostoevsky expresses the conviction that "the Yid is spreading with horrifying speed" over Russia. Russian liberals, Dostoevsky complains to Grishchenko, refuse to admit that "the Yid triumphs and oppresses the Russian" (*Pss,* 30.1:8).

57. Cassedy, *Dostoevsky's Religion,* 73.

58. Pattison and Thompson, *Dostoevsky and the Christian Tradition,* 11.

59. D. S. Merezhkovsky, "Prorok russkoi revoliutsii: K iublieiu Dostoevskogo." *Polnoe sobranie sochinenii D. S. Merezhkovskogo,* vol. 11 (St. Petersburg: M. O. Wolf, 1911). David Zaslavksii, "Dostoevskii o evreiakh (K stoletiiu so dnia rozhdeniia)," *Evreiskii vestnik* 1 (1 April 1922).

60. Nathan Rosen, review of *Dostoevsky and the Jews,* by David I. Goldstein, *Dostoevsky Studies* 3 (1982): 203.

61. Jones, "Dostoevskii and Religion," 158. For another eloquent exposition of this view, see Leonid Grossman, *Ispoved' odnogo evreia* [*Confession of a Jew*] (Moscow: Dekont and Podkova, 1999).

62. A. Boyce Gibson, *The Religion of Dostoevsky* (London: S.C.M.P., 1973), 3, 2.

63. Sergei Hackel, "F. M. Dostoevsky (1821–1881) Prophet Manque?" *Dostoevsky Studies* 3 (1982): 5–25, quotation at 22.

64. Louis Allains, for one, disputes the validity of separating Dostoevsky's art from his political views. Observing that many Dostoevsky scholars "feel that Dostoevsky's 'ideology' should in general be separated from, on the one hand, his 'true' artistic works, and, on the other hand, from his 'false,' or at any rate 'controversial,' journalistic works," Allains concludes that "it is difficult to agree with such approaches." Allains explains, "Their direct consequence is to remove from Dostoevsky's poetics its moral center. Dostoevsky's nationalism not only thoroughly suffuses his five novel-tragedies, but it also imparts to them a unique and intense pathos." Louis Allains, "Fyodor Dostoevsky as a Bearer of a Nationalist Outlook," in *The Search for Self-Definition in Russian Literature,* ed. Ewa M. Thompson (Houston: Rice University Press, 1991), 147. Edward Wasiolek likewise objects: "This view is not accurate. Dostoevsky did not keep his politics out of his novels. His politics and his psychology are inseparable and both are at the heartbeat of his talent." Edward Wasiolek, "Revolutionary Conservatism," in *Modern Age: A Quarterly Review* 9 (1965): 63.

65. Vadim Rossman, *Russian Intellectual Antisemitism in the Post Communist Era* (Lincoln: University of Nebraska Press for the Vidal Sassoon Center for the Study of Antisemitism [SICSA], Hebrew University of Jerusalem, 2002), 16.

66. Morson, "Apologetics and Negative Apologetics," 84.

CHAPTER 1

The quotation in the head comes from a letter Dostoevsky wrote to L. A. Ozhigina in February 1878 (*Pss*, 30.1:9).

1. T. A. Kasatkina, "Lazarus Resurrected: A Proposed Exegetical Reading of Dostoevsky's *Crime and Punishment,*" trans. Liv Bliss, *Russian Studies in Literature* 40, no. 4 (Fall 2004): 6–37, quotation at 7. From the Russian text in *Voprosy literatury* 1 (2003): 176–208.

2. In-depth analysis of Dostoevsky's anxieties regarding the efficacy of Zosima's rebuttal to Ivan can be found in Robin Feuer Miller, *The Brothers Karamazov: Worlds of the Novel,* ed. Robert Lecker, Twayne's Masterwork Studies (New York: Macmillan, 1992), 53–79.

3. *Pss*, 15:492. This view has only recently been eclipsed by enthusiasm for

Zosima. It was shared by many Anglophone critics such as Ernest Simmons, who writes, "Zosima's answer, however, is not convincing, for his philosophy of optimism is essentially one of stagnation. And there is much reason to believe that Dostoevsky himself was unconvinced by the answer which he put in the mouth of Zosima. In his own search for God his ambivalent nature led him into the same furnace of doubt that consumed Ivan." Ernest J. Simmons, introduction to *Notes from Underground, Poor People, The Friend of the Family: Three Short Novels by Fyodor Dostoevsky,* trans. Constance Garnett; Laurel Dostoevsky series (New York: Dell, 1960), 24.

4. Victor Terras and Jostein Børtnes advance a different, more sanguine view of the redemption plots shaping Dostoevsky's novels. "Resurrection," Terras writes, is "the theme that emerges triumphant at the end of the novel [*The Brothers Karamazov*]" (Victor Terras, "Narrative Structure in *The Brothers Karamazov,*" in Robin Feuer Miller, ed., *Critical Essays on Dostoevsky* [Boston: G. K. Hall and Company, 1986], 216; reprinted from Terras, *Karamazov Companion,* 100–10). Børtnes reads Dostoevsky's novels as successful adaptations of what he calls "the regeneration pattern" (Jostein Børtnes, "Religion," in *The Cambridge Companion to the Classic Russian Novel,* ed. Malcolm V. Jones, Robin Feuer Miller, and Lesley Milne [Cambridge: Cambridge University Press, 1998], 104–29, quotation at 112). Alyosha and Dmitry Karamazov undergo metamorphoses, Børtnes believes. He contends, "Like his brothers, Ivan is on the road to rebirth" (114). Avril Pyman, on the other hand, shares my perception of an entirely different contour to Dostoevsky's novels: "Again and again, Dostoevsky's characters pronounce their 'Hosannah' or strike up their underground hymn, and again and again their songs of praise are drowned out by the thunder of history, stamped back into earth by jack-booted realism, extinguished by doubt" ("Dostoevsky in Prism," 104).

5. Fyodor Dostoevsky, *Crime and Punishment,* trans. Constance Garnett, intro. Joseph Frank (New York: Bantam Classic, 1987), 8, 52 (hereafter cited in text as *CP* with page number).

6. Philip Rahv, "Dostoevsky in *Crime and Punishment,*" in Wellek, *Dostoevsky: Critical Essays,* 16–38, quotation at 36.

7. Frank, *Miraculous Years,* 146.

8. Robin Feuer Miller, *Dostoevsky and "The Idiot": Author, Narrator, and Reader* (Cambridge, Mass.: Harvard University Press, 1981), 51.

9. Ibid.

10. Frank, *Miraculous Years,* 147.

11. Miller, *Dostoevsky and "The Idiot,"* 51.

12. "Introduction to the Publication of the Translation of Hugo's *Notre Dame,*" *Pss,* 20:28.

13. The complex relationship between Dostoevsky's novels and journals

encompasses gestation, reflection, response, rebuttal, amplification, embodiment, and reinforcement, to name a few dimensions of the dialogue. My perception that Dostoevsky composes an intergeneric dialogue among his novels and journals is indebted to the extensive scholarship analyzing Dostoevsky the novelist together with Dostoevsky the essayist. Morson's attention to the effect of generic form on ideas has been especially valuable. See Morson, *Boundaries of Genre.* The work of William Mills Todd on serialization has been indispensable. See William Mills Todd III, "*The Brothers Karamazov* and the Poetics of Serial Publication," *Dostoevsky Studies* 7 (1986): 87–98. My notion of an intergeneric dialogue is indebted to Andrew Wachtel, who traces stages in "a specifically Russian literary tradition of intergeneric dialogue on historical themes." See Andrew Wachtel, *An Obsession with History: Russian Writers Confront the Past* (Stanford, Calif.: Stanford University Press, 1994), quotation at 219. I perceive the relationship between Dostoevsky's novels and journals as a nonhierarchical dialogue; this approach has been influenced by Joseph Frank, who emphasizes the intimate relationship between Dostoevsky's novels and journals. "Dostoevsky," he writes, "had never drawn any hard-and-fast line between his purely creative works and journalism, and his novels had been nourished by close scrutiny of the daily press" (Frank, *Mantle of Prophet,* 202). Many of Dostoevsky's Russian critics have emphasized the importance of his ideas about history, and his engagement in current affairs through his nonfiction, for his creativity. The Dostoevsky who emerges from the studies of scholars such as Volgin, Nechaeva, and Kirpotin is a man engaged in political life, an artist of the present whose creative work is nourished by his immediate environment. Nina Perlina advances the view that we can establish interpretive primacy, and she finds the novels privileged. *The Brothers Karamazov* quotes the *Diary,* Perlina argues, in order to repudiate, validate, or otherwise pass judgment on the ideas expressed in the journal. See Nina Perlina, *Varieties of Poetic Utterance: Quotation in "The Brothers Karamazov"* (Lanham, Md.: University Press of America, 1984). James Scanlan, on the other hand, believes that Dostoevsky's essays enjoy interpretive primacy over the novels and "provide unambiguous indications of what side he was on" (*Dostoevsky the Thinker,* 4). Dostoevsky's journals, Scanlan writes, provide us access to the writer's real thoughts about history. "With the nonfiction to guide us, we can establish his own beliefs with considerable confidence and can then treat the fiction selectively as providing elaboration of his views" (Scanlan, *Dostoevsky the Thinker,* 4). Scanlan thus turns the typical critical approach to Dostoevsky's novels and journals, as described by Wachtel and practiced by Perlina, on its head: the typical approach "assumes a hierarchical relationship between the two texts with interpretive priority given to the ultimate expression of an idea in the fiction" (Wachtel, *Obsession with History,*

124). Geoffrey Kabat adopts this approach. Kabat distinguishes between what he calls Dostoevsky's "imaginative" and "ideological" styles of thought. He relegates the "ideological" style, which "finds its ultimate expression in Dostoevsky's militant nationalism, his pan-Slavism, his xenophobia, and his antisemitism" in the *Diary*, to lesser status. See Geoffrey C. Kabat, *Ideology and Imagination: The Image of Society in Dostoevsky* (New York: Columbia, 1978), quotations at 12.

CHAPTER 2

1. V. V. Ermilov, *F. M. Dostoevsky* (Moscow: 1956), 256. Quoted in Pattison and Thompson, *Dostoevsky and the Christian Tradition*, 26.

2. Pattison and Thompson, *Dostoevsky and the Christian Tradition*, 26.

3. Robert Louis Jackson, "Alyosha's Speech at the Stone: 'The Whole Picture,'" in Jackson, *New Word on "Brothers Karamazov*," 236.

4. William W. Rowe, *Dostoevsky: Child and Man in His Works* (New York: New York University Press, 1968), 233. For the theme of children in nineteenth-century Russian culture, see Andrew Wachtel, *The Battle for Childhood: Creation of a Russian Myth* (Stanford, Calif.: Stanford University Press, 1990).

5. Jones, "Modelling Religious Dimension," 49.

6. Gary Rosenshield, "Western Law vs. Russian Justice: Dostoevsky and the Jury Trial, Round One" in *Graven Images* 1 (1994): 117–35, quotation at 125.

7. Is the worldview articulated in Dostoevsky's novels an essentially quietistic one, according to which seeming injustice must be accepted as part of an inscrutable order, or is it one of radical dissatisfaction? Some scholars adopt the first premise. Susanne Fusso, for example, believes that Dostoevsky focuses attention on the crimes of children against their fathers; in Dostoevsky's last three novels (*Demons, The Adolescent,* and *The Brothers Karamazov*), she writes, "the centre of attention becomes the sins of the sons, not the fathers." According to Fusso, Dostoevsky's art expresses the belief that children must love their fathers no matter how unworthy the fathers may be. See Susanne Fusso, "Dostoevskii and the Family," in Leatherbarrow, *Cambridge Companion to Dostoevskii,* 175–90, quotation at 182. Such a reading of the novels is vulnerable to serious objections; Dostoevsky himself was unequivocally opposed to such a vision. In a March 1878 letter to an anonymous correspondent, a mother who apparently wrote Dostoevsky seeking advice about child rearing, he explains that parents have the heavy burden of behaving in such a way that justifies their children's love. If the parents fail, and the children cease loving, the fault lies with the parents, Dostoevsky asserts (see *Pss*, 30.1:17). Vetlovskaia takes issue with readings such as Fusso's, which impute an essentially traditionalist religious mind-set to Dostoevsky. According to readings like Fusso's, Dostoevsky's novels affirm the necessity of loving even unworthy (paternal) authorities; Vetlovskaia's analysis,

on the other hand, asserts that the artist fully endorses Ivan's critique of injustice (originating with the heavenly father) and the subsequent need for radical change. "It is worth reemphasizing that Dostoevsky fully accepts and shares both Ivan's strongest argument (the suffering of children) and his idea about the necessity of reorganizing the world immediately," Vetlovskaia writes. "It testifies to the fact that the author of *The Brothers Karamazov,* which was written during the period of Dostoevsky's friendship with Pobedonostsev, decidedly did not share the latter's views" (Vetlovskaia, "Rhetoric and Poetics," 233). Vetlovskaia stresses this point. "Ivan's critique of traditional Christianity's teaching on the nature of human suffering (as the result of Original Sin and as a pledge of future, heavenly harmony) is presented in the novel as justified" (233).

8. Tikhomirov, "Dostoevsky on Children," 197.

9. Rowe, *Dostoevsky: Child and Man,* viii.

10. Tikhomirov, "Dostoevsky on Children," 200.

11. Rimvydas Silbajoris, "The Children in *The Brothers Karamazov,*" *SEEJ* 7, no.1 (Spring 1963): 26–38, quotation at 37.

12. Miller, *Worlds of Novel,* 96.

13. Silbajoris, "Children in *Brothers Karamazov,*" 37.

14. Jackson, "Alyosha's Speech," 237.

15. Rowe, *Dostoevsky: Child and Man,* 122.

16. V. Ivanov, *Freedom and The Tragic Life: A Study in Dostoevsky,* trans. Norman Cameron, ed. S. Konovalov, with an introduction by Robert Louis Jackson and foreword by Sir Maurice Brown (Wolfeboro, N.H.: Longwood Academic Press, 1989), 14.

17. Ibid., 151–52.

18. Miller, *Worlds of Novel,* 133.

19. Like E. F. Tiutcheva, Albert Camus decides that the novel is ultimately unable to assuage the doubts it elicits. Referring to Dostoevsky's well-known statement that the main concern of *The Brothers Karamazov* was his lifelong question about the existence of God, Camus concludes, "It is hard to believe that a novel sufficed to transform into joyful certainty the suffering of a lifetime." Albert Camus, *The Myth of Sisyphus and Other Essays,* trans. Justin O'Brien (New York: Vintage Books, Alfred A. Knopf and Random House, 1955), 82.

20. Tikhomirov, "Dostoevsky on Children," 197.

21. Ibid., 199.

22. Ibid., 200.

23. Ibid., 197.

24. Much contemporary Dostoevsky criticism tends toward a certain view of the problem of theodicy in Dostoevsky's novels, namely, the belief that Dostoevsky's writings articulate an ultimately affirmative, reconciled relationship with God. The basic position staked by Frank and Jackson—that Dostoevsky's novels teach acceptance of injustice—is widely shared. Donald Palumbo gives

this dominant view an interesting twist by arguing that Dostoevsky's novels show good emerging from seeming evil. Each novel, Palumbo writes, illustrates "the principle of the fortunate fall, the idea articulated in *Paradise Lost* that apparent evil results in real good, that Divine Providence operates through the means of the temporary, seeming triumph and flourishing of evil, which It permits, to achieve finally a lasting and good end. These novels thus reconcile the apparently meaningless suffering and injustice perceived by their protagonists with the idea of a living God." Donald Palumbo, "The Theme of the Fortunate Fall in Dostoevsky's *The Brothers Karamazov*: The Effective Counterargument to Ivan's Ambivalent Atheism," *CEA Critic: An Official Journal of the College English Association* 43, no. 4 (May 1981): 8–12, quotation at 8.

25. Robert Louis Jackson, *The Art of Dostoevsky: Deliriums and Nocturnes* (Princeton, N.J.: Princeton University Press), 201.

26. Caryl Emerson provides a provocative reevaluation of this problem. See "Zosima's 'Mysterious Visitor,'" 155–79.

27. Ibid., 166.

CHAPTER 3

1. Identifying with those whom he abuses poses a problem for Stavrogin. Richard Pope and Judy Turner point out that Stavrogin identifies with Matresha: they are both ill-treated by their mothers, "and in Stavrogin's unconscious," Pope and Turner argue, Matresha "mirrors himself as the unloved, uncared-for child. She is not only the victim to be exploited by Stavrogin's murderous rage, but also a victim with whom he can strongly identify." See Richard Pope and Judy Turner, "Toward Understanding Stavrogin," *Slavic Review* 49, no. 4 (Winter 1990): 543–53, quotation at 550. Richard Peace suggests viewing Stavrogin's marriage to Maria Timofeevna as "an act of self-identification." Through this union, the emotional cripple Stavrogin "is revealing an essential identity with the object." See Richard Peace, *Dostoyevsky: Examination of the Major Novels* (1971; reprint, Cambridge: Cambridge University Press, 1975), quotation at 199.

2. Joseph Frank provides extensive analysis of how time spent in Europe influenced Dostoevsky's creative and intellectual evolution. The effects of exile on Dostoevsky included "a growing antipathy toward European life in all its aspects," Frank writes (*Miraculous Years*, 248). David I. Goldstein identifies European experiences as a catalyst in the evolution of Dostoevsky's antisemitism: "it was, undoubtedly, the period of his prolonged and involuntary European exile—April 1867 to July 1871—that exerted a telling influence on the formation (or deformation) of Dostoevsky's thought and writing during the last fifteen years of his life" (*Dostoevsky and Jews*, 50). David Bethea and Gary Saul Morson each believe that a decisive transformation took place sometime between the mid-1860s and the *Diary*. Between *Winter Notes* and the *Diary*, Bethea writes,

"Dostoevsky had shifted his focus from individual to national salvation, from death as a personal apocalypse to revolution as a political one" (David Bethea, *The Shape of the Apocalypse in Modern Russian Fiction* [Princeton, N.J.: Princeton University Press, 1989], 70). During the mid-1860s, Morson writes, Dostoevsky understood "the promise of the millennium . . . only in a figurative sense," whereas during the *Diary* era, he "had apparently come to believe that the millennium might be both literal and immanent" (Morson, *Boundaries of Genre*, 37). Malcolm V. Jones provides a helpful assessment of the impact of his European travels on Dostoevsky's development in "Dostoevsky and Europe: Travels in the Mind," *Renaissance and Modern Studies* 24 (1980): 38–57.

3. Morson review of Frank, *The Mantle of the Prophet*.

4. Rahv, "Dostoevsky in *Crime and Punishment*," 18.

CHAPTER 4

The first epigraph is from Honoré de Balzac, *Eugénie Grandet*, trans. Marion Ayton Crawford (London: Penguin, 1955). The passage in Balzac reads as follows:

> Aie bien soin de tout. Tu me rendras compte de ça là-bas, dit-il en prouvant par cette dernière parole que le christianisme doit être la religion des avares.
> —Honoré de Balzac, *Eugénie Grandet*.
>   *Oeuvres Complètes M. de Balzac,* ed. Jean A. Ducourneau, vol. 5
>   (Paris: Les Bibliophiles de l'originale, 1965), 344

Dostoevsky alters this passage significantly in his translation, simply omitting the commentary on old Grandet provided by Balzac's narrator. He was apparently unwilling to repeat the narrator's words about Christianity being a religion for misers. Here is the entire passage from Dostoevsky's translation:

> Когда священникъ пришолъ къ нему съ святыми дарами, то почти-совсѣмъ угасшіе взоры его оживились при видѣ серебрянаго креста и паникадила. Онъ пристально посмотрѣлъ на все и шишка на носу его зашевелилась въ послѣдній разъ. Наконецъ, когда священникъ поднесъ крестъ къ устамъ его, старикъ сдѣлалъ тяжолое усиліе, чтобы вырвать его изъ рукъ священника. Это усиліе стòило ему жизни. Онъ вспомнилъ о Евгеніи въ послѣднія минуты свои, но не могъ уже видѣть ее. Евгенія стояла на колѣнахъ и омывала слезами похолодѣвшую руку его.
>   —Батюшка! благословите меня, сказала она.
>   —Старайся, заботься обо всемъ, береги золото! береги золото! я потребую у тебя отчота на томъ свѣтѣ.
> Это были послѣднія слова его. И вотъ Евгенія осталась одна въ опустѣломъ домѣ, одна съ Нанетой, единственнымъ существомъ, которое могло понимать ея горе и заботу, которое любило ее, и которому она могла повѣрить тайну свою. Нанета сдѣлалась другомъ Евгеніи.
> —Fyodor M. Dostoevsky, "Evgeniia Grandé," *Polnoe Sobranie Sochinenii,*
>   Kanonicheskie Teksty, ed. V. N. Zakharov, vol. 1 (Petrozavodsk: Petrozavodskogo Universiteta, 1995), 559

The second epigraph is from Charles Baudelaire, "Madame Bovary" (1857), in Gustave Flaubert, *Madame Bovary,* ed. Paul de Man (New York: W. W. Norton, 1965), 336–43, quotation at 339.

1. "Dostoevsky," his biographer Mochulsky writes, "never found any given amount of money sufficient. He lived freely" (*Dostoevsky: Life and Work,* 18). Discussing the impression Dostoevsky made on Dr. Riesenkampf, the writer's roommate during the 1840s, Mochulsky explains that Riesenkampf was struck by Dostoevsky's impractical largesse. "The honorable doctor went to great lengths to inspire his roommate with some principles of household economy, but without success. Dostoevsky lived in hopeless extravagance and disorder. Now he regaled the doctor with a 'sumptuous' dinner in fashionable Lerch's restaurant on Nevsky Prospect; then for several months he remained without a cent. Having received a thousand rubles from his trustee in Moscow, he promptly lost it at billiards. . . . He entered into conversations with Riesenkampf's patients and supplied them with money" (19). Jacques Catteau examines "the strange connections" between Dostoevsky's passions for writing and gambling, and he establishes the importance of gambling and the need for money for Dostoevsky's creativity in general. See Jacques Catteau, *Dostoevsky and the Process of Literary Creation,* trans. Audrey Littlewood, Cambridge Studies in Russian Literature (Cambridge: Cambridge University Press, 1989), quotation at 141.

2. The importance of debts in Dostoevsky's writings has been addressed by A. V. Andreevskaia: "In all of Dostoevsky's major works, the theme of debts arises one way or another." "Dolg glazami geroev Dostoevskogo," *Slovo Dostoevskogo. Sbornik statei,* ed. Iu. N. Karaulov (Moscow: Institut Russkogo Iazyka RAN, 1996), 187–94, quotation at 188.

3. Todd likewise provides invaluable analysis of the relationship between the profession of literature and Dostoevsky's creativity. See William Mills Todd III, "Dostoevskii as a Professional Writer," in Leatherbarrow, *Cambridge Companion to Dostoevskii,* 66–92.

4. Frank, *Mantle of Prophet,* 217.

5. Quoted in ibid.

6. Ibid.

7. Morson discusses the relationship between writing and gambling in "Writing like Roulette," introduction to *The Gambler,* trans. Constance Garnett (New York: Random House, 2003), xi–xliii.

CHAPTER 5

1. It was his first published work, with the exception of "Zuboskal," published under that pen name in 1845 in *Notes of the Fatherland.*

2. Frank likewise notes the coexistence of social and religious rebellion in Devushkin, writing that "earlier, Devushkin revolts explicitly only against the

injustices of the social hierarchy, [but] at the very end of the book there is the timid beginning of a revolt against the wisdom of God Himself" (*Seeds of Revolt,* 148).

3. F. M. Dostoevsky, *Poor Folk,* trans. and intro. Robert Dessaix (Ann Arbor, Mich.: Ardis, 1982), 22 (hereafter cited in text as *PF* with page number). See also *Pss* vol. 1, my translations.

4. In this discussion of the effects of suffering on Varvara Alekseevna, I draw on Belknap's analysis of the role of suffering in *Poor Folk* and on a study of Varvara Alekseevna provided by Rosenshield: Robert Belknap, "The Didactic Plot: The Lesson About Suffering in *Poor Folk,*" in Robin Feuer Miller, ed., *Critical Essays on Dostoevsky* (Boston: G. K. Hall and Company, 1986), 30–39; Gary Rosenshield, "Varen'ka Dobroselova: An Experiment in the Desentimentalization of the Sentimental Heroine in Dostoevskii's *Poor Folk,*" *Slavic Review* 45, no. 3 (Fall 1986): 525–33.

5. See also V. E. Vetlovskaia, "Religioznye idei utopicheskogo sotsializma molodoi F. M. Dostoevskogo," in *Khristianstvo i russakaia literatura,* ed. V. A. Kotel'nikov (St. Petersburg: Nauka, 1994).

6. The inappropriateness of Devushkin as a rebel figure has been discussed from a different angle by Terras in "Problems of Human Existence in the Works of the Young Dostoevsky," *Slavic Review* 23, no. 1 (1964): 79–91. Some of Dostoevsky's early characters, including Devushkin, "take upon themselves—or are given by fate—a role for which they are not fit, a role in which they must inevitably fail," Terras writes; he notes "a loud ugly dissonance between what a man is trying to be and what he is" in such characters (89, 90).

7. The problem of sexuality in *Poor Folk* is addressed in Joe Andrew, "The Seduction of the Daughter: Sexuality in the Early Dostoevsky and the Case of *Poor Folk,*" in *Neo-Formalist Papers: Contributions to the Silver Jubilee Conference to Mark 25 Years of the Neo-Formalist Circle, Mansfield College, Oxford, 11–13 September 1995,* ed. Joe Andrew and Robert Reid, Studies in Slavic Literature and Poetics (Amsterdam: Rodopi, 1998), 123–41.

8. "Series of Essays on Russian Literature: Introduction," *Pss,* 18:56.

9. "Subscription Announcement for the Journal 'Time' for 1861," *Pss,* 18:36.

CHAPTER 6

The quotation in the chapter head is from *Pss,* 3:429. All translations from *The Insulted and Injured* are my own.

1. "Two Camps of Theoreticians," *Pss,* 20:5.

2. "Subscription Announcement for 1861," *Pss,* 18:36; "Two Camps of Theoreticians," *Pss,* 20:18.

3. "Subscription Announcement for 1861," *Pss,* 18:35.

4. "Series of Essays on Russian Literature: Introduction," *Pss*, 18:50, 18:69.

5. Frank gives an authoritative presentation of the view that Siberia served as a transformative catalyst. Before exile, Frank writes, Dostoevsky believed that his "humanitarian, philanthropic ideals" had "been brought to Russian life by the progressive ideology of the Russian Westerners," but afterward he believed they "were actually embodied in the instinctual moral reflexes of the much-maligned Russian peasant" (Frank, *Years of Ordeal*, 144).

6. "Series of Essays: Introduction," *Pss*, 18:42.

7. Ibid., 18:54.

8. Ibid., 18:42.

9. See also Clarence Manning, "Alyosha Valkonsky and Prince Myshkin," *Modern Language Notes* 57, no. 3 (March 1942): 182–85.

CHAPTER 7

1. "Series of Lectures on Russian Literature: Bookishness and Literacy; First Essay," 1861, *Pss*, 19:7.

2. "Series of Essays: Introduction," *Pss*, 18:57.

3. Fyodor Dostoevsky, *Memoirs from the House of the Dead,* ed. Ronald Hingley, trans. Jessie Coulson (Oxford: Oxford University Press, 1965; 1992 edition), 32 (hereafter cited in text as *MHD* with page number).

4. My interpretation of *Notes* as a work of disappointed expectations—one that flouts expectations built by Dostoevsky's contemporaneous essays in *Time* and later writings—runs counter to an influential interpretive trend. Julie de Sherbinin's assessment of *Notes* as a successful redemption narrative represents a currently popular view of this work. "*Zapiski iz mertvogo doma* can be regarded as a sort of 'mystery play' in which the entire symbolic corpus of prisoners plays the hero, destined to descend into the depths of sin in order to reemerge, enriched by their suffering," Sherbinin writes; "Gorjanchikov, in turn, follows the pattern of the 'mystery play,' resurrected through his contact with the Russian people." Julie de Sherbinin, "Transcendence through Art: The Convicts' Theatricals in Dostoevskij's *Zapiski iz mertvogo doma*," *SEEJ* 35, no. 3 (1991): 339–51, quotation at 348. I find much of Sherbinin's evidence in favor of this thesis unconvincing, as will be discussed.

5. "Subscription Announcement for 1861," *Pss*, 18:37.

6. "Series of Essays: Introduction," *Pss*, 18:54.

7. Jackson identifies the superficial quality of the prisoners' Christianity. The convicts "respond only to the symbolism and ceremony of the Christian service; with few exceptions, faith as he may experience it does not shape his ethical and social consciousness" (*Art of Dostoevsky*, 140).

8. *MHD*, 343. Jackson is surely correct to insist upon the irresolvable nature of the narrator's identity. "Which is the real Gorianchikov?" he asks. "Is he the

broken man who is first shown in the 'Introduction' or is he the man of hope, rejoicing in 'new life' and in his 'resurrection' at the conclusion of his prison term? He is both one and the other," for the "opposition between hope and all the appalling facts of the human condition constitutes a dramatic tension in all of Dostoevsky's major works." See Robert Louis Jackson, "The Narrator in *Notes from the House of the Dead*," in *Studies in Russian and Polish Literature in Honor of Waclaw Lednicki* (The Hague: Mouton, 1962). Morson shows that the work can "play on its double status." See Gary Saul Morson, "Paradoxical Dostoevsky," *SEEJ* 43, no. 3 (1999): 471–94, quotation at 492. Dale Peterson and Jacques Catteau likewise maintain that the decision to use a frame and fictional narrator must have been artistically significant. See Dale Peterson, *Up from Bondage: The Literatures of Russian and African American Soul* (Durham, N.C.: Duke University Press, 2000); Jacques Catteau, "De la Structure de la Maison des Morts de F. M. Dostoevskij," *Revue des études slaves* 54, nos. 1–2 (1982): 63–172. For a helpful summary of the various positions critics have taken on the question of fiction versus autobiography, see Karla Oeler, "The Dead Wives in the Dead House: Narrative Inconsistencies and Genre Confusion in Dostoevsky's Autobiographical Prison Novel," *Slavic Review* 61, no. 3 (Autumn 2002): 519–34.

9. Morson and Frank reach very different assessments of the frame narration. "Dostoevsky can be accused of allowing a disturbing clash to occur between his theme as a whole and the frame narration in which it is contained," Frank argues (*Stir of Liberation*, 218–19). "For none of the consoling truths that the narrator has learned in the house of the dead; none of his discovery of the people and his triumph over his initial despair; none of the exuberance, the sense of hope, the possibility of beginning a new life that he felt on his release—none of these events are in accord with the character and fate of the Gorianchikov who is presumed to have written the manuscript we read" (219). There is only a "disturbing clash" if the "theme as a whole" is in fact what readers such as Frank and Sherbinin believe it to be: the reality of resurrection. If, on the other hand, the theme is the absence or extreme difficulty of resurrection, then there is harmony between the work's form and content. For Frank and Sherbinin to be correct, there must be a flaw in Dostoevsky's artistry. Oeler dismisses Frank's view that Gorianchikov is just a device for evading censorship. "Such dismissal of the preface is undermined by the fact that after its serial publication in *Russkii mir* and *Vremia*, *Notes from the Dead House* appeared in book form three times in Dostoevsky's lifetime, and although he altered the text for each republication, he never once changed the story of Gorianchikov given by the frame narrator" ("Dead Wives," 520). On the contrast between the two narrators—Gorianchikov and Dostoevsky himself as the shadowy autobiographical voice projected into the text—Morson writes, "So glaring is this contradiction that it seems inconceivable to attribute it to mere carelessness"; *Notes from the House of the Dead*

"seems to play deliberately on its double status" and "seems to resonate between two narratives subsisting within the same covers." See Gary Saul Morson, *Narrative and Freedom: The Shadows of Time* (New Haven, Conn.: Yale University Press, 1994), quotation at 129.

10. The view that his experiences in Siberia effected a dramatic revolution in Dostoevsky's outlook is well established. "The influence of the prison-camp years," Frank writes, was to establish Dostoevsky's faith in "the traditional Christian morality of the Russian peasant" (*Stir of Liberation,* 299). "It is precisely such peasants," Frank claims, "whom Dostoevsky singles out as the finest specimens of the Russian people" (224). "It is one of the anomalies of *House of the Dead* that Dostoevsky does not include an account of his conversion experience in its pages," Frank believes; it was twenty-six years later in "The Peasant Marey" that Dostoevsky allegedly "supplied the missing pages from his prison memoirs" (114). Dostoevsky's "religious faith was reborn and made whole again under the impression of the humble and devout faith of the prisoners," Vladimir Soloviev writes in *Three Speeches in Memory of Dostoevsky, 1881–83* (Berlin: 1925), 13. While in prison, Ernest Simmons asserts, Dostoevsky realizes that "many of these criminals possessed qualities of calm, courage, real goodness, and even a certain nobility of soul which he associated with the common people ... one can deduce Dostoevsky's growing faith in the masses" (*Dostoevsky: The Making of a Novelist* [London: Oxford University Press, 1940], 84). Edward Wasiolek, on the other hand, counters, "What courage, what goodness, and nobility? What religious faith? Almost without exception Dostoevsky saw them as pitiless, cruel, and emptied of any suggestion of moral feeling" (*Dostoevsky: The Major Fiction* [Cambridge, Mass.: MIT Press, 1964], 24). "Critics have persisted in having Dostoevsky discover the 'golden heart' of the Russian people in prison, but what he discovered was the soundless irrational depths of destruction," Wasiolek insists (23).

11. "Series of Essays on Russian Literature: The Latest Literary Phenomena; The Newspaper *Day,*" *Pss,* 19:59.

12. *Pss,* 28.1:170. Jackson points out the moral superiority of the educated elite in *Notes,* where an "educated, cultivated sensibility" makes a "developed conscience" in an individual more likely (*Art of Dostoevsky,* 131). "Personal conscience is an attribute (though by no means invariably) of a spiritually developed, educated consciousness" in *Notes,* Jackson contends (129). On the other hand, Jackson continues, the peasants in *Notes* are characterized by "a condonation of lawlessness and a de facto evasion of personal moral responsibility" (126), whereas the elite are the bearers of "moral codes, social norms and forms" (134). Frank maintains the opposite view, arguing that experiences in camp led Dostoevsky to ascribe moral degeneration to the elite, not the people. "Prison camp persuaded him that this was far more likely to occur among the educated elite than among the people," Frank writes (*Miraculous Years,* 127). Yet Frank also admits that Dostoevsky provides no examples of conscience in the people.

Dostoevsky, he concedes, "told Katkov that he had seen the inner need for punishment manifest itself 'even among very uneducated peasants, in the crudest circumstances.' In fact, however, he offered no examples of such a need among the peasant convicts, and had spoken of it only as an attribute of an 'educated conscience'" (66).

13. Acknowledging the existence of environmental factors, Jackson points out, is not equivalent to moral apologetics. The influence of the environment does not explain the existence of evil in human nature, for "to say that environment brings out the worst in people is not to say that environment creates the evil in us, that is, the proclivity toward evil" (*Art of Dostoevsky*, 110). Frank comes close to ascribing environmental reductionism to Dostoevsky. Dostoevsky, he writes, "unobtrusively sketches in a background revealing that the violence for which the peasant convicts had been condemned had been, more often than not, a reaction provoked by intolerable humiliation and mistreatment" (*Stir of Liberation*, 215).

14. V. A. Tunimanov likewise points out that Gorianchikov never achieves any final, decisive condition. *Notes from the House of the Dead*, Tunimanov believes, is characterized by complex, contradictory, incomplete processes. See V. A. Tunimanov, *Tvorchestvo Dostoevskogo, 1854–1862* (Leningrad: Nauka, 1980). Oeler also emphasizes the absence of a consoling conclusion. She insists on "the impossibility of representing within it a totalizing narrative—including a redemption narrative—that could produce a unity out of all the contradictions or redeem any of the injustices" ("Dead Wives," 534). The work's structure mitigates against reading *Notes* as a successful redemption narrative, she points out. "Readings that emphasize the progressive, linear redemption plot cannot account for the preface's wayward frame except by invoking circumstances external to the text" (522).

15. My interpretation of "Akulka's Husband" differs sharply from the readings offered individually by Jackson, Frank, and Rosenshield. "Akulka's death may be viewed as a sacrifice generating hope for the rescue of mankind," Jackson writes (*Art of Dostoevsky*, 96). Of this story, Frank writes, "It dramatizes the survival in the Russian common man, even in the midst of his worst excesses, of a strain of deep and pure humanity which, if not capable of redeeming his behavior, at least indicates a remorseful awareness of his own degradation" (*Stir of Liberation*, 226–27). Rosenshield's close reading of the story arrives at the conclusion that Akulka's death "underlines the greatness of her moral victory, the power of meekness, and the incarnation of the ideal in a world of brutality and hatred" (Gary Rosenshield, "Akul'ka: The Incarnation of the Ideal in Dostoevskij's *Notes from the House of the Dead*," *SEEJ* 31, no. 1 [Spring 1987]: 15).

16. My reading of this vignette is similar to that of Oeler. Any reading that finds positive meaning in Akulka's suffering, Oeler persuasively argues, must in a sense forget about or erase Akulka herself. "To read the murder of Akulka as

part of a redemption narrative and thus ultimately, in a larger context, as itself achieving a redemptive, regenerative meaning, is to repeat the elision of her perspective," Oeler writes ("Dead Wives," 533).

17. Jackson discerns a different significance to the relentless return of the same portrayed in *Notes*. "The continual cycle of death and resurrection . . . expresses the tragic optimism of *House of the Dead,* its triumph over the finite," he writes (*Art of Dostoevsky,* 6).

18. Miller, *Dostoevsky and "The Idiot,"* 15; F. M. Dostoevsky, *Polnoe sobranie khudozhestvennykh proizvedenii,* ed. B.V. Tomashevsky and K. I. Khalabaev, 13 vols. (Moscow: GIXL, 1926–30), 11:188).

19. The portrait of Bumstein is perhaps the earliest representation of a Jew in Dostoevsky's writings. The real-life prototype, Isai Bumstehl, was a jeweler imprisoned for murder, whipped and branded. The records say that he was a convert to Greek Orthodoxy. Goldstein notes that Gorianchikov uses the word "Jew" (*evrei*) rather than the term "Yid" (*zhid*), which occurs frequently in Dostoevsky's later writings (*Dostoevsky and Jews,* 15). There is some question as to whether the record stating Bumstehl's conversion is correct (169).

20. Sherbinin, who identifies the chapter on the theatricals as "the ideological nucleus of the work," reaches a different conclusion as to its meaning ("Transcendence Through Art," 339). This chapter, she writes, enacts the reality of resurrection, for here "Russian folk theater becomes the locus of transcendental experience" (344). Her interpretation of "Kedril" as a positive drama of resurrection is based on stretched speculation, however. The lanterns, or "bizarre heads" (Gorianchikov's words), of the devils who take away Kedril and his master, she writes, "are likely borrowed from the Polish and Ukrainian folk custom of parading paper lanterns, representing the sun, preceding *vertep* (puppet) performances of the Nativity"; and "the folk association of the lantern heads with the birth of Christ points to the seed of renewal within fallen man" (346). This odd mishmash of elements from Nativity plays and diverse, secular sources in Kedril may point to the opposite conclusion, however: far from hinting at the renewal of the fallen, it may emphasize the depth of their fall. This odd pastiche points to a total lack of understanding of the meaning of the Nativity, to a disjointed quality to the prisoners' inner lives. The distance between the original meaning of the paper lanterns in Nativity plays and their role here as devils may indicate a form of degeneration working against rebirth.

CHAPTER 8

1. Kasatkina offers a reading of the novel diametrically opposed to mine. I emphasize the religious doubts and questions raised in the novel, whereas Kasatkina reads the novel as an exercise in Orthodox theology, a fictional explica-

tion of doctrinal points. We can approach *Crime and Punishment,* she writes, by performing "a multilevel interpretation comparable to the exegesis of sacred texts," for the novel "has grown, as a crystal from its source, out of a Gospel text" ("Lazarus Resurrected," 9, 6). Kasatkina's approach to literature as a vehicle for theological exposition appears to be part of a post-Soviet "return to religion" with specific consequences for literary criticism. The "return to literary criticism as a form of religious philosophy means reading Dostoevskii as a fundamentalist, whose works are straightforward adaptions of the Gospels" (Harriet Murav, "From Skandalon to Scandal," 758).

2. Many others argue that the novel encourages readers to associate Raskolnikov with Christ. Jostein Børtnes, Alexandra Rudicina, and George Gibian, for example, each identify compelling textual evidence of parallels between Raskolnikov and Christ. A "whole series of biblical references scattered throughout the novel," Børtnes argues, including "allusions to Lazarus, to Golgotha, to the New Jerusalem," constitute "a system of parallelisms" linking Raskolnikov with Christ (Jostein Børtnes, "The Function of Hagiography in Dostoevskij's Novels," in Feuer Miller, ed., *Critical Essays on Dostoevsky,* 188–93, quotation at 191). By mingling "sacred" and "profane" registers, Børtnes argues elsewhere, Dostoevsky is "establishing a complex relationship of equivalence and difference between Christ's archetype and Raskolnikov's process of restoring his own self in the image of the archetype" ("Religion," 112). "By accepting Lizaveta's cross from Sonya," Rudicina writes of Raskolnikov, "he is consciously enacting his acceptance of the path to Calvary" (Alexandra F. Rudicina, "Crime and Myth: The Archetypal Pattern of Rebirth in Three Novels of Dostoevsky," *PMLA* 87, no. 5 [October 1972]: 1065–77, quotation at 1071). See also George Gibian, "Traditional Symbolism in *Crime and Punishment,*" *PMLA* 70 (1955): 979–96.

3. Several articles stress the importance of sacrificial and erotic love, and Raskolnikov's relationship with his mother and sister, for motivating the crime. See Edward Wasiolek, "Raskolnikov's Motives: Love and Murder," *American Imago* 31 (Fall 1974): 252–69; David Kiremidjian, "*Crime and Punishment*: Matricide and the Woman Question," *American Imago* 33 (Winter 1976): 403–33; Peter Marchant, "The Mystery of Lizaveta," *Modern Language Studies* vol. 4, no. 2 (Autumn 1974): 5–13; and Louis Breger, "*Crime and Punishment:* A Psychoanalytic Reading," *Dreamworks* 3, no. 1 (1982): 35–50.

4. Some find that the novel does successfully portray Raskolnikov's resurrection. Kasatkina, for example, writes, "*Crime and Punishment* ends at the moment when 'he that was dead came forth' and Jesus said, 'Loose him and let him go'" ("Lazarus Resurrected," 7). Børtnes writes that "the Gospel accounts of Lazarus' resurrection, and of Christ's death and Resurrection, form a pattern underlying the representation of Raskolnikov's descent into the hell of the Siberian prison, where in his dream about the plague Raskolnikov finally conquers the forces of evil that have transformed his mind into an inferno" ("Religion," 111). Works

critical of the epilogue include Lev Shestov, *Dostoevsky i Nitshe* (Berlin: Skify, 1923); M. M. Bakhtin, *Problemy poetiki Dostoevskogo*, 3rd edition (Moscow: Khudozhestvennaia literatura, 1972); and V. Shklovsky, *Za i protiv: zametki o Dostoevskom* (Moscow: Sovetskij pisatel', 1957). Ernest Simmons argues that the epilogue is "neither artistically plausible nor psychologically sound" (*Dostoevsky: Making of Novelist*, 153). See also Julius Meier-Graefe, *Dostojewski der Dichter* (Berlin: Ernst Rowahlt Verlag, 1926); Edward Wasiolek, "On the Structure of *Crime and Punishment*" *PMLA* 74 (1959), no. 1:131–36; and David Matual, "In Defense of the Epilogue of *Crime and Punishment*," *Studies in the Novel* 24, no. 1 (Spring 1992): 26–34. Positive assessments of the epilogue include: Donald Fiene, "Raskolnikov and Abraham: A Further Contribution to a Defense of the Epilogue of *Crime and Punishment*," *Bulletin of the International Dostoevsky Society* 9 (1979): 32–35; George A. Panichas, *The Burden of Vision: Dostoevsky's Spiritual Art* (Chicago: Gateway Editions, 1985); and Donald Palumbo, "Coincidence, Irony, and the Theme of the Fortunate Fall in *Crime and Punishment*," *University of Dayton Review* 18 (1987): 27–35. Rahv notes that the epilogue seems "implausible" to many readers for a good reason: "Sonia's faith is of a sort that offers no solution to Raskolnikov, whose spiritual existence is incommensurable with hers" ("Dostoevsky in *Crime and Punishment*," 36). Mochulsky dismisses Raskolnikov's regeneration as a "pious lie" (*Dostoevsky: Life and Work*, 312). Wasiolek argues that the epilogue is an artistic failure but necessary to complete the ascendance of Sonia's influence over Raskolnikov ("On Structure," 131–32). Cassedy offers an interesting view of the epilogue. "The whole debate is in a sense misdirected," he contends (Steven Cassedy, "The Formal Problem of the Epilogue in 'Crime and Punishment': The Logic of Tragic and Christian Structures," *Dostoevsky Studies* 3 [1982]: 171–90, quotation at 171). The novel is a "tragedy in the classical Greek mold and a Christian resurrection tale," Cassedy writes; as far as these are compatible, the two can be superimposed, but they diverge in the epilogue. The tragedy concludes with Raskolnikov's suffering, with his arrest at the end of part 6, "while for the Christian form suffering is merely an antecedent to another stage, namely, resurrection, and this requires the inclusion of the Epilogue" (171).

5. Frank voices the dissatisfaction many have felt with Svidrigailov's money as a solution. "The munificence of Svidrigailov disposes much too facilely of all the social misery that Dostoevsky has so unflinchingly depicted, and to sweep it away only through Svidrigailov's caprices causes a serious thematic imbalance that cannot be overlooked," he writes (*Miraculous Years*, 140). Liza Knapp, on the other hand, speculates that salvation through this financial windfall might exemplify a point of Orthodox theology. See Liza Knapp, *The Annihilation of Inertia: Dostoevsky and Metaphysics* (Evanston, Ill.: Northwestern University Press, 1996).

6. The complex associations linking Raskolnikov and Svidrigailov lie outside

the scope of this discussion. See V. Ia. Kirpotin, *Razocharovanie i krushenie Ro-diona Raskol'nikova. Kniga o romane Dostoevskogo 'Prestuplenie i Nakazanie'* (Moscow: Sovetskii pisatel', 1974).

CHAPTER 9

1. Recalling her husband's reaction to this image, Anna Grigorevna writes: "the painting had a crushing impact on Fyodor Mikhailovich. He stood before it as if stunned . . . his agitated face had a kind of dread in it" (quoted in Frank, *The Miraculous Years,* 221).

2. *Pss,* 9:246. Miller and Børtnes, among others, point out significant parallels linking Myshkin with Christ. Miller shows that Dostoevsky borrows techniques used to characterize Jesus in the Gospels for his representation of Myshkin (*Dostoevsky and "The Idiot,"* 84). Børtnes interprets events associated with Myshkin, as with Raskolnikov, as variations on the archetype of Christ. Discussing "a series of execution stories told by Myshkin and his interlocutors," for example, Børtnes argues, "these executions are all variations on the archetypal execution of Christ" ("Religion," 116–17).

3. For extensive discussion of Dostoevsky's notebooks for *The Idiot* and their relationship to the final novel, see *The Notebooks for "The Idiot,"* ed. and intro. Edward Wasiolek (Chicago: University of Chicago Press, 1967), and Miller, *Dostoevsky and "The Idiot,"* 46–89.

4. *Pss,* 9:242. Like the epilogue to *Crime and Punishment,* the final outcome of *The Idiot* has been the subject of intense and probably irresolvable debate. The poles of critical opinion are eloquently set forth by Børtnes and Thompson. For Børtnes, the novel affirms the reality of resurrection through Christ; the Christ who fails is a false one, the "all too human Christ of post-Hegelian Biblical criticism" ("Religion," 118). Børtnes sharply limits the scope of the novel's pessimism. "The story of Prince Myshkin demonstrates the impossibility of an *imitatio Christi* based on the particular image of Christ posited by nineteenth-century liberal theology," he contends (117). Thompson, on the other hand, discerns no such limits on the novel's pessimism about Christ. It is "a corpse," she argues, "which is the organizing symbol of the novel's tragic vision" ("Problems of Biblical Word," 75). Christ's Word of eternal life is definitely overcome in this novel, she maintains: "no one moves toward redemption or renewal through the Word," for "the Word is . . . disabled, rendered impotent, like the epileptic idiot hero, because it is not invested with sufficient countervailing force to resist, let alone stem, the avalanche of avarice, lies and malice which prevails in this novel's world" (75). *The Idiot,* she concludes, is "Dostoevsky's bleakest work, a claustrophobic tale of unmitigated tragedy for all its protagonists" (76). The different responses to the painting articulated by Myshkin and Ippolit are discussed in Miller, *Dostoevsky and "The Idiot,"* 212–13.

5. For more on the significance of this painting for the novel, see Sarah Young, "Kartina Gol'beina 'Khristos v mogile' v structure romana 'Idiot,'" in *Roman Dos-*

toevskogo 'Idiot.' Sovremennoe sostoianie izucheniia, ed. T. A. Kasatkina (Moscow: Nasledye, 2001). The different responses to the painting articulated by Myshkin and Ippolit are discussed in Miller, *Dostoevsky and "The Idiot,"* 212–13.

CHAPTER 10

1. "The Metropolis and Mental Life," in *The Sociology of Georg Simmel,* trans., ed., and with an introduction by Kurt H. Wolff (New York: The Free Press, 1950; 1964 edition), 414. Works that address the problem of money in Dostoevsky include Catteau's *Dostoevsky and the Process of Literary Creation.* "Next to epilepsy, money is the ruling power in Dostoevsky's creative environment," Catteau asserts; "the whole of his work," Catteau contends, "tells us that money is *a category of the knowledge of our social and spiritual being,* like space" (*Dostoevsky and Literary Creation,* 141, 153). See also Boris Christa, "Dostoevskii and Money," in Leatherbarrow, *Cambridge Companion to Dostoevsky,* 93–110; Sophie Ollivier, "Argent et revolution dans *Demons,"* *Dostoevsky Studies* 5 (1984):101–15.

2. Vladimir Seduro, "The Fate of Stavrogin's Confession," *Russian Review* 25, no. 4 (October 1966): 397–404, quotation at 401.

3. Fyodor Dostoevsky, *Demons,* trans. and annotated by Richard Pevear and Larissa Volokhonsky (New York: Vintage Classics, 1995), 696, 699 (hereafter cited in text as *D* with page number).

4. Kasatkina's assertion that "Stavrogin is the absolute ironist," one who doesn't understand "how they [values] can exist," is thus only partially correct. As she concedes, "Stavrogin in fact does seek an idea that could withstand his destructive analysis." See T. A. Kasatkina, "Emotsional'no-tsennostnaia ironii i ee voploshchenie v romane 'Besy' F. M. Dostoevskogo: Obraz Nikolaia Stavrogina," *Filologicheskie nauki* 2 (1993): 69–80, quotation at 77 (my translation).

5. Mochulsky, *Dostoevsky: Life and Work,* 459.

6. Sven Linnér, "Bishop Tichon in *The Possessed,"* *Russian Literature* 3 (1976): 273–84, quotation at 273.

7. Dolinin, "Stavrogin's Confession," 79.

8. Jacques Madaule, *Le Christianisme de Dostoïevski* (Paris: Bloud et Gay, 1939), 53; Sven Linnér, "Bishop Tichon," 277.

9. Pope and Turner, "Toward Understanding Stavrogin," 544.

10. Leonid Grossman, "The Stylistics of Stavrogin's Confession: A Study of the Chapter of *The Possessed,"* in Feuer Miller, *Dostoevsky: Critical Essays on Dostoevsky,* 148–58, quotation at 150; Mochulsky, *Dostoevsky: Life and Work,* 463.

11. Dolinin, "Stavrogin's Confession," 76. Vitalii Svintsov reevaluates the notorious legends about Dostoevsky's alleged sexual abuse of a child in light of the author's intense identification with his creation Stavrogin. While dismissing such legends as probable calumny, Svintsov offers an interesting take on how they might have acquired such tenacious longevity. Dostoevsky himself, out of his intense moral rigor, insisted on the fact that he too could be capable of the worst

crime; his insistence on his own potential culpability in the worst transgressions may have fostered such rumors, Svinstov speculates. See Vitalii Svinstov, "Dostoevsky i stavroginskii grekh," *Voprosy literatury* 2 (1995): 111–42. Translated by Laura Givens in *Russian Studies in Literature* 34, no. 4 (Fall 1998): 28–55.

12. Quoted in Frank, *Mantle of Prophet,* 462.

13. Tikhomirov, "Dostoevsky on Children," 202.

14. Matt. 12:32, 18:6 (King James version); Tikhomirov, "Dostoevsky on Children," 203.

15. Dolinin, "Stavrogin's Confession," 85.

16. Ibid., 89–90.

17. Frank notes that Stavrogin—whose name contains the Greek root for cross, *stavros*—is contending with Christ. Stavrogin, Frank writes, is tempted to compete with Christ for sanctity: "The temptation of sanctity is only the last and supreme test, the subtlest form taken by the sin of pride" (*Miraculous Years,* 378). Stavrogin does in fact usurp Christ's place as a figure of veneration and vehicle of regeneration for some characters. "'I dream of regeneration . . . Benefactor!'" Lebedyakin exclaims (*D,* 266). "'Before you, sir, it's like I'm before the True One,'" Fedka tells him (*D,* 259).

18. K. E. Golubov was one of the most important prototypes for the Prince. When Dostoevsky read about Golubov in an 1868 issue of the *Russian Messenger,* he became convinced that Golubov was a sign of a new era dawning for Russia. "Do you know who the coming Russian people are?" he asks Maikov in a December 1868 letter. Golubov, he answers, represents the "new Russian people" (*Pss,* 12:179; Frank, *Miraculous Years,* 345). In the notes for *Demons,* the Prince encounters Golubov and is impressed by him but does not derive his ideas from Golubov; he is an independent thinker and has come to similar ideas on his own.

19. To Norman Leer, Stavrogin's ascent in importance indicates the primacy of a moral-psychological drama over any sociopolitical dimensions to the novel. Dostoevsky himself, Leer argues, viewed Stavrogin as "the main character," who "both caused and took precedence over the political action" (Norman Leer, "Stavrogin and Prince Hal: The Hero in Two Worlds," *SEEJ* 6, no. 2 [1962]: 99–116, quotation at 99). Leer quotes a letter to Katkov in which Dostoevsky writes that the murder of Shatov and political intrigue behind it "is nevertheless only an accessory and background for the action of another figure who can really be called the main character of the novel" (99–100). Frank, on the other hand, emphasizes the national-historical dimensions of the novel and Stavrogin himself, finding contemporary social explanations for Stavrogin's condition. Stavrogin, Frank writes, is "a victim of the famous mal du siecle," the "ennui" suffered by nineteenth-century intellectuals (Joseph Frank, "The Masks of Stavrogin," *Sewanee Review* 77 [October–December 1969]: 683).

20. Pope and Turner offer a psychoanalytic explanation for his failure of redemption. "Since facing up to the ludicrousness and banality of his evil deeds is impossible, and since not doing so closes the road to expiation and reparation,

Stavrogin is lost and can never tolerate the burden of his guilt," they argue. He takes his own life when he is told, by Tikhon and Liza, that "he may be perceived as ridiculous" ("Toward Understanding Stavrogin," 552). Seduro gives this explanation: "failure of repentance" results from "overmastering pride and the striving for self-assertion, plus the complete victory of evil over good, predetermined the further downfall of Stavrogin and his final suicide" ("Fate of Stavrogin's Confession," 401–2).

21. As Dostoevsky originally composed the novel, "At Tikhon's" was chapter 9, following the chapter "Ivan Tsarevich." Yet "At Tikhon's" has been excluded from some significant editions, for example, F. M. Dostoevsky, *Sobranie sochinenii,* 10 vols. (Moscow, 1956–58). It is included in Dostoevsky, *Polnoe sobranie khudozhestvennykh proizvedenii,* where it appears as a supplement at the end of the novel. It was first published as an independent text in *Dokumenty po istorii russkoi literatury i obshchestvennosti,* no. 1 (Moscow, 1922); it subsequently appeared in *Byloe* 19 (Leningrad, 1922).

22. Pope and Turner, "Toward Understanding Stavrogin," 543.

23. Peace, *Dostoyevsky: Examination,* 211. See also Leonid Grossman, *Dostoevsky: A Biography,* trans. Mary Macklen (London: Allen Lane, 1974), 471–72.

24. F. M. Dostojewski, *Die Urgestalt der Brueder Karamasoff. Dostojewskis Quellen, Entwuerfe und Fragmente,* annotated by W. Komarowitsch (Munich, 1928), 76–90.

25. W. J. Leatherbarrow, "Misreading Myshkin and Stavrogin: The Presentation of the Hero in Dostoevskii's *Idiot* and *Besy,*" *Slavonic and East European Review,* 78, no. 1 (January 2000): 1–19, quotation at 14.

CHAPTER 11

1. Murav likewise draws attention to this aspect of Ivan's critique. "According to Ivan, the suffering of children enters some sort of economy: a logic of exchange takes over, and the suffering attains value as the means by which harmony is purchased. The logic of calculation, of damage done and compensated for, the basis of law and civil society, whose inadequacies religion tries to overcome—ends up reappearing within religion" (Murav, "From Skandalon to Scandal," 767).

2. Ivan's relationship to innocent suffering has come under criticism. Marina Kostalevsky, for example, argues that "his position can hardly be called ethical, since it derives not from compassion but precisely from his fixation on suffering, his fixation on pain. . . . Compassion generates a desire to help the other, that is, commit a life-asserting action, but fixation on suffering is fraught with the desire to understand the meaning of the phenomenon" (Marina Kostalevsky, "Sensual Mind: The Pain and Pleasure of Thinking," in Jackson, *New Word on "Brothers Karamazov,"* 200–9, quotation at 207).

3. Jackson, "Alyosha's Speech," 235.

4. Using mercantile language to speak about redemption is of course not original to Dostoevsky, who would have encountered it in the Bible. But we cannot assume that we understand the significance of such language for Dostoevsky's novel simply by referring to its presence in the Bible; the fact that Dostoevsky's use of such language may have been inspired by the Bible does not exhaust its potential implications. The mercantile language used within the world of *The Brothers Karamazov* may convey meanings that are very different from their original biblical significance.

5. Archpriest George Florovsky, *Puti russkogo bogosloviia* 2nd ed., with an introduction by Archpriest Meiendorff (Paris: YMCA Press, 1981), 300.

6. In Caryl Emerson's compelling reading, the story of Zosima's mysterious visitor encapsulates the perhaps irreconcilable conflict of interest between transgressors seeking forgiveness and those associated with them. "In my judgment," Emerson writes, "there is no moral dilemma anywhere in Dostoevsky's final novel that can match this little story in efficiency and hopelessness. It is a portrayal of the 'right thing' accomplished, but where all parties were guaranteed to lose—and only the criminal, at the last minute before his death, selfishly reaps relief" ("Zosima's 'Mysterious Visitor,'" 162). After acknowledging attempts by Roger Anderson and Rudolf Neuhäuser to find Zosima compelling, Emerson concludes, "Such spiritually anchored discussions of Dostoevsky's final novel cannot be faulted in their wisdom or their correctness. But they cannot, in my view, walk us barefoot through the killing fields as Dostoevsky, his Ivan Karamazov, or the anguished mysterious visitor would have us walk" (166).

7. Palumbo, "Fortunate Fall," 10.

8. Ibid., 11.

9. Nathan Rosen, "Style and Structure in *The Brothers Karamazov*," *Russian Literature Triquarterly* 1, no. 1 (1971): 352–65. Reprinted in Matlaw, ed., *The Brothers Karamazov*, 861–70, quotation at 846.

10. Harold Bloom, introduction to *Fyodor Dostoevsky's "The Brothers Karamazov,"* ed. and intro. Harold Bloom (New York: Chelsea House Publishers, 1998), 1–5, quotation at 4.

11. For a recent affirmation of this view, see Cassedy, who writes that Zosima "remains within mystery" (*Dostoevsky's Religion,* 100). Miller offers moving discussion of what she identifies as the mysterious bases of Zosima's faith (*Worlds of the Novel,* 75).

12. Their lack of attention to victims forms an intriguing parallel between Zosima and his mysterious visitor. Emerson points out the odd locus of the mysterious visitor's guilt: he, a murderer, does not express much guilt about the victim whose life he took away, preferring instead to speak at length about the horrors of social isolation ("Zosima's 'Mysterious Visitor,'" 161). She draws attention "to the vexed, not the blessed, side of Zosima's behavior" (160). One could gain the impression, she writes, that Zosima lacks regard for victims, for "Zosima's portrait— so full of affirmation and tears of joy—might well seem a case of salvation solely

for the strong and serene at heart" (158). Readings that affirm Zosima's behavior in the mysterious visitor story, Emerson observes, "are liable to downplay the external costs" of sinners' reconciliation with God (160). Zosima's "Final interaction as a layperson," his encouragement of the murderer to confess, causes "universal confusion, pain, disbelief, . . . the ruin of his family, his own death" (162). "Morally righteous decisions—as both Tolstoy and Dostoevsky affirm—can be astonishingly selfish, and neither novelist would have us forget it" (160). Such evidence leads Emerson to speculate: Does this little story in fact invite us to judge Zosima and "perhaps even the 'living God' into whose fearful hands the criminal has fallen?" (160). "It is up to the reader to decide whether a 'delay in the operation of grace' is sufficient compensation for the survivors," she concludes (162). A "delay in the operation of grace" is identified by Belknap as a "central theme" in the novel. See Robert Belknap, *Structure of "The Brothers Karamazov"* (1967; reprint, Evanston, Ill.: Northwestern University Press, 1989), 66.

13. Vladimir Golstein points out that Ivan glaringly overlooks the mistreatment of a real child in his life, his own probable half-brother Smerdiakov. See Vladimir Golstein, "Accidental Families and Surrogate Fathers: Richard, Grigory, and Smerdyakov," in Jackson, *New Word on "Brothers Karamazov,"* 90–106. Olga Meerson argues that the universal neglect of Smerdiakov—committed by all characters, including Alyosha and the narrator-chronicler—forms the central moral quandary of the novel. See "The Fourth Brother," in Meerson, *Dostoevsky's Taboos,* Studies of the Harriman Institute (Dresden–Munchen: Dresden University Press, 1998), 183–218.

14. Frank, *Mantle of Prophet,* 607.

15. Silbajoris, "Children in *Brothers Karamazov,*" 27.

16. E. H. Carr, *Dostoevsky: A New Biography* (New York: Houghton Mifflin, 1931), 289.

17. Mochulsky, *Doestoevsky: His Life and Work,* 615.

18. Miller, *Worlds of Novel,* 75.

19. Vladimir Kantor, for example, writes, "Dostoevsky's hero demands vengeance and retribution," and quotes Ivan saying, "'I need retribution, otherwise I will put an end to myself.'" See Vladimir Kantor, "Pavel Smerdyakov and Ivan Karamazov: The Problem of Temptation," in Pattison and Thompson, *Dostoevsky and the Christian Tradition,* 195.

20. Terras, "Narrative Structure in *The Brothers Karamazov,*" in *Karamazov Companion,* 127.

21. Ibid., 219. "Through these three children," Miller writes of Liza, Kolya, and Ilyusha, "each of whom the reader cares for, Dostoevsky offers the reader different and painful examples of his belief that children are not exempt from the temptation and allure of evil" (*Worlds of Novel,* 112–13). Liza's condition, Diane Thompson writes, is one of "self-corruption" and illustrates "evil inherent in the soul" ("Lise Khokhlakova: *Shalunia/besionok*" in *O Rus! Studia litteraria slavica in honorem Hugh McLean* [Berkeley, Calif.: Berkeley Slavic Specialties, 1995],

281–97; quotation at 293). "Tension between childhood innocence and childhood guilt is at the heart of the novel," Anne Hruska writes (Anne Hruska, "The Sins of Children in *The Brothers Karamazov*: Serfdom, Hierarchy, and Transcendence," in *Christianity and Literature* 54, no. 4 [Summer 2005]: 471–95, quotation at 471). "The child's sweetness and goodness are often, unlike in Dickens, tempered by the impulsive, the corruptible, and even the perverse," Rowe writes. "At times, Dostoevsky's children are playfully or even vindictively malicious." Yet they also display "unambivalent pity" and "a natural goodness almost entirely lacking in his adults" (Rowe, *Dostoevsky: Child and Man*, 230–31). These readings impute theological accuracy to Dostoevsky—adherence to the doctrine of original sin through the portrayal of children—precisely where some other critics, such as Tikhomirov, find it lacking.

22. The story first appeared in 1860 in *The Bell*.

23. Attempts to find Ivan conclusively discredited have become more frequent in recent years than in previous periods of Dostoevsky scholarship. Such readings often resort to incomplete or misleading argumentation, as exemplified by Vetlovskaia's discussion. Vetlovskaia unconvincingly finds only "hatred and profound contempt" for others in Ivan ("Rhetoric and Poetics," 226). She lumps Ivan together with Fyodor Pavlovich and Smerdiakov as characters who "all tell lies" (224). As an example of Ivan's lies, she cites his statement to Alyosha that he will watch over their father. To call this statement a simple lie is an oversimplification; Ivan's feelings regarding his father are complex, and his own intentions are unclear even to himself. Vetlovskaia accepts Smerdiakov as an unproblematic source of truth about Ivan, taking this highly unreliable character's accusation that Ivan is the real murderer as the simple truth (226). Any reading that uses statements characters make about one another as evidence would have to include Zosima's and Alyosha's very positive words about Ivan as well. Jackson likewise draws only selectively from unreliable characters in order to discredit Ivan. "'Ivan loves nobody,'" Jackson quotes Fyodor Pavlovich saying ("Alyosha's Speech," 238). There is no textual evidence to support Jackson's contention that the sad face Ivan has while speaking of suffering children is merely "a theatrical gesture" rather than the result of inward emotion (238).

24. Rosen argues that the lyric, emotional power of Zosima's language indicates the preeminence of his faith over Ivan's rebellion, yet a similar argument could be made about Ivan's language. The wrenching, emotional power of Ivan's descriptions of innocent suffering are buttressed by the power of Dostoevsky's parallel rhetoric in the *Diary*. Rosen, "Style and Structure in *The Brothers Karamazov*."

25. Kantor draws a similar conclusion from this passage. "In ascribing these words to Ivan, Dostoevsky simply *forgets himself* for a minute, revealing to us, that he himself speaks on behalf of Ivan," he asserts. "There is too much of Dostoevsky in Ivan to vouchsafe an antagonistic attitude to him," Kantor writes; "in making up our minds about Ivan's destiny, we would be making up our minds

about Dostoevsky." Vladimir Kantor, "Whom Did the Devil Tempt and Why?" *Social Sciences* 33, no. 4 (2002): 81.

26. Morson, *Boundaries of Genre*, 59.

27. *BK*, 241. Intimate connections such as these make it impossible to agree with Vetlovskaia's assertion that Dostoevsky's relationship to Ivan is one of "respectful distance" ("Rhetoric and Poetics," 232).

28. When Jackson points to the fact that Ivan draws his examples of suffering children "from scattered news accounts" and assumes the role of "an 'observer'" as evidence against this character, he is citing evidence that cuts two ways (Jackson, "Alyosha's Speech," 238). The Russian public knew that Dostoevsky himself was a voracious reader of newspapers who drew inspiration from media accounts of current events. Reading newspapers and observing injustice are just as likely to associate Ivan positively with his creator as to condemn him.

29. Dolinin points to similarities between Ivan's rejection of God on the basis of the injustices he permits and some of the positions adopted in "Idealist and Positivist Methods in Sociology," read in the winter of 1848 to the Petrashevsky circle by N. S. Kashkin. See A. S. Dolinin, "Dostoevsky sredi Petrashevtsev," *Zven'ia*, vol. 6, 523; quoted in *Pss*, 15:403.

30. *Pss*, 15:470. English translation here quoted in Frank, *Mantle of Prophet*, 429.

Index

Fictional characters are indexed under the name by which they are best known (e.g., Raskoni-kov, Sonia) and followed by the name or abbreviation of the book in which they appear. This index uses the following abbreviations:

BK   *The Brothers Karamazov*
CP   *Crime and Punishment*
FD   Fyodor Dostoevsky
Notes   *Notes from the House of the Dead*

231

Index

Index

Index

Index

messianic nation. *See* Russian messianism

Miretsky (*Notes*), 97, 102

money
  and leveling of differences, 144–45, 223n1
  and poverty, 83
  transformative power of, 58
  see also merchant God; windfalls as salvation

moral accountability
  abdication of, 100, 104, 107
  Jewish non-accountability, 191
  and political authorities, 184, 185–86

moral flaws in prisoners in *Notes*, 112

mothers, 181

Muslims in *Notes*, 109–11, 113

Myshkin (*Idiot*)
  as central character, 135–37
  and Christ, 134–35, 222n2
  and common people, 92
  in Europe, 138–39
  faith and doubt, 27
  and man on scaffold, 136, 140, 160
  and national resurrection, 141
  and sanctity of children, 34
  and separation criticism, 17
  as spokesman for FD, 14

mysterious visitor (*BK*), 226n12

Napoleon, 121, 128

Natasha Fillipovna (*Idiot*), 139, 140

national messianism. *See* Russian messianism

national redemption
  community as an object of redemption, 28–29, 78–79, 93, 134
  in FD's late works, 141, 143
  mediation through the people, 94, 154
  need for, 78–79
  Russia as vehicle, 14–15, 30, 140–41
  see also Russian self-sacrifice

national resurrection, 134, 154–55

Nechaev, Sergei, 153

Nelli (*The Insulted and Injured*), 32, 73, 79–80, 85–89

Notes from the House of the Dead, 90–116
  conscience in prisoners, 92, 96, 97, 100–101, 104–5, 112
  disappointed expectations, 90, 93–97
  evasion of moral accountability, 100, 104, 107

expectations of Christmas, 103–4

Jews, 92, 111–13, 117, 219n19

narrative frame of, 108–9

and need for communal redemption, 78–79

redemption narratives, 28, 99–100, 108–9

resurrection, failure of, 116

Russian people, 90–93, 95–97, 107–8

suffering, 102–3

victims and victimizers, 106–7

see also "Akulka's Husband"; Bumstein; Isaiah Fomich; Gorianchikov

Notes from the Underground, 27

novels in dialogue with journalism, 29, 43–44

Nurra (*Notes*), 110, 113

Original Sin, 36, 169, 210n7, 227n21

Orlov (*Notes*), 96

other-sacrifice, 108, 121
  see also child sacrifice; self-sacrifice; suffering of innocents

panhumanism, 79
  see also unity of humanity

parents and children, 80–81, 84–85, 86
  see also fathers and children

particularism, 52
  see also unity of humanity

Passion, 35–36, 39, 89, 133–34, 157–58

"The Peasant Marey" (*Diary*), 24, 94, 97–100, 102, 217n10

Petrov (*Notes*), 98, 99, 104, 116

Poland, 51–52

Poor Folk, 69–77, 213n1
  child abuse, 71, 75
  and *Diary*, 72–73, 74, 76–77
  and *The Insulted and Injured*, 79–80, 83
  reader response to, 69, 83
  rebel characters, 74–75, 214n6
  Russian abuse of children, 180
  Russia's mission to Europe, 75, 76, 89
  and *Time*, 76
  victims and victimizers, 70
  see also Devushkin; Varvara Alekseevna

"positive" characters in FD's works, 32
  see also Alyosha Karamazov; Sonia; Tikhon; Zosima

Index

Russia and the West, 48–50, 138–39,
  182–83
  see also Russian mission to Europe
Russian hero, 151
Russian idea
  chosen people elected to defeat the Jew-
    ish Antichrist, 7
  and the Crucifixion, 10
  expressed in art, 79
  and individual morality, 184
  and Ivan Karamazov, 173–74, 228n23
  origins in *Poor Folk,* 69
  and problem of redemption, 29
  and *Time,* 82
  and unity of humanity, 15
  and victims of history and harmony,
    192
  see also Russian messianism; Russian
    self-sacrifice
Russian messianism, 133–43
  development of idea, 89, 152–53
  in *Idiot,* 140–41
  and redemption, 29
  vs. Jewish messianism, 203n36
Russian mission to Europe
  and *Idiot,* 140–41
  and moral accountability, 185–86
  Poor Folk, 75, 76, 89
  in *Time,* 92
  see also Russia and the West
Russian Orthodox Christianity
  and the Crucifixion, 8–9, 202n34
  failure in *Idiot,* 139
  FD relation to, 3–5, 200n6
  moral equivalence with Jews in *Notes,* 92
  necessary for salvation, 153
  refusal to participate in sacrificial ex-
    change logic, 194
  and reprisals against atrocities, 173
Russian people
  absence of union with, in *Notes,* 102
  capacity for self-sacrifice, 12–13, 89,
    195–96, 204n45
  depravity of, in *Notes,* 95–97
  as distinct from Jews, 15–16
  FD's criticism of after prison release,
    94–95
  moral state of, 99
  in *Notes,* 90–93, 107–8
  poor treatment of, 86

as risk takers, 58, 65
  see also elites and common people; Rus-
    sian society
Russian prisoners, depravity of, 109, 113
Russian self-hatred, 76
Russian self-sacrifice
  national redemption, 30
  redemptive imitation of Christ's self-
    sacrifice, 12–13, 204n45
  and Russian idea, 15
  in *Time,* 75
  vs. other-sacrifice, 89, 121, 195–96
  Winter Notes on Summer Impressions,
    51
  see also Russian idea; Russian
    messianism
Russian society
  and capital punishment, 138
  cost-benefit logic of, 123, 124
  split between elites and common people,
    80–81
  and utilitarianism, 117
  see also elites and common people; Rus-
    sian people
Russian soil and resurrection, 154–55
Russians and Jews
  distinctions between, 63–65, 134
  similarity between, 92, 117

sacrifice. *See* child sacrifice; other-sacrifice;
    self-sacrifice; suffering of innocents
sacrificial exchange logic
  absence of alternatives to, 131–32
  in *Crime and Punishment,* 118–19, 129,
    137
  Crucifixion, 120, 158–59, 197–98
  in *Demons,* 145
  Jewish idea, 192
  and Job, 165–66
  and Providence, 130–31
  redemption as economic transaction,
    157–58
  and Russian society, 124, 194
  West (Europe), 120
  Zosima, 163–65
  see also authorities, political and spiri-
    tual; utilitarianism
salvation
  gambling as, 62–63, 120–21
  through risk taking, 58

Index